DEFERRED DREAMS, DEFIANT STRUGGLES

The Collegium of African American Research (CAAR) was founded at the University of the Sorbonne Nouvelle in 1992 and incorporated at the University of Rome later that year. From its inception, it has worked to stimulate research in African American Studies in Europe and beyond. CAAR promotes intellectual collaboration through the creation of an international and interdisciplinary research and teaching network. CAAR organizes bi-annual conferences, sponsors local symposia, helps to create research networks, and supports publications, most prominently its FORECAAST (Forum for European Contributions in African American Studies) series.

The first volume of the FORECAAST series was issued by Lit Verlag in 1999, and for its twentieth volume the series moved to Liverpool University Press. Begun as an occasional publication of monographs and themed, selected conference papers, the series has always sought to highlight the best recent scholarship in the field. In 2013, FORECAAST became an annual publication of CAAR, reflecting the growth of the organization and the richness of the scholarship produced by its members.

SERIES EDITORS:

Professor Cynthia S. Hamilton, Liverpool Hope University and Professor Alan Rice, University of Central Lancashire

Deferred Dreams, Defiant Struggles

Critical Perspectives on Blackness, Belonging, and Civil Rights

Edited by
Violet Showers Johnson, Gundolf Graml,
and Patricia Williams Lessane

Liverpool University Press

First published 2018 by
Liverpool University Press
4 Cambridge Street
Liverpool
L69 7ZU

Copyright © 2018 Liverpool University Press

The rights of Violet Showers Johnson, Gundolf Graml, and Patricia Williams Lessane to be identified as the editors of this book have been asserted by them in accordance with the Copyright, Designs and Patents Act 1988.

All rights reserved. No part of this book may be reproduced, stored in a retrieval system, or transmitted, in any form or by any means, electronic, mechanical, photocopying, recording, or otherwise, without the prior written permission of the publisher.

British Library Cataloguing-in-Publication data
A British Library CIP record is available

ISBN 978-1-78694-033-9

Typeset by Carnegie Book Production, Lancaster
Printed and bound by CPI Group (UK) Ltd, Croydon CR0 4YY

In memory of Andrzej Antoszek (1971–2013),
outstanding scholar of African American Studies in Poland
and a dedicated member of the Collegium for African
American Research.

Contents

List of Illustrations ... ix

Acknowledgments ... x

List of Contributors ... xi

1 Introduction: Deferred Dreams, Defiant Struggles ... 1
 Violet Showers Johnson, Gundolf Graml, and Patricia Williams Lessane

DIASPORA, DISPLACEMENT, MARGINALIZATION, AND COLLECTIVE IDENTITIES

2 Josephine Baker's Routes and Roots: Mobility, Belonging, and Activism in the Atlantic World ... 11
 Katharina Gerund

3 Beyond the Ethnographic Other: Pan-African Activism at the Turn of the Twentieth Century ... 33
 Thomas E. Smith

4 Black Sojourners in the *Métropole* and in the Homeland: Challenges of Otherness in Calixthe Beyala's Loukoum: *The "Little Prince"* of Belleville and Myriam Warner-Vieyra's *Juletane* ... 57
 Philip Ojo

PERFORMING IDENTITIES, RECLAIMING THE SELF

5 Staging the Scaffold: Criminal Conversion Narratives of the Late Eighteenth Century ... 77
 Carsten Junker

6 The Plays of Carlton and Barbara Molette: The Transformative Power of African-American Theater ... 94
 Silvia Pilar Castro-Borrego

MOVED TO ACT: CIVIL RIGHTS ACTIVISM IN THE US AND BEYOND

7 "Together We Can Build a Nation of Love and Integration": The 1965 North Shore Summer Project for Fair Housing in Chicago's Northern Suburbs   117
Mary Barr

8 Redrawing Borders of Belonging in a Narrow Nation: Afro-Chilean Activism in the Hinterlands of Afro-Latin America   137
Sara Busdiecker

9 Lowcountry, High Demands: The Struggle for Quality Education in Charleston, South Carolina   154
Jon Hale and Clerc Cooper

Index   175

Illustrations

3.1 American Negro Exhibit – Plan of Installation
Reprinted from *Report of the Commissioner-General for the United States to the International Universal Exposition, Paris, 1900 Volume II* (Washington, DC: Government Printing Office, 1901)   37

3.2 African American Man – American Negro Exhibit
Library of Congress, Daniel Murray Collection: African American Photographs Assembled for the 1900 Paris Exhibition Reproduction Number LC-USZ62-116617   39

3.3 Savage South Africa – Empress Theater
Reprinted from the *Official Catalogue of the Greater Britain Exhibition* (London: Spottiswoode & Co., 1899)   44

3.4 War Dance of Cape Lopez Blacks – Darkest Africa, Pan-American Exposition of 1901
Reprinted from Richard H. Barry, *Snap Shots on the Midway of the Pan-Am Expo* (Buffalo, NY: Robert Allan Reid, 1901)   49

3.5 Three "Culled Gemmen" – Old Plantation, Pan-American Exposition of 1901
Reprinted from Richard H. Barry, *Snap Shots on the Midway of the Pan-Am Expo* (Buffalo, NY: Robert Allan Reid, 1901)   50

6.1 Rosalee Pritchett (photo by Carlton Molette)   103

Acknowledgments

We would first like to thank the authors in this volume for responding to our call and working hard in revising their CAAR 2013 conference papers to the appropriate standards required for an anthology of this caliber. The anonymous peer reviewers played an important role in helping the contributors attain these standards. We are grateful for their queries, comments, and suggestions. Thanks to Cindy Hamilton and Alan Rice, general editors of the FORECAAST series. Special thanks to Cindy for her careful and patient editing of several drafts of the manuscript. Finally, we must acknowledge our families for kind words and best wishes as we plodded through the many stages of the creation of this collection. Particular thanks to P.J., Violet's son, the artist of the cover image.

Contributors

Mary Barr is the author of *Friends Disappear: The Battle for Racial Equality in Evanston* (University of Chicago Press, 2014), in which she writes about a group of childhood friends growing up in the Illinois suburb during the 1960s and '70s at the very height of local civil rights activism. She recently began archival research that examines integration efforts made by Chicago's all-white northern suburbs during the same period. Grants from the Congregational Library in Boston and libraries at the University of Wisconsin and the University of Virginia have supported this research. Previously, she has received fellowships from the National Endowment for the Humanities, Black Metropolis Research Consortium, and American Council of Learned Societies. Her areas of interest include twentieth-century African-American history, educational inequalities, and race and racism. Dr. Barr is an Assistant Professor of Sociology at Kentucky State University. She received her PhD in sociology and African American studies from Yale University.

Sara Busdiecker holds a PhD in anthropology from the University of Michigan. She is co-director of the African Diaspora Studies Program and faculty member in the International Studies Program at Spelman College in Atlanta, Georgia. Her research and publications focus on contemporary Afro-Latin America, with a particular emphasis on the intersections of Afro-descendant identity, collective organizing, performance, representation, and space/place in the contexts of Bolivia and Chile. She regularly teaches courses on Latin America and the global African diaspora. In the spirit of bridging scholarship and advocacy, she served as regional coordinator for the Andean Project for the Promotion of Afro-descendant Human Rights in Bolivia, Ecuador, and Peru, an effort sponsored by the UN Office of the High Commissioner for Human Rights in La Paz, Bolivia in 2009–2010.

Silvia Pilar Castro-Borrego is Lecturer of English and North American literature and culture at the University of Málaga, Spain. She has edited the volume *The Search for Wholeness and Diaspora Literacy in African American*

Literature (Cambridge Scholars, 2011), and published the articles "Re(claiming) Subjectivity and Transforming the Politics of Silence through the Search for Wholeness in *Push*" in *Atlantis* (2014) and "Integration, Assimilation, and Identity in Lorraine Hansberry's *A Raisin in the Sun* and Barbara and Carlton Molette's *Rosalee Pritchett*" in *Revista Canaria de Estudios Ingleses* (2015). Recent publications include the article "Claiming the Politics of Articulation through Agency and Wholeness in Two Afro-Hispanic Postcolonial Narratives" in JIWS (2016). In June 2017 she organized the twelfth CAAR conference at the University of Málaga under the theme "Diasporic Encounters, Subjectivities in Transit: Race, Gender, Religion and Sexualities in the African Diasporas" and is now a member of the research project "Bodies in Transit" at the universities of Huelva and Vigo (ref. FFI2013-47789-C2-1-P) http://bodiesintransitproject.com.

Clerc Cooper graduated *summa cum laude* from the College of Charleston, where she majored in history and African American studies. Her undergraduate research focused on public and Catholic school desegregation in Charleston, SC and New Orleans, LA. She is currently pursuing her Juris Doctor at Tulane University Law School.

Katharina Gerund is an assistant professor of American studies at Friedrich-Alexander-Universität Erlangen-Nürnberg, in Germany. She is the author of *Transatlantic Cultural Exchange: African American Women's Art and Activism in West Germany* (transcript Verlag, 2013) and the co-editor, with Alexandra Ganser and Heike Paul, of *Pirates, Drifters, Fugitives: Figures of Mobility in US Culture and Beyond* (Winter Verlag, 2012) and, with Frank Adloff and David Kaldewey, *Revealing Tacit Knowledge: Embodiment and Explication* (transcript Verlag, 2015). Katharina has lectured and published widely in the fields of African-American literature and culture, popular culture, Americanization, and cultural mobility as well as gender and diaspora studies. She is currently working on a monograph tentatively titled *Happy Home Front Heroines? Army Wives in US Literature and Culture*.

Gundolf Graml is Associate Professor and Director of German Studies as well as Faculty Coordinator for Global Learning at Agnes Scott College. His research interests focus on the role of travel, tourism, and space in the formation of identity narratives, on whiteness and German identity, and on the role of cultural narratives in the Anthropocene. His articles include "Black Bodies on White Snow: Revisualizing Germanness as Whiteness in Luis Trenker's *Prodigal Son* (1934)" and the forthcoming "'What had not happened in Chicago would finally happen in Berlin': Racial and Sexual Re-Mappings of Berlin in Darryl Pinckney's *Black Deutschland* (2016)." He is currently finishing a monograph titled *Revisiting Austria: Tourism, Space, and National Identity, 1945–2000*. He teaches the language, culture, and history of the German-speaking countries through courses such as Afro-German history and culture and faculty-led study abroad seminars in Germany, Austria, and Hungary.

Jon Hale is an associate professor of educational history at the University of South Carolina. His research focuses on the history of student and teacher activism, grassroots educational programs, and the role of southern black high schools during the civil rights movement. His publications include: *The Freedom Schools: A History of Student Activists on the Frontlines of the Mississippi Civil Rights Movement* (Columbia University Press, 2016) and (with William Sturkey) *The Freedom School Newspapers: Writings, Essays and Reports from Student Activists During the Civil Rights Movement* (University Press of Mississippi, 2015). His teaching focuses on the history of American education, the history of the civil rights movement, a history of student activism, and equity in education policy. Dr. Hale currently serves as the executive director of the Charleston Freedom School and co-director of the Quality Education Project.

Violet Showers Johnson is Associate Dean and Professor of History in the College of Liberal Arts at Texas A&M University. Her research focuses on the history of immigrants and refugees of African descent in the United States. She has authored and co-authored books and articles on the experiences of African and Afro-Caribbean immigrants. Her publications include: *The Other Black Bostonians: West Indians in Boston* (Indiana University Press, 2006) and (with Marilyn Halter) *African & American: West Africans in Post-Civil Rights America* (NYU Press, 2014). She has taught courses on race, ethnicity, and immigration in the United States, African-American history, African history, and the history of the African Diaspora. She is currently working on a monograph tentatively titled *Black While Foreign: African and Afro-Caribbean Immigrants and Race and Racism in Late 20th-Century America*. Dr. Showers Johnson is president of the Collegium for African American Research (CAAR).

Carsten Junker is Visiting Professor and Acting Chair of American Literature at the Institute for American Studies at Leipzig University. Previously, he was Assistant Professor of English-speaking Cultures/American Studies at the University of Bremen. For research on his second book on early abolition, he received the Christoph Daniel Ebeling fellowship, jointly sponsored by the German Association for American Studies and the American Antiquarian Society. Junker was visiting professor at the American Studies Center at the University of Warsaw in 2012. He obtained his doctorate in North American literature and culture from the Humboldt-Universität, Berlin, with a study on the essay as genre of cultural critique. His recent publications include *Patterns of Positioning: On the Poetics of Early Abolition* (Universitätsverlag Winter, 2016), co-edited with Sabine Broeck, *Postcoloniality—Decoloniality—Black Critique* (Campus, 2014), and, with Marie-Luise Löffler, *Black Studies—Paradigm Shifts*, a special issue of *Zeitschrift für Anglistik und Amerikanistik—A Quarterly of Language, Literature and Culture* (De Gruyter, 2017).

Patricia Williams Lessane is the Executive Director of the College of Charleston's Avery Research Center for African American History and Culture, where she is a tenured faculty member in the library. Dr. Williams Lessane is currently co-editing *We Carry These Memories Inside of We: Celebrating Daughters of the Dust and the Blacks Arts Aesthetic of Julie Dash*, under contract with University of South Carolina Press. Her 2015 *New York Times* editorial "No Sanctuary in Charleston" gave personal and social commentary on African-American life in Charleston following the massacre at Mother Emmanuel Church. In 2016, she was a Fulbright scholar at University of Málaga, Spain.

Philip Ojo is Ashe Professor of French and Francophone Studies at Agnes Scott College. His research focuses on francophone literature with a concentration on Africa and the Caribbean. He is also interested in global issues, particularly migrant experience, as well as expressions of identities and social conditions in popular culture as a platform for criticism, change, and nation building. He has published on the articulation of these issues in fiction, music, cartooning, cinema, and drama. He is currently working on a project on the role of African communities in the transformation of the landscape of European mega-cities. Ojo also maintains http://philipaojo.agnesscott.org/, a website aimed at promoting the understanding and study of French and francophone cultures worldwide.

Thomas E. Smith is an associate professor of history at Chadron State College. His research focuses on the history of the modern Atlantic world, including Pan-Africanism and reform. He teaches courses on modern Africa, the history of the diaspora, and the history of the Atlantic world. He has published articles in the *Journal of Colonialism and Colonial History* and the *Journal of Transatlantic Studies*. He is currently working on a manuscript titled *Crowning Abolitionism: The Pan-African Search for Racial Equality at the Turn of the Twentieth Century*.

1
Introduction: Deferred Dreams, Defiant Struggles

Violet Showers Johnson (Texas A&M University),
Gundolf Graml (Agnes Scott College),
and Patricia Williams Lessane (College of Charleston)

The Collegium for African American Research marked the fiftieth anniversary of the March on Washington by holding its biennial conference in Atlanta, a bulwark of the civil rights movement and the birthplace of Martin Luther King, Junior. This volume has grown out of that conference. It acknowledges the defiant struggles and deferred dreams of African Americans while accepting the challenge offered by that anniversary to take stock, interrogating the Black experience across epochs and locations. At the March on Washington on August 28, 1963, Martin Luther King delivered his iconic "I Have a Dream" speech. It is a speech that continues to resonate because of King's articulation of the optimism of African-descended people in the midst of continuing exclusion from an American polity that they themselves had helped to construct. In his speech, King indicts America while affirming the resolve of African Americans to hold the republic to its "promissory note to which every American was to fall heir" but on which "America has defaulted […] insofar as her citizens of color are concerned. Instead of honoring this sacred obligation, America has given the Negro people a bad check." King demanded that his country "cash this check, a check that will give us upon demand the riches of freedom and security of justice." King's rhetoric encapsulates two fundamental themes addressed by the 2013 Biennial Conference of the Collegium for African American Research (CAAR)[1] and of the present volume: the persistent dashing of the dreams and aspirations of African-descended peoples for inclusion, equality, and justice around the world; and the equally relentless resolve of Blacks to fight for civil and human rights for themselves and others.

---

[1] The Collegium for African American Research is a Europe-based organization that was formed by a group of European scholars of African American studies. By its twentieth year, in 2013, CAAR had become one of the biggest international organizations devoted to Black studies.

The civil rights movement in America and contemporaneous black struggles elsewhere have made significant gains, but important aspirations remain unrealized and some dreams newly born out of the freedom struggles of the 1950s and 1960s remain unfulfilled. Even in the twenty-first century, racialized discrimination and direct assaults on blackness continue to be pervasive, to the extent that, as Michelle Alexander famously noted, there has emerged "a new Jim Crow" (2010). The modern civil rights movement has assumed international proportions, but the United States is still its epicenter, continuing to expose the enduring legacies of slavery, of Jim Crow, of political, economic, and legal injustices. The American civil rights movement forged black protest strategies that have had international impact. "We Shall Overcome," the "Negro protest rallying song," became a universal anthem of protest (see Redmond, 2014, esp. Chapter 4; Bobetsky, 2014). The movement in the United States continues to highlight the centuries-old deferred dreams.

Nonetheless, the struggle has always been international, responding to a racism that has proved to be as pervasive as it is pernicious. Brazil, which received the largest number of slaves in the Atlantic trade, embarked on a denial of blackness, even as it touted its supposed racial democracy. In Honduras, racist and exclusionary policies toward Afro-Caribbean immigrants were adopted from the late nineteenth century to the mid-twentieth century, even as these immigrants' labor was exploited in the development of that nation (see Chambers, 2010). In Mexico, racial bigotry enabled Spanish colonial elites to construct a caste system of racial subtypes (Overmyer-Velázquez, 2013, 11). So entrenched had this racist positioning become by independence that postcolonial revolutionaries were unsuccessful in distancing themselves from the colonial-era racial constructs. In their insistence on a unified national *mestizo* race, they embraced the notion that people of African descent were "a negative stain on racial progress," ignoring the vital roles that Blacks had played in the establishment and formation of Mexico since the colonial era (Overmyer-Velázquez, 12; see also Bennett, 2009).

Even recognition for glaringly obvious Black accomplishments has been deferred. Almost a century after the Haitian Revolution resulted in the establishment of the second republic in the western hemisphere, that nation struggled for recognition. In his "Lecture on Haiti" delivered at the World's Fair, Jackson Park, Chicago on January 2, 1893, Frederick Douglass bluntly exposed the reason for the disrespectful treatment of Haiti, then the "only self-made Black Republic in the world": "Haiti is black, and we have not yet forgiven Haiti for being black or forgiven the Almighty for making her black."

The worldwide struggle for recognition and justice has been maintained in every epoch when hopes and dreams were dashed by the realities of captivity, oppression, suppression, misrepresentations, and exclusion. Queen

Elizabeth I made two attempts to deport African-descended people to Spain and Portugal. The fact that the deportation never happened, because recalcitrant masters were concerned about the economic implications of losing their black workers, should not preclude recognition of the racial factors that influenced the queen's "economic" initiative. In her first request in 1596, the queen complained of the "divers blackmoores brought into this realme, of which kinde of people there are already here too manie" ("Queen Elizabeth," 16–17). In 1601, she objected to the "great numbers of Negars and Blackamoors" who had "crept into this realm," describing them as infidels with no understanding of Christ or his Gospel (qtd. Jones, 1971, 20–21). Centuries later, during the reign of Elizabeth II, Enoch Powell's blatant and vicious racism found expression in his notorious "Rivers of Blood" speech delivered to a Conservative Association meeting in Birmingham, England, April 20, 1968. Lamenting the deterioration of Great Britain, he blamed society's woes on the influx of Commonwealth immigrants, specifically from South Asia and the West Indies, immigrants whose children had been inculcated with the tactics of the freedom struggle ("Enoch Powell's 'Rivers of Blood' Speech," 2007).

Other European "mother countries" exhibited similar racial xenophobia towards immigrants from former colonies in Africa and the Caribbean, rejecting populations in a way that did not preclude exploitation. Under the Bureau pour le développement des migrations dans les départments d'outre-mer, France sought to ensure an uninterrupted supply of cheap, compliant labor for her industries by regulating migration from her "overseas departments," former colonies primarily in the Caribbean, but also in Africa. Similar histories of extensive black migration, labor exploitation, and anti-black racism span Western Europe as people of African descent arrived in the European metropolises in unprecedented numbers from former colonies. Surinamese immigrants who arrived and settled in the Netherlands,[2] and Congolese and Rwandan immigrants in Belgium,[3] suffered a similar fate.

Even on the African continent itself, blackness has been under assault. Race was at the center of the conquest, colonization, and arbitrary partitioning of Africa. The disrespect for most things African and the audacious attempts to eradicate and replace them with things European did not originate only from nationalistic superiority but fundamentally from an ethnocentricy that presumed the inherent inferiority of blackness. Wole Soyinka, Chinua Achebe, Ngugi Wa Thiong'o, and Ousmane Sembene have tackled the racial

---

[2] For a concise but insightful account of the Black Surinamese presence in the Netherlands, see Deogratias, Singleton, and Wojtalewicz (2017).
[3] For a simple but useful synopsis of the presence of francophone Africans in Belgium, see Kano (2009).

and racist dimensions of the European colonial project on the continent. In two world wars, Africans were coerced to fight, but did so also in the hope of full, more respectful inclusion into European empires. The subsequent unfulfilled promises led to African nationalism and independence after the Second World War.[4] Nowhere was the racist insidiousness of colonialism more overt than in southern Africa, in Rhodesia (Zimbabwe), South Africa, and German Southwest Africa (Namibia).

Nonetheless, the new millennium began with high hopes. African nations celebrated half a century of independence, the reintroduction of multiparty political systems and efforts at expanding democracy, even as some of them continued to deal with civil wars. The United States elected its first Black president. Few were more optimistic about a post-racial America than Barack Hussein Obama during his candidacy and the first year of his presidency. But there were too many unresolved faults in the centuries-old structure to allow for the rapid relegation of race and racism envisioned by Obama and others. As sociologist Eduardo Bonilla-Silva has pointed out, a new form of racism—color-blind racism that employed more subtle pronouncements and tactics to sustain and justify racial inequities—had emerged, as insidious as the one it replaced.[5]

But many of the pronouncements and tactics of enduring discrimination and racism have been less subtle. A rash of violent and deadly encounters with law enforcement agencies in the United States mark the rise of a brutal, officially sanctioned racism: Eric Garner died from a police chokehold on July 17, 2014; Fergusson, Missouri exploded after the killing of Michael Brown by a police officer on August 9, 2014; Tamir Rice, 12 years old, was gunned down by Cleveland, Ohio police officers on November 22, 2014; Walter Scott was hunted down and killed by a North Charleston police officer on April 4, 2015; Freddie Gray died in Baltimore Police custody one week later, on April 12; Sandra Bland died in custody, possibly by suicide, in Hampstead, Texas on July 13; and the list goes on. Prior to these encounters with the police, Trayvon Martin was killed by a vigilante in Sanford, Florida on February 26, 2012; his killer, George Zimmerman was subsequently acquitted in July 2013. These incidents and many others, which became *causes célèbres*, highlighted the continuation of the black struggle in post-civil rights America.

Such overt racism was certainly not confined to the United States. In the Dominican Republic, the ruling of the Dominican Constitutional Court retroactively stripped citizenship from those born after 1929 to parents without

---

[4] For examples of African contributions to the two world wars and the activism that followed, see Killingray and Omissi (1999) and Killingray and Plaut (2010).

[5] Eduardo Bonilla-Silva (2003) expounds on this discourse comprehensively in his multi-edition work *Racism without Racists*.

Dominican ancestry, a ruling which overwhelmingly affected the descendants of black Haitians. In Israel, Blacks from Ethiopia were labeled as a different kind of Jew. Germany, France, and Great Britain saw the rise of extreme right-wing movements seeking to exclude non-whites from full citizenship. No other issue brought this reality to the forefront as much as the backlash against immigration. Contemporary bloggers and tweeters disseminated sentiments reminiscent of Enoch Powell's anti-immigrant diatribe, demonstrating that twenty-first-century assaults on blackness, though exhibiting their own unique characteristics in the age of technology, have not changed.

The essays collected here do not present a continuous story of oppression and protest, nor do they chronicle the denial and curtailment of the rights and freedoms of African-descended people. Instead, they explore the dynamic interrelationships of hope, disappointment, and struggle. Part I, "Diaspora, Displacement, Marginalization, and Collective Identities," investigates deferred dreams and struggles in a transnational and global context. Drawing on the concept of mobility studies, Katharina Gerund's essay sheds new light on the role of Josephine Baker as transnational activist. As singer and entertainer, as member of the French *résistance* and spy against the Nazis, as participant activist in the March on Washington, and as "model mother" of her so-called "rainbow tribe" residing in a French *château*, Baker has occupied roles that have repeatedly defied easy reconciliation because of apparently contradictory elements. Thus, Josephine Baker exemplifies the transnational flow of black activist ideas and demonstrates the shifting form of the struggle in different national contexts at different times. Thomas Smith examines pan-African ideas in the context of turn-of-the-century World's Fairs. He argues that while these exhibitions initially failed to challenge the concept of a "global color line," the contradictions exposed by them ultimately generated a more militant pan-African protest movement. Philip Ojo looks at the way African immigrants' experience of marginalization in metropolitan Paris is presented in the work of Cameroonian Calixthe Beyala's *Loukoum: The Little Prince of Belleville* (1995) and in Guadeloupean Myriam Warner-Vieyra's *Juletane* (1987). Ojo analyzes the complex intercultural tensions that shape migrants' experiences in these texts. Taken together, these three essays demonstrate that while unfulfilled promises are a global issue, deferred dreams cannot be discussed without an awareness of place. As cultural geographer Doreen Massey phrases it, only an understanding of places as "open and porous networks of social relations" will lead to a situation whereby places, even marginalized ones, are able to generate their own simultaneous but different histories that can ultimately challenge still dominating imperialist historical narratives (1994, 121).

Part II, "Performing Identities, Reclaiming the Self," recognizes the need for Black speakers to disrupt and reconstruct socially constructed discourses of blackness through artistic and religious performativity. Carsten Junker examines the tradition of "dying speeches" wherein Black, mainly male, criminals confessed their transgressions. Ostensibly intended to provide a redemptive means for the condemned to enter the community of saved Christians, these dying confessions, berating and indicting the speaker's blackness, further excluded those whose confessions were recorded. By exposing the complicated interplay of enslavement, law, religion, and abolition, Junker suggests the deeper levels of political disenfranchisement that lurk behind the social construction of Black criminal identities. Silvia Castro-Borrego examines the Black Nationalist playwrights Carlton and Barbara Molette, situating their work within "the theater of experience." Rejecting assimilation, the Molettes' characters embody African retentions and cultural sensibilities, demonstrating the importance of African-centered thought in the struggle for Black liberation, rejecting notions of empire as concomitant with expressions of Black identity, and invoking Black power both as subject matter and as a tool of resistance.

Part III, "Moved to Act: Civil Rights Activism in the US and Beyond," tells the story of the civil rights movement through lesser known, yet vitally illuminating, struggles. The essay by Jon Hale and Clerc Cooper uses Charleston, South Carolina to illuminate the complex struggle for racial equality in education. Hale and Cooper demonstrate that access to high-quality public education in Charleston has remained racially unequal. In defiance of this system, Blacks have sought ways of providing a meaningful and effective education for their children. From the early twentieth century, the National Association for the Advancement of Colored People (NAACP) directly confronted, through the courts, institutionalized, systemic injustice, and local grassroots activists attacked the flawed implementation of "equalization" and agitated instead for desegregation.

Mary Barr recounts a little-known, but significant story in the struggle to desegregate housing in Chicago through community mobilization. Barr concentrates on the Summer Project of 1965, which brought together a diverse group of activists employing a range of strategies to expose and defy discrimination in housing. Student volunteers, supervised by seasoned civil rights activists, took an inventory of housing discrimination in Chicago's North Shore suburbs in a campaign that ultimately fell short of its hoped-for impact. Barr reminds us that the progress of the civil rights movement has been uneven and that its history in the United States is not merely a history of the American south.

Sara Busdiecker sheds much-needed light on the neglected presence of African-descended people in Chile. The activists Busdiecker studies have attempted to reclaim ancestry on their own terms, emphasizing "descent over race" and claiming a non-racial ancestry even as they embrace their

African descent. Busdiecker assesses the rationales and activities of those who confront the challenge of rallying behind a non-racial African descent while inhabiting bodies perceived as White or *Mestizo*.

Taken as a whole, this volume seeks to promote a more nuanced understanding of the dynamics of the struggle against racism in its many guises. Studying the particularities of aspects of that struggle within specific historical and intellectual contexts not only displays the vicissitudes of the fight for equality and the hydra-headed nature of racism, but also the fortitude and creativity of those who have fought and continue to fight against injustices. Case studies such as those on offer here help to build critical frameworks for a fuller understanding of the origins and evolution of present-day challenges and accomplishments in the lived experiences of people of African descent.

Works Cited

Alexander, Michelle. *The New Jim Crow: Mass Incarceration in the Age of Colorblindness.* New York: The New Press, 2010.
Bennett, Herman. *Colonial Blackness: A History of Afro-Mexico.* Bloomington, IN: Indiana University Press, 2009.
Bobetsky, Victor. *We Shall Overcome: Essays on a Great American Song.* New York: Rowman & Littlefield, 2014.
Bonilla-Silva, Eduardo. *Racism without Racists: Color-Blind Racism and the Persistence of Racial Inequality in the United States.* New York: Rowman & Littlefield, 2003.
Chambers, Glenn. *Race, Nation, and West Indian Immigration to Honduras, 1890–1940.* Baton Rouge, LA: Louisiana State University Press, 2010.
Deogratias, Benedicta, Kyera Singleton, and Casey Wojtalewicz. "Race in the Netherlands: The Place of the Surinamese in Contemporary Dutch Society." *Humanity in Action.* Dec. 29, 2017. https://www.humanityinaction.org/knowledgebase/372-race-in-the-netherlands-the-place-of-the-surinamese-in-contemporary-dutch-society. Accessed June 1, 2015.
Douglass, Frederick. "Lecture on Haiti." http://www2.webster.edu/~corbetre/haiti/history/1844-1915/douglass.htm. Accessed May 15, 2015.
"Enoch Powell's 'Rivers of Blood' Speech." *Telegraph.* Nov. 6, 2007. http://www.telegraph.co.uk/comment/3643823/Enoch-Powells-Rivers-of-Blood-speech.html. Accessed May 14, 2015.
Jones, Eldred. *The Elizabethan Image of Africa.* Charlottesville, VA: University of Virginia Press, 1971.
Kano, Sibo. "Afro-Europe: Black People in Contemporary Belgium." *Afro-Europe.* Apr. 26, 2009. http://afroeurope.blogspot.com/2009/04/black-people-in-contemporary-belgium.html. Accessed Jun. 1, 2015.

Killingray, David, and David Omissi, eds. *Guardians of the Empire: The Armed Forces of the Colonial Powers, 1700–1964*. Manchester: Manchester University Press, 1999.

Killingray, David, and Martin Plaut. *Fighting for Britain: African Soldiers in the Second World War*. London: James Currey, 2010.

Massey, Doreen. *Space, Place, and Gender*. Minneapolis, MN: University of Minnesota Press, 1994.

Overmyer-Velázquez, Mark. "Good Neighbors and White Mexicans: Constructing Race and Nation on the Mexico-U.S. Border." *Journal of American Ethnic History* 33.1 (Fall 2013): 5–34.

"Queen Elizabeth to the Lord Mayor et al. July 1596." In *Acts of the Privy Council of England*. Ed. John Roche Dasent. London: Mackie, 1902: 16–17.

Redmond, Shana. *Anthem: Social Movements and the Sound of Solidarity in the African Diaspora*. New York: New York University Press, 2014.

DIASPORA, DISPLACEMENT, MARGINALIZATION, AND COLLECTIVE IDENTITIES

2

Josephine Baker's Routes and Roots: Mobility, Belonging, and Activism in the Atlantic World

Katharina Gerund (FAU Erlangen-Nürnberg)

I. Introduction[1]

Josephine Baker is probably best remembered for her flamboyant performances as singer, dancer, and actress. In popular representations as in scholarly discourse, her image has been dominated by the iconography of her early dance acts and particularly the (in)famous banana skirt which is "forever associated with her name" (Glover, 2007–2008, 2). In the 1920s and 1930s, the time of her meteoric rise to international stardom, Baker came to represent American culture for European audiences and, simultaneously, European modernism for American audiences. In both contexts, she was frequently understood as an embodiment of a "primitive" culture lost to modern Western societies. For Europeans she was a foreign novelty, "representative of all that was the opposite of European urban modernity" (Nenno, 1997, 150). She represented their "stranger within" so that European audiences could imaginatively explore their "internal Africa" without, ultimately, destabilizing racial boundaries or challenging their white superiority (Dayal, 2004, 41). Baker became a "floating signifier" for "just about any kind of racial, ethnic, or national otherness" (Ngai, 2006, 166) or, at least, a "slippery signifier in the racial and sexual spectacles of Jazz Age popular culture" (Borshuk, 2001, 55). As a cultural icon, she was highly mobile and apparently easily appropriated and commodified in different contexts: in Weimar Germany, for example, her beauty secrets were revealed in women's magazines, Baker dolls were sold in stores as early as 1926 (Nenno, 1997, 157), and her life inspired Josef Sternberg's 1932 film *Blonde Venus*, which stars Marlene Dietrich and retells Baker's story in "almost perfectly symmetrical 'reversal'" (Ngai, 2006, 149). Baker was

---

[1] I would like to thank the editors of this volume as well as my anonymous reviewer for crucial feedback and helpful remarks.

imitated, for example, by the African-American dancer Ruth Bayton, who posed in a banana costume and was consequently called the "Josephine Baker of Berlin," or "German comedian Ilse Bois [who] did her grotesque dances and ironic comments on the jazz craze [...] 'Afro'-hairstyled and banana-girded at the Kabarett der Komiker in Berlin" (Naumann, 1998, 103). Baker herself contributed to her currency as an icon and to her successful commodification. Andrea Barnwell even claims that she "was always the principal agent of her reception, compelling her audience to examine the binary oppositions she created" (1997, 88).

As Janet Lyon aptly points out, "the kaleidoscopic nature of her public life has left a fractured composite portrait. [...] 'Josephine Baker' never coheres into a stable historical identity" (2001, 30).[2] Consequently, she "has always been treated as an enigmatic figure by cultural critics" (Lyon, 2001, 29). Baker helped to create this elusive public persona through several autobiographies and by making contradictory statements about her biography.[3] Though she may have had some degree of agency over her image, Baker was never able to overcome the powerful iconography of her early career, which continues to overshadow her (later) career and persona. Her enigmatic image may help to explain why, for example, her engagement in political and humanitarian activism, anti-racist work, and the black liberation struggle have not received intensive scholarly attention. Baker is enshrined in France's collective memory and cultural imaginary; and she is honored particularly for her dedication to the French resistance during the Second World War. Monuments and public places commemorate her work, art, and activism, and she is even considered a potential candidate for the Panthéon.[4] Despite her visibility in France and French-language scholarship, most anglophone studies tend to focus on her dance and film performances and their cultural impact. Overall, the scholarship on Baker in cultural history and criticism has so far largely neglected significant aspects of Baker's later career and the political dimensions of her work as artist and activist.[5] The 2007–2008

---

[2] I agree with Bennetta Jules-Rosette that it is more fruitful to explore the "constructed images and nested narratives that constitute her persona and the social strategies that she used to bring these images to life" than to search for the "true" Baker (2007, 4–5).

[3] Baker's autobiographies certainly merit a systematic analysis in order to establish a more comprehensive picture of her politicization, her discursive agency, and the development of her thinking. The exploration of these lines of inquiry lies beyond the scope of this article, which is interested more in Baker's situatedness and/or marginalization in specific scholarly fields than in her diverse narratives of her life and career.

[4] The idea has been prominently promoted by philosopher Régis Debray in a 2013 article in *Le Monde* and has sparked a broad debate in French and international media.

[5] In her excellent study *Josephine Baker in Art and Life: The Icon and the Image*, one of the most notable exceptions in this regard, Jules-Rosette asserts that several studies dealing with

special issue of *The Feminist and Scholar Online* on Baker is a case in point. Guest editor Kaiama L. Glover emphasizes that the volume "considers the big picture of Baker's life" and focuses "on the many ways in which her trajectory coincided and intersected with some of the most significant artistic and political phenomena of the last hundred years" (2007–2008, 2). Yet most of the contributions (essays, talks, performances) focus on the beginnings of Baker's career in Paris, her audiences, her performances on stage and on screen, the artistic and political dimensions of her dance and her body, as well as her continuing cultural reverberations. Baker's political activism receives little attention beyond the well-known debates about her agency, the political aspects of her performances, and the spectacle of her black female body—all of which are interpreted differently by critics and located somewhere between (implicit) subversive resistance and self-Orientalization or (commodified) exoticism. Anthea Kraut points out that writing about Baker, "one inevitable confronts the question of agency" (2007–2008, 1)—not only with regard to her performances as dancer, singer, and actress but also concerning her political activism and her public persona. Baker, in fact, even "staged her private life for public consumption, performing a vast array of personae in many different locations: as star of stage and film, as modernist muse, femme fatale, primitive savage, [and later] international spy, transnational antiracist activist, and as an icon of motherhood" (Scheper, 2007, 73). The diverse roles and potential subject positions which Baker occupied on and off stage and screen need to be analyzed in their interconnectedness and in their sociocultural and historical contexts.

For the purpose of this essay, however, I am less interested in the (implicit) political dimensions of Baker's artistic work and (the contexts of) her rise to stardom than in her role as an activist in the French resistance and in the US-American civil rights movement as well as her self-fashioning as mother, head of state, and humanitarian at Les Milandes—the French *château* she turned into both her stage *and* her home during her later life, an elaborate public tourist site and her domestic refuge. Like Baker the artist and cultural icon, Baker the political activist was highly mobile—culturally, socially, and geographically—in the Atlantic world; yet, somewhat in contrast to her stage personae, which functioned as signifier of "Otherness" in so many contexts, Baker also navigated multiple and shifting affiliations and modes of belonging and—again—turned herself into a projection screen for various desires, anxieties, and hopes. These aspects of Baker's life have

---

"Baker's life as performer end with the peak of her early career in 1935" (2007, 183). Matthew Pratt Guterl's *Josephine Baker and the Rainbow Tribe* strives to set the record straight and offers "an attempt [...] to reimagine Baker as a serious and determined, if wildly iconoclastic, thinker and activist in the age of modern revolutions" (2014, 6).

not yet received sufficient attention. Matthew Pratt Guterl observes: "As a historical subject, Baker resists any easy approach. Recognizable but relatively unknown or misunderstood, she appears—usually as a casual reference—across the widest spectrum of cultural and historical narratives. [...] it is remarkable how little sustained attention has been given to Baker's life and political practice" (2009, 40). Considering that Baker can be regarded an exemplary figure of the "Black Atlantic" (Paul Gilroy), that her life can be interpreted as a transnational case study of cultural mobility and, arguably, of Cold War black protest (which unsettles the very parameters of the dominant understandings of this protest), and that her social experiment at Les Milandes can be analyzed as a "utopian" version and vision of cosmopolitanism, it seems quite astonishing that Baker does not appear prominently in any of these flourishing fields (Guterl, 2009, 40).[6] The goal of my essay is twofold. First, I will zoom in on Josephine Baker's political activism, particularly in the French resistance and the civil rights movement in the context of transnational black activism in the mid-twentieth century and with an eye to its perception, dismissal, or appropriation in scholarly and public discourses. Second, I will analyze (the constructions of) Baker's shifting and sometimes conflicting affiliations in the transatlantic world—to nation-states, communities, and political purposes—and focus on her (cultural) mobility in connection with her different forms of belonging and her attempts to create a home. Overall, I hope to provide some tentative thoughts on how current research paradigms (particularly mobility studies and transnational American studies) may offer new perspectives on Baker's art, life, and activism and how she might, in turn, offer an interesting case study within these paradigms. In the context of the present volume, this focus on Baker's political life and travels allows for a (re)consideration of civil rights activism within a transatlantic frame as well as a negotiation of diasporic modes of belonging and marginalization. It sheds light on how Baker's changing positionalities, mechanisms of inclusion and exclusion in different social contexts, and experiences of displacement and exile partially determined her political work and how she was simultaneously constructed by these discourses.

---

[6] Guterl's observation holds true in the context of English-language research in American and cultural studies but might appear in a different light if one accounts for the French-language scholarship and Baker's popularity in France. Similarly, my own reading of her activism, national belonging, and cultural mobility is informed by the scholarship in these fields and responds to a blind spot specifically within this disciplinary discourse.

II. Mobility, Resistance, and Civil Rights

"J'ai deux amours" (1930), one of Josephine Baker's signature songs, already indicates her (at least) double affiliation—to France and the US—that shaped not only her life narrative but also her political activism. Margo Jefferson claims that "Wherever she was, wherever she went, Josephine was a foreign body; she never belonged fully to anybody or any body politic" (2007–2008, 1). Narratives of her life frequently depict Baker as not only searching for a home, a place, or a community where she could belong but also constantly (though one could argue not always voluntarily) on the move in several senses: she was geographically mobile as she crisscrossed the Atlantic and toured the world, she was socially mobile as she became an established international star moving confidently in different social circles and milieus, and she was culturally mobile as she navigated her affiliations to black traditions, white cultural institutions, and audiences from diverse cultural contexts. One could even say that she "made her life a spectacular traveling production; she found new roles and plotlines for herself (military spy, political activist, global mother)" (Jefferson, 2007–2008, 5). Yet her life story might not only be read as a quest for home and belonging or a traveling production but also as "a series of flights" from "toil, fitful maternal care, sexual bargins [sic] struck and marriages made too soon […] toward safety, […] pleasure, […] and glory" (Jefferson, 2007–2008, 5).

Baker's life story—whether in her own accounts or in scholarly, journalistic, and essayistic narratives—is essentially shaped by her transatlantic routes and her attempts to establish roots. Considering that mobility can be "both central to power and a threat to it" (Cresswell, 2012, 8), Baker's movements across geographical, social, and cultural spaces are revealing of the power structures that shape established routes and safeguard their boundaries and thus make some forms of mobility "ideologically sound" while stigmatizing others (Cresswell, 2006, 58). The proclaimed "mobility turn" (Hannam, Sheller, and Urry, 2006, 1) or the so-called "new mobilities paradigm" (see Urry 2007) in the social sciences have recently (re)directed scholarly attention to issues of mobility, movement, immobility, and motility.[7] This development corresponds to a "new critical attention paid to space and geographical as well as cultural mobility" in American studies (Paul, Ganser,

---

[7] Mimi Sheller elaborates that "critical mobilities research advances a relational basis for social theorizing that puts mobility, immobility and their associated power relations at its center; it proposes a research agenda around the study of various complex systems, assemblages, regimes and practices of (im)mobility; and at times involves a normative emphasis of addressing the future of mobility in relation to ecological sustainability and mobility justice" (2013, 2).

and Gerund, 2012, 16), even though, as Mimi Sheller claims, it has not yet gained a strong foothold in the field of transnational American studies (2013, 1). In transnational American studies, however, as put forth most prominently by Shelley Fisher Fishkin, mobility plays a central role. Fisher Fishkin elaborates that this emerging field will, among other things, focus on "historical roots of multidirectional flows of people, ideas, and goods and the social, political, linguistic, cultural, and economic crossroads generated in the process," "investigations of [...] cultural crossroads shaping the work of border-crossing authors, artists, and cultural forms that straddle multiple regional and national traditions," and "chapters of African American history lurking in archives outside the United States as well" (2005, 22, 32, 28). Josephine Baker's life, work, and activism could be a case study *par excellence* in this context and at the same time showcase some of the limitations of transnational American studies: most of her letters and notes included in the Henry Hurford Janes-Josephine Baker Collection housed at Yale University's Beinecke Rare Books and Manuscripts Library are written in French, a lot of the scholarly work on Baker is published in English, and studying her reception in diverse places such as Germany, Cuba, Japan, or Argentina requires not only a sufficient knowledge of those different languages but also a certain degree of cultural literacy. Baker can easily fall through the cracks of American or French studies (with their respective national foci) and she can readily be marginalized in African American and black studies (due to her seemingly marginal role in civil rights activism, her early iconography, and her controversial artistic and political performances). Yet her life and activism might exemplarily expose conflicting cultural and political forces within the black diaspora (and draw special attention to the genealogies and developments within the African American expatriate community in France); the structures and strictures of gendered, racialized, and national discourses and belongings; and the difficult task of taking "adequate" political and activist measures against discrimination, racism, and marginalization—particularly from a position of relative privilege, including a high degree of mobility, social and economic capital, and star status.

Baker used her privileged mobility and her celebrity status to transgress boundaries and to challenge established paths. She openly supported several political agendas, particularly the French resistance during the Second World War and the civil rights movement in the United States in the 1950s and 1960s. According to Bennetta Jules-Rosette, Baker's life as political activist can be structured around four roles: "(1) the spokeswoman; (2) the warrior and spy; (3) the militant and martyr; and (4) the head of family and state. These roles were interconnected across four stages of her political career, and each built on the other, creating her total political persona" (2007, 215). Baker's political consciousness was raised during her international tours in the late 1920s; upon her return to the US, she felt driven to act as a spokeswoman for equality and civil rights. During the war years, she was active for the French counterintelligence and resistance, and later became an ardent crusader against racism and segregation. Her political affiliations and activism have been variously received and commemorated. In the US context, her contribution to the civil rights movement is largely marginalized, while in France, Baker is predominantly cast as "une ardente patriote" who immediately and without hesitation signed up to support the French resistance, and as a "Gaulliste de la première heure" (Onana, 2013, 64, 74). Finally, Baker stayed in France and, at Les Milandes, fashioned herself as head of her own state and family.

According to Lynn Haney, it was The Night of the Broken Glass (*Reichskristallnacht*, November 9–10, 1938) which "radicalized [Baker], who remembered the storm troopers hurling ammonia bombs at her and shouting 'Go back to Africa' when she had performed in Germany and Eastern Europe in the late 1920s" (1981, 215).[8] In 1938, Baker had already officially and legally become a French citizen through her marriage to Jean Lion the previous year. She ultimately became part of the French resistance against the Nazis and "deployed her divadom as a political weapon, given that it provided her with both a cover and the privilege of mobility" (Scheper, 2007, 83). After the Allies declared war against Germany in 1939, Baker volunteered for the Red Cross, started to write letters to soldiers, and performed for the French troops deployed at the German frontier (see Haney, 1981, 216). Most of her biographers emphasize her steadfast patriotism and loyalty to her husband's country—as Baker herself often did in her life narratives, statements, and performances. Jean-Claude Baker and Chris Chase, for example, affirm that "she was ready to go all the way for her adopted country" (2001, 225). Jacques Abtey,[9] an officer working for the French military intelligence service, enlisted her as a spy, one of the "Honorable Correspondents who could travel around without attracting attention, and who would be able to report on what they saw" (Abtey qtd. in Baker and Chase, 2001, 226).[10] Baker's first "mission" was to visit the Italian

---

[8] Baker joined the International League against Racism and anti-Semitism after *Reichskristallnacht*, which may have had a personal dimension for her because her husband at the time, Jean Lion, was Jewish (see Wood, 2000, 212–213).

[9] In 1948, Abtey published *La guerre secrète de Joséphine Baker*, which detailed her wartime activities. As Phyllis Rose points out, her story could be enlisted by the "Gaullists in their postwar efforts to rewrite history, making France look as though it had been united behind de Gaulle in active resistance, and in their political struggle to hold on to the colonies in North Africa and the Middle East." But, as Rose also confirms, Baker's heroism was "real" and her Croix de Guerre "well-deserved" (1991, 182).

[10] He had no budget and therefore could not hire professionals. The enlisted patriots had to work for "la gloire et la patrie" alone (Baker and Chase, 2001, 226).

embassy and acquire information about Italy's possible involvement in the war; and, apparently, she was quite successful in that endeavor (see Onana, 2013, 64). She received several assignments from the Deuxième Bureau while she was also involved in entertaining the troops (see Baker and Chase, 2001, 227). When the Germans occupied Paris, Baker left for the countryside and, ultimately, Abtey and Baker used her cover as an international celebrity in order to travel abroad and to get important information to Britain (see Baker and Chase, 2001, 229–235; Rose, 1991, 185–187). Early on, Baker refused to perform in German-occupied France—she allegedly said that "As long as there's a German in France, Josephine won't sing"—but she would go on stage in the unoccupied zone (see Rose, 1991, 189). She continued to perform in several countries and to work for the French military intelligence, particularly in North Africa. There, she regularly entertained Allied soldiers (despite severe health issues), and she continued to promote Free France and Charles de Gaulle (see Rose, 1991, 200–202).[11] In fact, she was coopted as a "mobile demonstration of Free France's respect for people of color and, as such, an important part of the campaign to hold on to the African colonies" (Rose, 1991, 202). When Paris was liberated, Baker left for France with a unit of air force women (she was a member of the Ladies' Auxiliary for the French air force) and "came back a heroine of the resistance" (Baker and Chase, 2001, 260–261). While her motives and dedication to the French resistance have been doubted and criticized due to her uncritical embrace of French politics under de Gaulle (including colonial politics), Baker's image as heroine of the resistance prevailed and was bolstered by the official and military honors bestowed upon her for her wartime efforts, including a Croix de Guerre and, in 1957, her nomination as Chevalier de la Légion d'honneur (see Onana, 2013, 111–128, 181). Moreover, Baker's Second World War experiences may have been the "catalyst that brought out [her] political and humanitarian dimensions" (Haney, 1981, 246) and, as Phyllis Rose claims, "In the American struggle for civil rights, she saw a continuation of the war she had fought to free the world from racism" (1991, 208).

Throughout her career, Baker remained outspoken against fascism and racism alike:

[A]s a vocal critic of racial discrimination, Baker spoke out internationally about the lives of African Americans and other people of color in the US. [...] Later she would draw explicit connections between fascism, apartheid, and racism in different national contexts. [...] Using the moral

---

[11] In 1943, Baker performed at the opening of the Liberty Club, a service club at Marrakesh, for an audience of African-American servicemen in the segregated US army (see Baker and Chase, 2001, 251). For an account of her actions in North Africa, see also Onana (2013, 77–109).

authority of a global perspective and the publicity machine of a star, Baker was able to shame America for its racism. (Scheper, 2007, 83)

Baker had experienced US racism first-hand growing up in St. Louis, Missouri and returning to different parts of the US on her tours. During her stay in the mid-1930s, she "learned that she would never be as welcome in her home country as she had been in France" and that in American society, her status would be determined by her skin color rather than her success or personality (Wood, 2000, 201). Jefferson reflects on Baker's 1936 New York performances in the *Zigfield Follies*:

> She was treated like a second-tier performer not a headliner [...]. The reviewers gloated as they dismissed and belittled her. She was not supposed to act like an international star and a citizen of France, she was supposed to act like a lower-caste American Negro glad to be home again. (2007–2008, 6)

Even though she was not yet legally a French citizen at this point, Baker struck American audiences as "foreign" and was unfavorably received by viewers and critics (see Schroeder, 2006, 51). It was also her "American experience [which] led Josephine Baker to her role as a leading player in the theater of race struggle" (Jefferson, 2007–2008, 7).

Baker became increasingly active in the struggle for racial equality, particularly after the Second World War: she refused to perform for segregated audiences in the US and vigorously opposed racial discrimination, especially in the US South. During a US tour with her fourth husband Jo Bouillon in the late 1940s, the interracial couple was faced with hostility, racism, and segregation. An event which became known as the "Stork Club incident" specifically attests to Baker's confrontation with racist practices. On October 16, 1951,[12] she was allegedly refused service at the well-known Stork club in New York City and strove to publicize this act of discrimination. Baker expected another patron of the club, conservative journalist Walter Winchell from the *Daily Mirror*, to support her as a witness. The writer, however, "retorted with a blistering media attack": he denounced Baker as a communist sympathizer and accused her of being anti-American. Winchell also sent this information to J. Edgar Hoover and, ultimately, "triggered FBI surveillance of Baker's activities over a seventeen-year period" (Jules-Rosette, 2007, 70). Moreover, his accusations led to the termination of Baker's US contracts. Winchell's media slander was not the only opposition Baker encountered; the State Department and the FBI had a strong interest to silence Baker's criticism of US race relations and were supported even by

---

[12] Baker announced this tour as primarily politically motivated and categorically refused to perform for segregated audiences at any venue (see Jules-Rosette, 2007, 221).

African Americans—perhaps most prominently congressman Adam Clayton Powell, Jr. (Jules-Rosette, 2007, 224–225). Mary Dudziak regards Baker as a victim of Cold War politics and draws attention to the fact that since Baker was no longer a US citizen, the US government could not resort to the standard measures it would have taken against civil rights activists, such as withdrawing a passport to prevent the person from traveling internationally. Therefore, Baker was a threat *and* "special problem for the government" (Dudziak, 1994, 546). At the same time, her French citizenship provided her with a degree of protection from the US government and thus facilitated her participation in civil rights activism.

Beyond the symbolic political act of demanding desegregation, at least temporarily for her performances, Baker supported, for example, the case of Willie McGee, a young black man who was convicted of raping a white woman in Mississippi and executed in 1951. She "defended the integration of housing in Cicero, Illinois, amid a violent riot and supported the Trenton Six," a group of African-American men accused of murdering a white shopkeeper in New Jersey. Moreover, Baker was well aware of the problematic media representations of African Americans and wrote a protest letter to the National Association of Radio and Television regarding its hiring practices and "the use of racial stereotypes in the media" (Jules-Rosette, 2007, 222). To some degree, Baker "was welcomed by African Americans [at that time] because she declared her readiness to fight for the Civil Rights Movement and boycotted performances for segregated audiences" (Dayal, 2004, 49). She was even named Most Outstanding Woman of the Year by the National Association for the Advancement of Colored People (NAACP) in 1951.

In 1963, Baker participated in the March on Washington, where she appeared in her French air force uniform[13] and gave a short speech in which she contrasted the racialized and racist structures in the US—the country of her birth—with her adopted home, France. She specifically referred to her experience of coming to Atlanta: "it was a horror to me. And I said to myself, My God, I am Josephine, and if they do this to me, what do they do to the other people in America?" Jules-Rosette describes Baker's brief speech at the March on Washington as paradigmatic for her political activism. It relied on her personal story with its reiterated Cinderella motif, represented France as safe haven, a "fairyland place" (Baker qtd. in Jules-Rosette, 2007, 237), and presented herself as a heroic vocal protester for justice and equality. The speech "recapitulated the terms of her own idiosyncratic battle

---

[13] The uniform not only very obviously identified her as French citizen (and no longer an American) but also marked her as a decorated heroine engaged in yet another war, that of the race struggle in the US.

against racism, which, while it was encouraging and uplifting, was also somewhat marginal to the discourse of the collective civil rights struggle" (Jules-Rosette, 2007, 237). While Baker may have been marginal to the civil rights mainstream due to her idiosyncrasies and her strong identification with and unquestioning glorification of France, it is often claimed that she was the only woman to address the crowd at the March on Washington and the online magazine *The Root* recently listed her as one of the March's "unsung heroes" (Daniels, 2013). However, her appearance in Washington vividly displayed how her (voluntary) association with France had at that point long triumphed over her connection to the US. Nonetheless, she supported the civil rights struggle and thus enacted an affiliation with the black diaspora in the US and showcased her humanitarian convictions. In the same year, for example, she also gave a benefit concert for several civil rights organizations—the NAACP, the Student Nonviolent Coordinating Committee (SNCC), and the Congress of Racial Equality (CORE). Baker was allegedly proud to be part of the movement but her participation in these events may not have been completely selfless because it also helped her gain publicity and much-needed financial support for Les Milandes (see Wood, 2000, 285–288). Despite her involvement in civil rights activities and her role as a heroic figure for a new generation of African Americans, Baker could not identify with the radical agenda of the emerging black power movement; she was "increasingly out of sympathy with [these] new crusading attitudes evolving" (Wood, 2000, 305). Nevertheless, her international political agenda, though never free of contradictions and not always coherent, may be read as an equally valuable contribution alongside the interventions of civil rights and black power activists.

III. The Rainbow Tribe, Motherhood, and Belonging

In terms of national belonging, Baker stayed in France until her death in 1975, made the country her "home," and wholeheartedly and seemingly uncritically embraced her French identity. Guterl describes her funeral ceremony in Paris as an event akin to a parade: "Within the church, [was] something rather like a state funeral […], full of military honors and with an audience of ministers, celebrities, and cast members of *Josephine*" (2014, 189–190).[14] The public recognition signaled by Baker's funeral indicates her importance within the French collective memory and cultural imaginary as well as her broad acceptance as a French citizen, and this recognition continues to echo in the contemporary memorial and tourist culture surrounding her persona. While

---

[14] According to Bob McCann, Baker was "the first American-born woman to receive French military honors at her funeral" (2010, 31).

she did no longer associate herself primarily with the "imagined community" (see Anderson, 1983) of the United States, her civil rights activism may indicate her connection to the black diaspora in the US. This connection to the "black community" in the US had been highly contested, both at the very beginning of her career, but also, more recently, in the short duration of her fleeting visit to Washington in 1963. Early on, objections had been raised in the US that she "had removed herself from the black community, and had become a sort of ersatz white" (Wood, 2000, 172; see also Baker in Gates, 1985, 599).[15] On the contrary, Michel Fabre claims that Baker, as a "cultural beacon," has been a "role model for other African-American artists" and that her "very [name] evoke[s] a feeling of racial pride and 'togetherness' on a worldwide scale" (1994, 122). These contradictory assessments indicate how Baker was (and continues to be) constructed differently within the discursive realms of African-American and European activist and intellectual circles. Against the backdrop of this controversy, Baker's creation of her "utopian" family at Les Milandes as an "ultimate embrace of domesticity as the locus of her politics in the 1950s" (Dudziak, 1994, 569) may appear, at first glance, to be a turn away from black activist politics, not least because this community was made possible by its clearly demarcated boundaries, by its relative isolation from the outside world, and by the stereotypical "casting" of children as representatives of different races and cultures in their "purest" form. Les Milandes was a "commune," a "royal home," and a tourist site; it can be viewed as a "postnational dream, a utopian fairy tale, and a sort of colony" (Guterl, 2009, 46). Baker's construction of her own family/state in which diverse races, cultures, and religions could peacefully live together poses a striking contrast, at first glance, to the increasing radicalization and transnationalization of the black freedom struggle in and beyond the US. "The transformation of Baker's life, and her reinvention of motherhood, reflected an ascendant, seriously held utopian politics, quite different from the American radical traditions of the Black Power and the New Left, and just as distinct from the bourgeois integrationism of the mainstream civil rights movement" (Guterl, 2009, 39). Yet to read her construction of an autonomous familial realm in France as a retreat into the domestic sphere does not do justice to Baker's politics and philosophy. Following Guterl, I propose that it is more useful to regard her concept of motherhood as "radical" and to rethink the meaning of radicalism to account for Baker's activism as "an equally important provocation" alongside the civil rights and black power protests in the 1950s and 1960s (2009, 50). Baker's "humanistic

---

[15] When Baker was asked to be the Queen of the Colonies at the Colonial Exposition in 1931, *The New York World-Telegram* ran the headline "Queen, Where Is Yo' Kink?" (see Wood, 2000, 172).

project" at Les Milandes could be interpreted not in contrast to her political activism in the US but rather, as Jonathan Eburne suggests, as a change in her "political tactics" (2007–2008, 1).

Her performance of motherhood; her adoption of children with different religious, racial, and cultural backgrounds; and her construction of Les Milandes' "state fantasy" (see Pease, 2009) of universal brotherhood have to be situated in this political context. Within the context of her life story, they also must be read alongside Baker's mobility as an attempt to create "roots." In a 1973 interview, she reflected on her exile and acceptance in France and the relative absence of racial prejudice: "The French adopted me immediately. [...] I felt liberated in Paris" (Gates, 1985, 597). Asked whether she felt guilty for leaving the United States, especially during the civil rights era, Baker emphasized that she felt she could not have accomplished much in the US but often felt like "the Wandering Jew with my twelve children on my arms"—however, she also claimed that she "belong[ed] to the world now" (Gates, 1985, 600; 599). Les Milandes can be interpreted as a public sign of Baker's cosmopolitan worldview and a "touristic simulation of Baker's multiple private and public images, her idyllic narrative, and her life" (Jules-Rosette, 2007, 35), but also as her private effort to establish a home and family for herself and an aspect of her idiosyncratic self-fashioning. Such a multilayered analysis of Baker's project at Les Milandes can be approached through a (cultural) mobility studies lens in order to connect it to her activism and mobility in the Atlantic world. Revisiting Baker's project through this lens allows for negotiating another dimension of transnationalism: not just as scholarly practice but as political intervention.

In 1990, James Clifford prominently critiqued cultural analysis and especially ethnography because it "has privileged relations of dwelling over relations of travel" and called for a "comparative cultural studies approach to specific histories, tactics, everyday practices of dwelling *and* traveling: traveling-in-dwelling, dwelling-in-traveling" (1997, 22, 36). Clifford challenged monolithic notions of fixity and belonging, and made a claim for including mobility and travel into cultural analysis. Stephen Greenblatt has now prominently claimed that "cultural mobility studies" need to examine "*the sensation of rootedness*," the "allure [...] of the firmly rooted" (2010, 252–253; emphasis original). Both Clifford and Greenblatt mark the interdependence between routes and roots, mobility and immobility, that is also central to the "mobilities paradigm" as outlined by Kevin Hannam, Mimi Sheller, and John Urry (2006). This nexus offers a productive framework through which to approach Baker's life and activism. Throughout her highly mobile life, Baker attempted several times to start a family and to create a home, that is, to build a community and find a place where she belonged. Her multiple forms of mobility—literal and metaphorical—highlight the *"tension between individual agency and structural constraint"* that, following Greenblatt, cultural mobility studies should account for (2010, 251). Baker's project to establish a transnational, cosmopolitan community/family not only addresses the pleasure of rootedness but also the "contact zones" which *"mobility studies should identify and analyze"* (Greenblatt, 2010, 251; emphasis original). Baker's *château* can be regarded as an artificially and purposefully created contact zone where different cultures, religions, and languages could coexist and intermingle. Throughout her careers on stage, in the military, and at Les Milandes, Baker moved within existing contact zones but also opened up new ones as she carefully moved between and beyond national and regional cultures. She drew on different cultural repertoires in her performances and adapted them for her European audiences, used her diva status as a cover to move in different circles as a spy for the French resistance, and relied on her French citizenship to participate in the civil rights struggle in the US relatively safe from governmental repression.

There are contradicting accounts of when Baker actually acquired her *château* in the Dordogne. Rose claims that Baker had bought Les Milandes as early as 1936 (1991, 185); Eburne holds that she bought it in 1947, shortly before she invited several members of her family (her mother, sister, and brother-in-law) from St. Louis to join her at her new home in France (2007–2008, 1); and Baker suggests that she first came to Les Milandes in 1939 (1964, 1). These divergent accounts are typical for Baker's life story which, like the literature about her, never coheres into a single narrative. However, I am less interested in the historical accuracy of individual events than in their ideological and political ramifications within Baker's publicly constructed life narrative and the relevance of this life narrative to black protest in the 1950s and 1960s. According to Fabre, "her activism, her services during the war, and her adoption of children of many ethnic backgrounds won her universal esteem," adding to her earlier fame and recognition in and beyond France (1994, 128).

Baker adopted her first children, Akio Yamamoto and Teruya (later renamed Janot) Kimura, two so-called "occupation children," during a 1954 tour in Japan, where she gave fundraising performances to support "mixed-race" children and lectured on behalf of the International League Against Racism and Anti-Semitism (LICRA) (see Ara, 2010, 3, 11). She continued to bring back children from her travels. Next, she adopted Jari from an orphanage in Helsinki and Luis from Colombia. Rose's account of Baker's adoptions is telling of the essentialist logics that shaped her calculated plan for her seemingly multicultural family: "She now had four children—two Orientals, a Caucasian, and a black. Jari was Protestant, Akio Buddhist, Luis Catholic, and Janot Shinto. According to plan, she needed an American Indian. [...] It occurred to her that, given the difficulty of finding Indians, a

Jew might do" (1991, 233). The children were carefully selected according to their racial, religious, and national identities and their symbolic potential. From a 1956 tour she brought back two children, Marianne and Brahim, who were found together, the "sole survivors of a massacre during the Algerian war." Even though Bouillon and Baker had agreed to only adopt boys, Baker diverged from their plan as she was tempted by the "symbolic meaning" (Rose, 1991, 235). The selection of children and deliberate planning of the "Rainbow Tribe,"[16] as she called her children, are highly problematic, particularly in their fundamentally colonialist and exploitative undercurrents. Yet Baker's "social work" was informed by her belief "that the children's early environment and education would create a new kind of human being, as it were, who would not be conscious of racism or skin color" (Ara, 2010, 3). Les Milandes, in this context, can be understood as an experiment in education; Baker's plan ultimately included building a "College of Universal Brotherhood" to educate the future citizens of a multicultural world (see Jules-Rosette, 2007, 238–239). Her plans for an autonomous educational institution never fully materialized, but they were already implicitly present when she adopted her first children.

There are several theories as to her motives and motivations for establishing her Rainbow Tribe, including that she was unable to have children or had suffered several miscarriages. In any case, adoption was, at this point, "The only way of realising her dream of creating a household full of children" and "the only means of turning her dream of having a family of three or four children of different skin tones into a reality" (Ara, 2010, 10). By 1962, the Rainbow Tribe comprised 12 children. Not only were they selected and sometimes even named for their "ability to represent ethnicities and religions that were manifestly divided," but Baker wanted all of them to be "tutored in their native languages" and to be "reintroduced to their native lands by age 12" so that the Rainbow Tribe in fact stabilized and preserved cultural and racial differences (Eburne, 2007–2008, 2). Eburne suggests that in this light, Les Milandes appears "more like the neocolonial small world of Walt Disney than the domestic embodiment of the United Nations" (2007–2008, 2). Although her project can easily be criticized for its colonialist logics and essentialist taxonomy, Baker's adoption of 12 children harbors a symbolic and political potential. In any case, her project should be understood as more than "just" a domestic practice: "not only did the performer's massive international celebrity render such domestic practices public, but Baker herself mobilized this celebrity as a means for establishing the rainbow

[16] Jules-Rosette claims that to some degree the Rainbow Tribe "was not a family at all, but a social and quasi-utopian movement in which the concept of the primal family was used as a metaphor" (2007, 185).

tribe's symbolic value as what might be considered a depoliticized form of political intervention" (Eburne, 2007–2008, 2). She fashioned her village as a model United Nations, alluding to the iconography of the UN headquarters in New York on one of the posters for Les Milandes, a parallelism that was eagerly taken up by the international press. In Eburne's assessment, the "rainbow tribe mobilized both multiracial adoption and Frenchness in an effort to extend, through symbolic means, her civil rights activism of the early 1950s" (2007–2008, 2). Conceptually, Baker merged "French notions of fraternity and republicanism with American ideals of equality and redressive justice that came to fruition in the civil rights movement" (Jules-Rosette, 2007, 230). Baker's practices of adoption—both of her French nationality and of the Rainbow Tribe—can be understood as a critique of race relations in the postwar United States. Far from being a naïve enthusiast, Baker turns out to have had a "theory of adoption" that was a "calculated, albeit compromised form of symbolic militancy against the politics of segregation" (Eburne, 2007–2008, 3). It constitutes, in fact, a political act that should be included into the history of the black liberation struggle in the US as more than merely a footnote. When, in 1963, Martin Luther King, Jr. famously expressed his hope that his "four little children will one day live in a nation where they will not be judged by the color of their skin but by the content of their character" (2004, 109), Baker had already tried to turn her own dream of equality and freedom into reality and had built a "little world of her own, where all races would be received as equal" (Wood, 2000, 270). Of course, she did so in the comparatively risk-free, idiosyncratic, and remote rural French context of Les Milandes but, I would argue, this does not in itself render her acts of desegregation and of creating a "universal brotherhood" politically insignificant.

To be sure, Baker's Rainbow Tribe could not overcome the paradox of affirming the very categories of difference (nation, religion, culture, race) it intended to transcend; and her "social experiment" relied on its reclusiveness in rural France, its financial privilege, and Josephine Baker as its central figure and "Maman du monde" (Baker, 1964, n. pag.). Furthermore, for all her criticism of US segregation and racism, Baker never criticized her adopted homeland; her "allegiance to French nationalism in the midst of colonial warfare reveals, at best, her naïveté toward French politics, and, at worst, the ideological proximity of the rainbow tribe to the assimilationist tactics of French colonialism" (Eburne, 2007–2008, 5). Les Milandes revolved around Baker.[17] It was at the same time her private home and part

---

[17] Jules-Rosette views Les Milandes as the "totalizing symbol of the successes and struggles of Josephine Baker's later life," just as the equally ideologically loaded "banana skirt was for her youth" (2007, 36).

of her carefully staged public appearance, with a political agenda, but also an idiosyncratic dimension. Over the years, it became a home for her family as well as a tourist attraction with its own flags, postage stamps, and a wax museum, the "Jorama," depicting key scenes of Baker's life and career. Baker used Les Milandes to fashion her public persona and to stage her own version of motherhood. In the matriarchal organization of the Les Milandes, "Josephine was the boss" and the Rainbow Tribe reflected her "performative persona by representing the multiple national and cultural identities that she had assumed on stage, on film, and in song" (Jules-Rosette, 2007, 191–192). Even though Baker's "family experiment" may have succeeded in creating "a genuine atmosphere of solidarity, harmony and mutual tolerance of difference among the children" (Jules-Rosette, 2007, 207), it ultimately failed to survive as an institution, particularly after Jo Bouillon left, because Baker was no longer able to raise enough money to sustain it. Her forceful eviction from the property in 1969 generated an (almost) iconic media image which presented Baker on the doorstep of her *château*, poor, worn-out, and broke, an image in stark contrast to the glamorous and divaesque images of her early career. The rescue of Baker's family by Princess Grace of Monaco could be incorporated in the fairy tale-like master narrative of Baker's life and career, motherhood, and her "ideal of universal brotherhood" represented by the Rainbow Tribe (Jules-Rosette, 2007, 191).

Though the ultimate financial disaster of Les Milandes and the problematic premises of the Rainbow Tribe are not to be underestimated, they symbolize Baker's dream of a transnational community and her personal longing for a home and a "better" world. One could argue that Baker's Rainbow Tribe and the Les Milandes philosophy were at the time "little short of fantastic" (Ara, 2010, 16) or even a "quixotic" endeavor (Eburne, 2007–2008, 3). Yet they may be read as echoing Randolph Bourne's famous call for a "transnational America" destined to be a "federation of cultures" where distinctive national and cultural qualities are not "washed out into a tasteless, colorless fluid of uniformity" (1916, 90). Of course, Baker's "experiment" in France cannot simply be read as an attempt to create a model United States, but the parameters of her "imagined community" correspond to some central aspects of Bourne's social, political, and cultural vision of a transnational America.[18] Bourne's notion (like Baker's dream of a "utopian" community at Les Milandes) is steeped in exceptionalist, exclusionary, and colonialist logics

---

[18] Baker herself described the United States as representing her own cosmopolitan spirit: "people coming from all over to make a nation. But America has forgotten that. I love all people at the same time. Our country is people of all countries. How else could there have been an America? And they made a beautiful nation. Each one depositing a little of his own beauty" (Gates, 1985, 599–600).

and is inflected by discourses of (American) exceptionalism. However, just as Bourne's polemic still resonates in various ways in contemporary transnational American studies, Baker's proclaimed "VILLAGE DU MONDE, Capitale de la Fraternité" (Baker, 1964, 5) provides an instructive case study, a philosophical intervention, and practical provocation in relation to racial, national, religious, cultural, and gender politics. To be clear, I am neither suggesting that Baker would ultimately emerge as one of the major political agents in the black liberation struggle, nor that we should uncritically subscribe to her self-fashioning (and the corresponding media images) as a glorified French heroine or crusading black activist. Rather, I hold that the prevalent (and justified) critique of Baker's performances and her (sometimes dubious) political motifs should be balanced with an eye to the (representational) politics of her engagement in the French resistance, the civil rights struggle, and her (public) familial realm of Les Milandes—to name only the major arenas of her political interests and activism.

IV. Conclusion: A Revolutionary Diva?

Margo Jefferson says that she is "tired of thinking of women artists like Baker as divas," and instead asserts that "the great [women] we call divas [...] are conquerers [sic] and liberators" (2007–2008, 7). Kimberly N. Brown's concept of the "revolutionary diva" seems to be a promising way to bring together the many aspects of Baker's persona, including those of the diva and the political activist, and to acknowledge the other "important face" largely ignored by researchers and biographers alike: "the face of an activist who challenged racism; of a fighter, a humanitarian and an idealist" (Ara, 2010, 16). Though Baker does not figure prominently in Brown's seminal *Writing the Black Revolutionary Diva*, she certainly qualifies for the label (2010, 167). Baker enacted *"revolutionary diva subjectivity"* by "forc[ing] the audience to re-examine their assumptions of blackness and black womanhood," both in her performances and through her political activism; she was never a victimized black woman "just surviving, but [someone] truly *living* in all senses of the word" (Brown, 2010, 5, 21; emphasis original).

If we take Baker's political activism seriously and account for her shifting affiliations to nation-states like France and the US as well as to transnational formations like her Rainbow Tribe and the black diaspora, we have to acknowledge that she was more than a diva and show star acting out white fantasies and catering to white audiences. Her political involvement may have been "one of performance," but its "content of antiracism and multiculturalism consist[ing] of complex and textured messages" (Jules-Rosette, 2009, 230) was nonetheless politically relevant. Her contribution necessitates a reconsideration of Baker's life and activism within a broadened understanding of radicalism and revolutionary politics. It requires an examination of Baker's roots and routes in the Atlantic world, of the different cultural, social, and political settings within which she operated and the narratives of black protest and transnational black liberation struggles to which she contributed. And, moreover, it requires that we read her cosmopolitan vision as a political intervention with important theoretical implications. This is the case whether Les Milandes is seen as post-racial utopia or postnational community; as familial, social, and educational experiment; or as neocolonial and Disneyfied showcase of "universal brotherhood." Several scholars have begun to take up this project,[19] but Baker's contribution is still seen as marginal. Using research paradigms from mobility studies, black diaspora studies, and transnational American studies helps to create a more differentiated picture of the many facets of Baker's career as artist and activist. Baker may be an elusively mobile figure with shifting alliances who easily evades disciplinary matrixes, but she does not belong merely to the margins of current debates about (trans)national affiliations and cosmopolitanisms, (cultural) mobilities and immobilities, and political activism in the black diaspora.

Works Cited

Anderson, Benedict. *Imagined Communities: Reflections on the Origin and Spread of Nationalism.* New York: Verso, 1983.

Ara, Konomi. "Josephine Baker: A Chanteuse and a Fighter." *The Journal of Transnational American Studies* 2.1 (2010): 1–17.

Baker, Jean-Claude, and Chris Chase. *Josephine: The Hungry Heart.* New York: Cooper Square Press, 2001.

Baker, Josephine. "Josephine Baker's Children's Village." 1964. Letter and Exposé. JWJ MSS 89. Box 34. Beinecke Rare Manuscripts and Archives. Yale University.

Barnwell, Andrea B. "Like the Gypsy's Daughter; Or, Beyond the Potency of Josephine Baker's Eroticism." In *Rhapsodies in Black: Art of the Harlem Renaissance.* Ed. Joanna Skipwith. London: Hayward Gallery with the Institute of International Visual Arts; Berkeley: University of California Press, 1997. 82–89.

Borshuk, Michael. "An Intelligence of the Body: Disruptive Parody through Dance in the Early Performances of Josephine Baker." In *EmBODYing Liberation: The Black Body in American Dance.* Ed. Dorothea Fischer-Hornung and Alison D. Goeller. FORECAAST 4. Münster: LIT, 2001. 41–57.

Brown, Kimberly N. *Writing the Black Revolutionary Diva: Women's Subjectivity and the Decolonizing Text.* Bloomington: Indiana University Press, 2010.

---

[19] Most prominently, perhaps, Bennetta Jules-Rosette and Matthew Pratt Guterl.

Bourne, Randolph. "Trans-National America." *The Atlantic Monthly* 118 (July 1916): 86–97. http://www.swarthmore.edu/SocSci/rbannis1/AIH19th/Bourne.html. Accessed Dec. 4, 2013.

Clifford, James. *Routes: Travel and Translation in the Late 20th Century.* Cambridge, MA: Harvard University Press, 1997.

Cresswell, Tim. *On the Move: Mobility in the Modern Western World.* New York: Routledge, 2006.

Cresswell, Tim. "Foreword: Desire Lines." *Pirates, Drifters, Fugitives: Figures of Mobility in the US and Beyond.* Ed. Heike Paul, Alexandra Ganser, and Katharina Gerund. Heidelberg: Winter, 2012. 7–10.

Daniels, John. "March on Washington's Unsung Heroes." *The Root.* Aug. 20, 2013. https://www.theroot.com/march-on-washingtons-unsung-heroes-1790868338. Accessed Oct. 1, 2013.

Dayal, Samir. "Blackness as Symptom: Josephine Baker and European Identity." In *Blackening Europe: The African American Presence.* Ed. Heike Raphael-Hernandez. New York: Routledge, 2004. 35–52.

Debray, Régis. "Et si Joséphine Baker entrait au Panthéon?" *Le Monde.* Dec. 16, 2013. http://www.lemonde.fr/idees/article/2013/12/16/josephine-baker-au-pantheon_4335358_3232.html. Accessed Feb. 1, 2016.

Dudziak, Mary L. "Josephine Baker, Racial Protest, and the Cold War." *The Journal of American History* 81.2 (1994): 543–570.

Eburne, Johnathan P. "Adoptive Affinities: Josephine Baker's Humanist International." *Josephine Baker: A Century in the Spotlight.* Special issue of *The Feminist and Scholar Online* 6.1–2 (2007–2008). http://sfonline.barnard.edu/baker/eburne_01.htm. Accessed Jan. 16, 2014.

Fabre, Michel. "International Beacons of African-American Memory: Alexandre Dumas Père, Henry O. Tanner, and Josephine Baker as Examples of Recognition." In *History and Memory in African-American Culture.* Ed. Geneviève Fabre and Robert O'Meally. New York: Oxford University Press: 1994. 122–129.

Fisher Fishkin, Shelley. "Crossroads of Cultures: The Transnational Turn in American Studies—Presidential Address to the American Studies Association, Nov. 12, 2004." *American Quarterly* 57.1 (2005): 17–57.

Gates, Henry Louis, Jr. "An Interview with Josephine Baker and James Baldwin." *Southern Review* 21 (1985): 594–602.

Glover, Kaiama L. "Introduction: Why Josephine Baker?" *Josephine Baker: A Century in the Spotlight.* Special issue of *The Feminist and Scholar Online* 6.1–2 (2007–2008). http://sfonline.barnard.edu/baker/glover_01.htm. Accessed Jan. 16, 2014.

Greenblatt, Stephen. "A Mobility Studies Manifesto." In *Cultural Mobility: A Manifesto.* Ed. Stephen Greenblatt, Ines Županov, Reinhard Meyer-Kalkus, Heike Paul, Pál Nyíri, and Friederike Pannewick. Cambridge: Cambridge University Press, 2010. 250–253.

Guterl, Matthew Pratt. "Josephine Baker's 'Rainbow Tribe:' Radical Motherhood in the South of France." *Journal of Women's History* 21.4 (2009): 38–58.

Guterl, Matthew Pratt. *Josephine Baker and the Rainbow Tribe*. Cambridge, MA: Belknap, 2014.

Haney, Lynn. *Naked at the Feast: The Biography of Josephine Baker*. London: Robeson, 1981.

Hannam, Kevin, Mimi Sheller, and John Urry. "Editorial: Mobilities, Immobilities and Moorings." *Mobilities* 1.1 (2006): 1–22.

Jefferson, Margo. "Josephine Baker: An Intelligent Body, An Erotic Soul, A Kinetic Mind." *Josephine Baker: A Century in the Spotlight*. Special issue of *The Feminist and Scholar Online* 6.1–2 (2007–2008). http://sfonline.barnard.edu/baker/jefferson_01.htm. Accessed Jan. 16, 2014.

Jules-Rosette, Bennetta. *Josephine Baker in Art and Life: The Icon and the Image*. Urbana, IL: University of Illinois Press, 2007.

King, Martin Luther, Jr. "I Have a Dream." *The Norton Anthology of African American Literature*. Ed. Henry Louis Gates and Nellie McKay. 2nd ed. New York: Norton 2004: 107–109.

Kraut, Anthea. "Whose Choreography? Josephine Baker and the Question of (Dance) Authorship." *Josephine Baker: A Century in the Spotlight*. Special issue of *The Feminist and Scholar Online* 6.1–2 (2007–2008). http://sfonline.barnard.edu/baker/kraut_01.htm. Accessed Jan. 16, 2014.

Lyon, Janet. "Josephine Baker's Hothouse." *Modernism, Inc.: Body, Memory, Capital*. Ed. Jani Scandura and Michael Thurston. New York: New York University Press, 2001. 29–47.

McCann, Bob. *Encyclopedia of African American Actresses in Film and Television*. Jefferson, NC: McFarland, 2010.

Naumann, Christine. "African American Performers and Culture in Weimar Germany." *Crosscurrents: African Americans, Africa, and Germany in the Modern World*. Ed. David McBride, Leroy Hopkins, and C. Aisha Blackshire-Belay. Columbia, SC: Cambden House: 1998. 96–105.

Nenno, Nancy. "Femininity, the Primitive, and Modern Urban Space: Josephine Baker in Berlin." *Women in the Metropolis: Gender and Modernity in Weimar Culture*. Ed. Katharina von Ankum. Berkeley, CA: University of California Press, 1997. 145–161.

Ngai, Sianne. "Black Venus, Blonde Venus." *Bad Modernisms*. Ed. Douglas Mao and Rebecca L. Walkowitz. Durham, NC: Duke University Press, 2006. 145–178.

Onana, Charles. *Joséphine Baker contre Hitler: la star noire de la France Libre*. 2nd ed. Paris: Éditions Duboiris, 2013.

Paul, Heike, Alexandra Ganser, and Katharina Gerund. "Introduction." *Pirates, Drifters, Fugitives: Figures of Mobility in the US and Beyond*. Ed. Heike Paul, Alexandra Ganser, and Katharina Gerund. Heidelberg: Winter, 2012. 11–27.

Pease, Donald E. *The New American Exceptionalism*. Minneapolis, MN and London: University of Minnesota Press, 2009.

Rose, Phyllis. *Jazz Cleopatra: Josephine Baker in Her Time*. New York: Vintage, 1991.

Scheper, Jeanne. "'Of la Baker, I Am a Disciple': The Diva Politics of Recognition." *Camera Obscura* 65 22.2 (2007): 72–101.

Schroeder, Alan. *Josephine Baker: Entertainer*. New York: Chelsea House, 2006.

Sheller, Mimi. "Aluminum across the Americas: Caribbean Mobilities and Transnational American Studies." *The Journal of Transnational American Studies* 5.1 (2013). https://escholarship.org/uc/item/7bb5c9j6. Accessed Jan. 22, 2014.

Urry, John. *The Mobilities Paradigm*. Cambridge: Polity, 2007.

Wood, Ean. *The Josephine Baker Story*. London: Sanctuary, 2000.

3

Beyond the Ethnographic Other: Pan-African Activism at the Turn of the Twentieth Century

Thomas E. Smith (Chadron State College)

In the late nineteenth and early twentieth century, World's Fairs were an especially popular forum that lauded Euro-America as central to global connectivity and progress.[1] Inaugurated with the 1851 Crystal Palace Exhibition in London, World's Fairs celebrated technological advancements that helped order the modern world and articulated ideational standards that set progress according to Western measures. World's Fairs often confirmed confidence in Euro-American leadership and superiority through the demonstration of racial difference—the display of the "ethnographic other." This display usually took place on the popular Midway entertainment sections of the Fairs and was often staged in stark dichotomies of "savage" and "civilized." This perpetuation of the ethnographic other at World's Fairs was part of the projection and maintenance of difference which, as argued by Frederick Cooper and Ann Stoler, "justified different intensities of violence" in an imperial world (1997, 4). A rich literature demonstrates how World's Fairs were profound cultural sites that contributed to the Euro-American control of others in the pursuit of empire.[2]

Historically, there was perhaps no more readily available platform upon which to construct stark racial difference than peoples of African descent. The construction of the savage against the backdrop of the civilized provided a rationale for both pronounced and everyday Euro-American violence against peoples of African descent. This violence occurred throughout the long sweep of slavery and continued post-emancipation into the late

---

[1] Emily Rosenberg comments that World's Fairs "constituted one of the most important nodes" in the transnational connections of the period 1870–1945 (2012, 887).
[2] Seminal works include Rydell (1984, 1993), Greenhalgh (1988), Corbey (1993), Lindfors (1999), and Wright (2002). Munro (2010) gives a historiographical overview of the field and demonstrates how World's Fairs extended outside of Europe and the United States, but retained a similar emphasis on the standards of progress.

nineteenth and early twentieth century with, for example, the proliferation of lynching in the American South. Further, this creation of difference provided an apologetic for the ongoing denial of equality and rights to peoples of African descent subject to Euro-American control.

However, a continuum of difference always accompanied dichotomies of savage and civilized. In the imperial world of the late nineteenth and early twentieth century, the most notable "complement" was the progressive zeal for uplift.[3] The imperial mission of uplift relied upon *both* the positioning of colonized people as inferior and the belief that this inferior status could be corrected. Hence, while World's Fairs invariably depicted people of color in subordinate positions, the very nature of a progressive scale implied that racial difference was not inherent or stable. Of course, this imperial progressivism rarely escaped its paternalist moorings long enough to consider this implication in terms of racial equality. The proliferation of imperial progressivism in transatlantic reformer discourse, however, did provide opportunities for differing interpretations and emphases. Turn-of-the-century Pan-African actors interrogated the promise of progress embedded in the continuum of racial difference and implied by the end logic of imperial progressivism to broach discussions of racial equality. In the summer of 1900, at the American Negro Exhibit held at the Exposition Universelle in Paris and at the contemporaneous Pan-African Conference held in London, Pan-African activists staged their own international challenge to the harsh dichotomy of the ethnographic other that was a staple of World's Fairs.

This Pan-African activism did not stop the characterization of peoples of African descent as ethnographic others, let alone halt intensive or quotidian racialized violence. By denouncing stark depictions of the ethnographic other, however, by claiming subjectivity for African peoples and critiquing the promise of inclusion by making direct calls for political rights, this protest contributed to an international discourse that questioned the faith in imperial progressivism. In doing so, Pan-Africanism at the turn of the twentieth century kept alive a struggle that clamored for the recognition of humanist equality and denounced the open-ended deferment of its realization.

---

[3] As Duncan Bell argues, "binaries" such as civilized and savage were "complemented, supplanted, and occasionally undermined by other attempts to classify and order the world" (2006, 283).

Paris, the United States, and the American Negro Exhibit

The 1900 Exposition Universelle in Paris was a definitive expression of the modern world and the highest attended World's Fair, receiving almost 50 million visitors. Like all World's Fairs, imperialism was central to the showcasing of the modern experience, and L'Exposition Universelle included exhibits from the colonial encounter, including those dedicated to the viewing of the ethnographic other.[4] However, Paris did more than uncritically celebrate Euro-American mastery of the modern world. Burgeoning late nineteenth-century progressivism, a reform movement, saw itself as providing solutions for social problems and Paris was the first World's Fair to dedicate an entire building—the Musée Social—to transatlantic progressivism's response to the dislocations of modernity. Situated prominently in the Musée Social, Thomas Calloway's and W.E.B. Du Bois's American Negro Exhibit challenged stark depictions of the ethnographic other.

The American Negro Exhibit was only one aspect of the United States' participation at the Fair. Notably, in a visible international venue on European soil, the United States affirmed its imperial standing through its exhibits on Cuba and Hawaii in the Colonial Hall. The United States Department of War granted 25,000 dollars to prepare the Cuban exhibit and the US government had a direct role in the preparation, sending a Lieutenant-Commander Baker to verse the Cubans in charge, Commissioner Gonzalo de Chuesada and Secretary Ricardo Diaz Albertini, about the nature of the exhibition, which ultimately included items regarding primary instruction in arithmetic, exercises in grammar, study guides to the history of the United States, a treatise for the pronunciation of English, and assorted essays by Cuban authors on the arts, medicine, and sociology. The exhibit also had a substantial section dedicated to the progress of the agriculture, mineral, and chemical industries on the island. W.G. Irwin, under the auspices of the Territorial Governor of Hawaii, Sanford B. Dole, oversaw the creation of the Hawaiian Exhibit, which concentrated on themes similar to the Cuban section. Both exhibits produced representations of the US "official mind," advertising the United States as a modern, progressive imperial power (*Report of the Commissioner-General*, 1901, 249–252).

As the United States formally announced itself as a colonial power at Paris, it also participated in the exposition's Musée Social. The Musée Social is considered the crowning display of how the transatlantic progressive movement navigated the dislocations of modernity (see Rodgers, 1998).[5]

---

[4] Included in the displays of native village exhibits at Paris was the oft-replicated African Dahomey village. See *Report of the Commissioner-General* (1901, 112).
[5] Daniel Rodgers (1998) uses the Musée Social at Paris 1900 as an entry point for his

The Musée Social set the United States alongside other European nations displaying a series of exhibits demonstrating advances in issues of the "social economy." Thomas Calloway's and W.E.B. Du Bois's American Negro Exhibit was placed as one of the first exhibits in the United States Space. It connected to the ethos of social advancement evinced in the hall by documenting African Americans' post-emancipation progress. Race relations in the United States, most often labeled the "negro question," had long been viewed with interest by Europe: as imperialism drew the world closer together, race relations were a significant international question.[6] As the United States trumpeted its imperialism in the Colonial Hall exhibit at Paris, enthusiasm for the American Negro Exhibit furthered its claims on progressive imperialism. The "successful" handling of the "negro problem" could stand as a model for positive international race relations.

Exhibit organizer Thomas J. Calloway, shamed by images of lynching that, he argued, made the "Old World" conceive of the American black as a "mass of rapists," saw the exhibit as a chance to change the perceptions of European audiences ("The American Negro Exhibit," 2).[7] While Calloway did not detail his reasoning, his exaggerated description—"mass" of rapists— suggests that his purpose was in line with an established counter-narrative that lambasted lynching apologists who endorsed the violent act through a gendered argument condemning the black male as a savage, sexual threat.[8]

---

seminal work on the connective dimensions of transatlantic reform. He argues that the dramatic expansion of industrial capitalism pushed this connectivity and that a shared sense of common history and underlying kinship also forced social reform across political boundaries.

[6] Race relations in the United States had long been important to Europe, most notably Great Britain. Race "theorists" saw commonality in the struggles of the Morant Bay rebellion against the British Empire and the struggles of Reconstruction in the United States. Comparative race relations was an important strand of thought throughout the remainder of the nineteenth century as continued imperialism brought issues of the global "color line" front and center. The "progress" of post-emancipation peoples in the United States was often the foil for the (overwhelmingly negative) evaluation of other race relations. Indicative of this focus was race "expert" James Bryce's widely referenced 1902 Romanes Lecture, "The Relations of the Advanced and Backward Races of Mankind" (1903).

[7] The first page of this issue of the *Colored American* presents a full-page picture of Calloway sitting in the main entry of the American Negro Exhibit. The issue contains significant commentary on the exhibit from Calloway as well as notes of affirmation from some leading African Americans, including Mary Church Terrell and T. Thomas Fortune.

[8] Calloway correspondent, the prolific African-American journalist John Bruce, wrote a scathing denunciation of the gendered apologies for lynching in his *The Blood Red Record* (1901). He explicitly argued that accusations of rape were a cover for the political reasons underlying lynching: "The charge of rape is exceedingly diaphanous when applied to the Negro as the cause of opposition to him in those communities where he is most in evidence and most ambitious to enjoy, in common with white men, his constitutional rights and

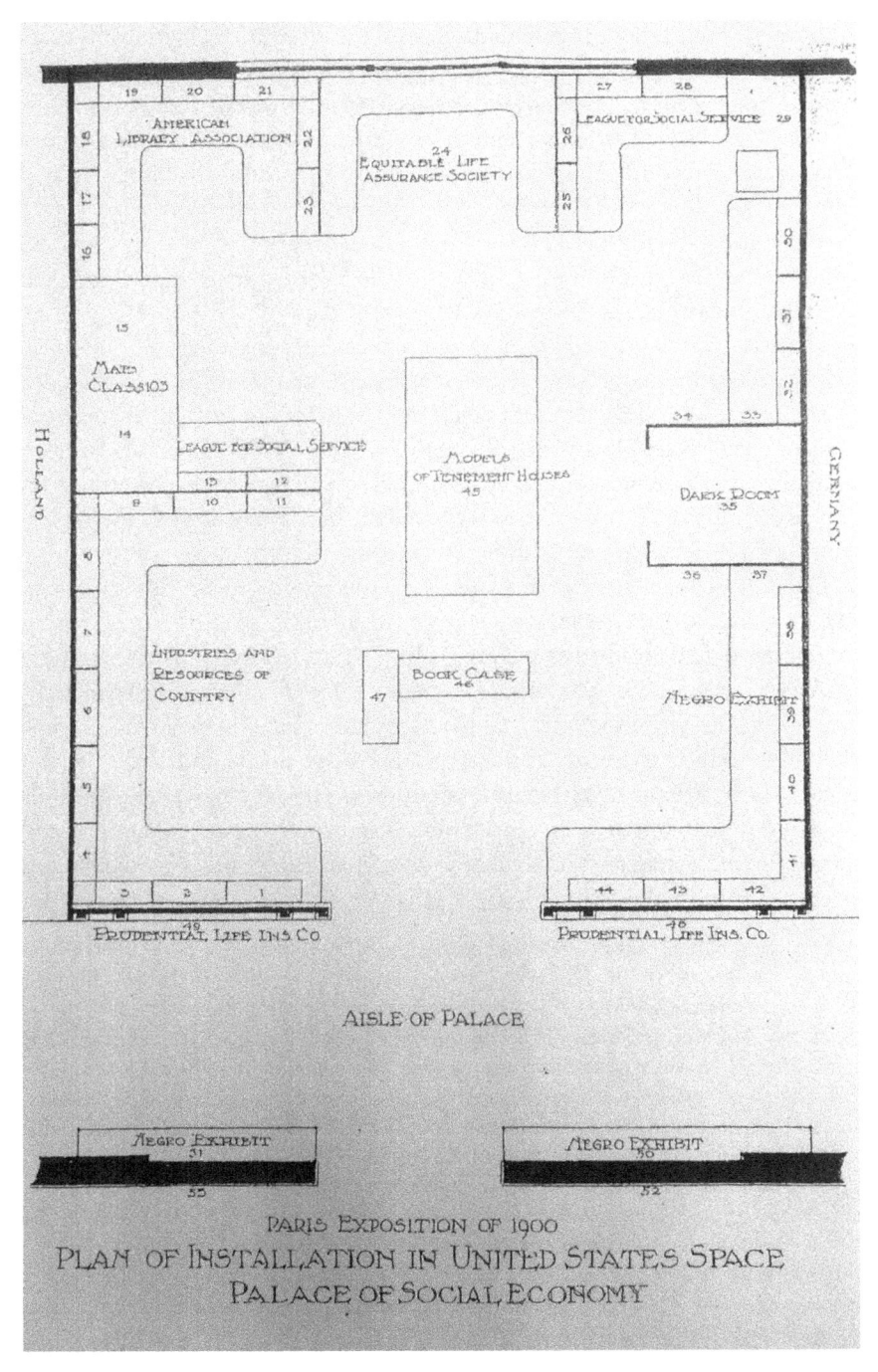

Figure 3.1 American Negro Exhibit – Plan of Installation

Calloway's international demonstration of the post-emancipation progress of African Americans in trade, industry, and education certainly helped the United States tout its "successful" race relations. However, Calloway's effort can also be read as an endorsement of African-American progress *despite* deep-seated prevailing racism that perpetuated sensationalist international impressions.[9] On a fundamental level, Calloway and the American Negro Exhibit gave an alternative view that discredited scales of progress and complicated the generalized template of the World's Fairs that objectified ethnographic others, often in stark hues of "savagery."

The use of images at Paris was one of the first instances of Du Bois's articulation of the concept of double consciousness.[10] For Du Bois, the idea of the "negro" as a problem that could be fixed was not only at the heart of racism, but also deeply affected the ability of those objectified as a problem to realize their own subjectivity. Du Bois challenged the objectification rife in World's Fairs by creating an exhibit that "encourag[ed] viewers to participate in new ways of looking and seeing" (Smith, 2004, 112).

Du Bois's engagement with sociological theory influenced this approach. He emphasized that sociology was not an abstract science but instead a practical tool to help advance society.[11] His portrayal of the statistical progress of African Americans was offered as more than just abstract information. These statistics were, to Du Bois, proactive pieces that documented progress; they were akin to the other exhibits in the Musée Social and could be read as tools to rectify the distorted gaze of difference based on savagery. Du Bois (1900) commented that, while the exhibit certainly documented progress and development, it was most important to note that, "above all," the exhibit was

---

prerogatives" (1901, 6). Ida B. Wells (1970) led the most noteworthy protest of the lynching and its apologetics, which included two anti-lynching tours to Great Britain. There is substantial literature on Wells, of which Bedermen (1996) is an important work.

[9] Shawn Michelle Smith has a different reading of Calloway, arguing that he was firmly in the accommodationist camp and, thus, she comments on his effort at the American Negro Exhibit: "rather than celebrating African-American resistance to overwhelming U.S. racism, Calloway sought to congratulate the United States on a triumph of racist paternalism" (2004, xxxvii). My central point is that Calloway and the American Negro Exhibit fundamentally resisted the stark portrayal of the ethnographic other and made claims about the basic equality of African peoples through an appeal to the very logic of the progressivism that defied control, despite its paternalist origins. For more on Calloway, see Travis (2004).

[10] Shawn Michelle Smith provides a particularly insightful discussion of the visual work crucial to Du Bois's concept and negotiation of double consciousness in *Photography on the Color Line*.

[11] Rebecka Rutledge Fisher (2005) argues that Paris was a crucial moment in Du Bois's ongoing critique of the field of sociology. She argues that he used the American Negro Exhibit to challenge what he saw as the abstract and conservative nature of traditional sociology.

Figure 3.2 African American Man – American Negro Exhibit

"made by themselves," meaning that black people shared in its creation. Du Bois explicitly noted that one of the exhibit's goals was to show the "history of the American Negro" in which achievements receive recognition and the subjectivity obscured by the lumping of African peoples and history into Dark Africa is restored.

The most striking aspect of the exhibit is the pictorial section, where dozens of photographs denied the objectifying gaze of the viewer and asserted that black peoples had similar levels of conscious awareness. The American Negro Exhibit gave African Americans a "multivalent aesthetic" that denied the timeless portrayals of the savage, of the ethnographic other, and projected a subjectivity that demanded inclusion in modernity (Fisher, 2005, 757, 764–765). In other words, Du Bois's goal at the American Negro Exhibit—and, more broadly, in his long career as a reformer—was to declare the equality of man and assert the subjectivity and agency of African peoples.

The London Pan-African Conference of 1900

The momentum of the American Negro Exhibit carried over to another important historical signpost of activism: the London Pan-African Conference of 1900. Organized by British Trinidadian Henry Sylvester Williams, the London Pan-African Conference of 1900 attracted many notable figures. As leading African-American public figures, both Calloway and Du Bois played major roles in the conference and Booker T. Washington attended an early preparatory meeting (*Report of the Pan-African Conference*, 1900, 2). The conference was a gathering of leaders of African descent and its agenda was decidedly international. Its official report lauded the meeting as the "first assembling of members of the African race from all parts of the globe," and while the conference's stated subject was the controversial South African War, its message was much more than an observation on the conflict (*Report of the Pan-African Conference*, 1900, 3). The Pan-African Conference (beyond the obvious signification of its name) overtly demonstrated the international nature of its activism, targeting practices in Africa, the Caribbean, and the United States (*Report of the Pan-African Conference*, 1900, 9).

As evidenced by Du Bois's "To the Nations of the World" address (which was sanctioned by the conference and signed by its officers), participants at the conference linked race relations to the construction of the global color line.[12] Often overlooked by scholarship, the Pan-African conference

---

[12] On Du Bois's understanding of the "negro problem" as a "local phase of a world problem," see Kelley (1999, 1054). Du Bois felt that African Americans had a special role in combating the color line: "the advance guard of the Negro people [is] the eight million people of Negro blood in the United States of America" (1897, 78).

also elaborated correctives to battle the color line. Some aspects of these strategies reflected tenets of the paternalist strains of imperial progressivism. The conference (perhaps cognizant of the South African War) supported the idea of benign British civilization: "There are good friends in England yet, and though we wade through the mire of the evil curses of civilisation in the Colonies, their voices will blend with ours, that righteousness and justice will be the ruling words of British civilisation" (*Report of the Pan-African Conference*, 1900, 5). The proceedings of the Pan-African Conference also evoked religious arguments that had long characterized activism with regard to African peoples. They twice noted that the reform was "for Christ and humanity" and the conference dates were deliberately chosen to follow on the heels of the World's Christian Endeavor Conference (*Report of the Pan-African Conference*, 1900, 7, 2). The Pan-African Conference also issued an official memorial to the Reverend Bishop James Johnson of Lagos, hoping that all could follow his example and "glorify the cause of our common Master, Jesus Christ" (*Report of the Pan-African Conference*, 1900, 4). Last, the conference also thanked the Society of Friends for their efforts to teach Africans "a true sense of civilisation calculated to bring them to Christ" (*Report of the Pan-African Conference*, 1900, 8).

However, Du Bois's "To the Nations of the World" demanded that the "cloak of Christian missionary enterprise" no longer provide a cover for exploitation. He invoked the pantheon of abolitionism—Wilberforce, Clarkson, Garrison, and Douglass—suggesting a moral ethos while stressing the need to "crown" abolitionism with political rights (*Report of the Pan-African Conference*, 1900, 10–11). While this call retained certain aspects of paternalist narratives of progress, it reflected the emphasis of the American Negro Exhibit and used African-American achievements to press for the consideration of the rights of subjects and citizens. Combined with the conference's denunciation of color as a distinction amongst men and, thus, as the basis for the global color line, the invocation of political rights marked a crucial moment in the evolution of Pan-African protest.

This invocation of political rights was made against a backdrop of dramatic changes affecting reformers on both sides of the Atlantic.[13] As the late nineteenth century brought a new sense of the modern, an emphasis on secular change affected reformer strategies. In connection to marginalized peoples, this emphasis worked to augment earlier protest based primarily on religion and equality before God. Hence, while Pan-Africanism, at times, invoked older allusions to religion, looked to strategies of uplift, and supported "good imperialism," it also began to connect the struggle across

---

[13] On these changes, see Kloppenberg (1986), Freeden (1978), and Rodgers (1998).

boundaries and began to appeal to the rights-based script connected to the secularizing modern moment of the late nineteenth and early twentieth century. The documentation of progress, the invocation of subjectivity, and the call for political rights provided a stark contrast to the crass hues of the ethnographic other at the turn of the century.

Savage South Africa

Yet the expressions of subjectivity and calls for political rights that flowed from a Pan-African reading of imperial progressivism faced formidable obstacles. The two World's Fairs that bookended the summer of 1900 are reminders that stark depictions of African peoples as ethnographic others were only too readily available and often trumped other understandings.

Less than four miles from the Pan-African Conference's location at Westminster Town Hall in London was the Empress Theatre at Earl's Court Arena. Earl's Court and the Empress staged a host of exhibitions and performances in the 1890s that catered to imperial sentiment.[14] In July of 1899, one year before the Pan-African Conference, the Greater Britain Exhibition opened. The gathering followed the World's Fair template, offering evidence of material progress in the British Empire, presenting visual spectacles and catering to patriotic imperial sentiment. With an emphasis on "loyalty to the Mother Country," the exhibition sought to legitimize the empire by creating a sense of unity between colonial peoples and those from the metropolis.

This unity was not one of equality, however, as the Greater Britain Exhibition constructed clear racial hierarchies that sought to order the imperial moment by constructing exactly what Du Bois would articulate at the Pan-African Conference: a global color line elevating a standard of whiteness.[15] The British Empire had long fielded calls for autonomy from its settler colonies. Charles Dilke's 1868 work *Greater Britain*, the establishment of the Dominion of Canada in 1873, and Gladstone's Home Rule Bill for Ireland in 1886 informed the dominion movement of the late nineteenth century. Sitting astride the dominion push was the perception of the rising threat of the "lower races" in the international racial struggle.[16] Proponents of this movement argued that colonies with sufficient British settlers deserved greater latitude regarding local rule as well as distinction

---

[14] For background on Earl's Court and the construction of the Empress Theatre, see Shepard (2003, 36–38).

[15] Lake and Reynolds (2008) demonstrate the transnational assertion of whiteness.

[16] For more on this line of thinking, see Lake and Reynold's analysis of Charles Pearson's 1892 work, *National Life and Character: A Forecast* (2008, 75–94).

from other non-Anglo imperial possessions.[17] The dominion movement argued that unity in empire should follow the same contours defined by deeply racialized worldviews and that "whiteness" linked the imperial vision and guaranteed aspects of self-rule in the colonies. While the Greater Britain Exhibition did not articulate an official position on the dominion movement or elaborate upon the exact meaning of its title, it did contain disproportionate testaments to advances in Australia, the most recent area to lobby for a realignment of the colonial relationship.[18]

As the exhibition lauded the advances of Britain's Australian cousins, it also affirmed Anglo loyalty and racial hierarchies through the depiction of the ethnographic other; the twice daily show *Savage South Africa* was the main attraction at the Empress Theatre. The theatre was situated at a prominent location in the exhibition, and the performances were well attended.[19] These performances (the only display at the exhibition that was acted out as a show) reinforced the stark line between civilized and savage and constructed a narrative of white domination in the colonial encounter. Central to the show was the reenactment of the 1896 Matabele War in Rhodesia. This included a depiction of a Matabele massacre of a white homestead and Chief Lobengula (reportedly played by the real chief's son) calling for the annihilation of the white man. The performance ended with the famous Rhodesian settler column defeating the Matabele and restoring white order (see Shepard, 2003, 76–79).

This trumpeting of difference *vis-à-vis* the replication of war and violence took on a charged jingoist tint as Great Britain was in the midst of the South African War. In connection to the conflict, the exhibition took another liberty with constructions of the ethnographic other. *Savage South Africa* included Boer peoples within the visual display of essentialized difference. The show's handbill promised: "A sight never previously presented in Europe; a horde of savages, direct from the kraals, comprising 200 Matabeles, Basutos, Swazies, Hottentots, Malays, Cape and Transvaal Boers."[20] The Greater Britain Exhibition not only sought to affirm the dichotomy of savage and civilized through the common trope of Africa and its peoples, but also

---

[17] On the dominion movement, see Darwin (1999, 64–87). For a deeper understanding of the concept of Greater Britain, see Bell (2007).
[18] On May 9, 1899, *The Times* (London) announced that the Greater Britain Exhibition was a "high-sounding title" for an exhibition dominated by collections from Australia.
[19] "Frank Filliss's Savage South Africa" is listed on the map of the exhibition grounds as being performed in the Empress Theatre. No other performance or exhibit is noted. See *The Official Catalogue of the Greater Britain Exhibition* (1899, 4–5).
[20] There are several full-page advertisements for *Savage South Africa* in the *Official Catalogue of the Greater Britain Exhibition* that were surely posted to the public.

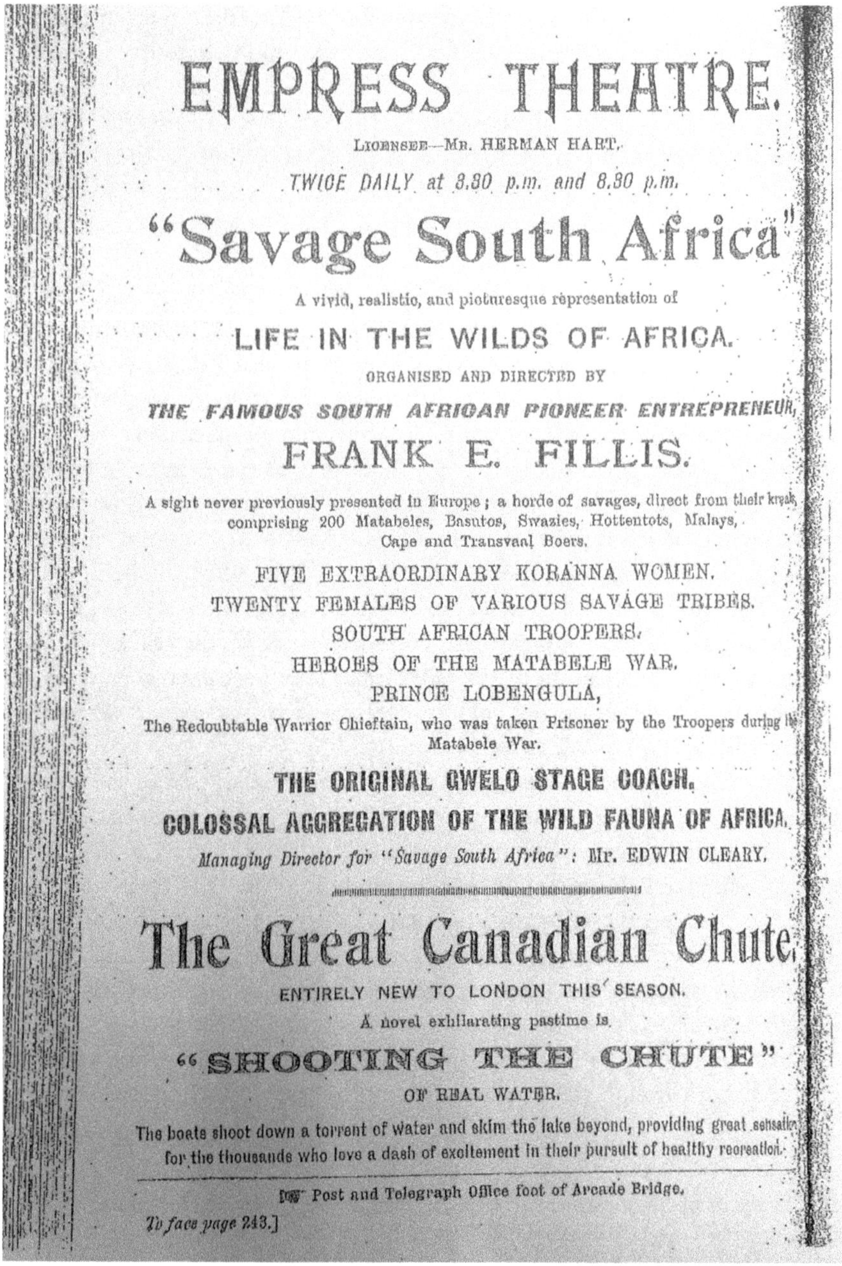

Figure 3.3 Savage South Africa – Empress Theater

used this platform to specifically drum up support for British efforts against the Boers in the South African War.

Savage South Africa gained immediate notoriety in the press. The majority of the coverage focused on one of two concerns: the welfare of the native Africans brought to perform in the show and the fear that "savage" natives would threaten London society. Pan-Africanist Henry Sylvester Williams only addressed the first concern and, in a letter written to the Colonial Office, argued that the native Africans taken from their "primitive homes" to perform at the exhibition should be introduced to the benefits of civilization during their stay in England. Operating within the tenets of progress, Williams endorsed Great Britain's civilizing mission. During the South African War, many touted British imperial rule as a dramatic improvement over Boer authority for African peoples. Perhaps the context of the war affected Williams's appeal to have African peoples introduced to the civilizing norms of British society, but it also exposes his acquiescence to the paternalistic overtones of imperial progressivism. There is no question, however, that Williams was deeply offended by the crass ethnographic other represented by *Savage South Africa*. In the same plea to the Colonial Office, Williams explicitly protested *Savage South Africa* as a "spectacle of constant ridicule and caricature" (see Shepard, 2003, 80–81).

Colonial critic J.A. Hobson also denounced the caricatures displayed at exhibitions such as *Savage South Africa* and his insights remain one of the seminal discussions of the ethnographic other. According to Hobson, the projection of difference in the stark dichotomies of civilized and savage fueled the spectator's "primitive lust" for domination and pushed the jingoism of empire (1902, 224–228). Hobson also had a particular interest in the South African War and spent the summer and autumn of 1899 in the country gathering material for his work *The War in South Africa: Its Causes and Effects* (1900). In this work he further echoed Williams, asserting that stereotypical representations of Africans such as those perpetuated in the Earl's Court show gave a skewed understanding of the "native question" (1900, 285). Yet Hobson also argued that metropolitan "praiseworthy sentiments of freedom and justice" were equally misguided in seeking to rescue the natives of South Africa from the racist Boer through good imperial practice (1900, 283). In line with his diatribe against the "rand capitalists," Hobson asserted that the horrendous conditions in the mines where native workers were subjected to "despotic and degrading restrictions on their liberty" destroyed any benign dimensions of the civilizing work ethic (1900, 287). Furthermore, any hope that the imposition of British imperial control could minimize the power of capital interests and accompanying abuse was denied by the historical record of empire. Justice and equality would also founder because of the shared racial attitudes of white people in South Africa. "Both white races are strongly opposed to the liberation and elevation of the native, and the British are no more likely to carry out an Exeter Hall policy than the Dutch," Hobson explained. "There is virtual unanimity among white South Africans that the natives must be kept down" (1900, 288, 289).[21] He continued: "Educated niggers are not more popular with the British in South Africa than they are with the British in India; there is not, either among the British or the Dutch, any real growth of liberal feeling upon native question" (1900, 291).

The conflation of Boer with black African in the performance of *Savage South Africa* might have generated jingoism in a metropolitan audience. But this construction could not have been further away from the realities on the ground. Despite the cottage industry of writing on the antipathies between British and Boer, the commonality of whiteness—the construction of the global color line—united them in southern Africa. After British victory in the South African War, the Treaty of Vereeniging did not signal a new phase of imperial progressivism and improved race relations but, instead, witnessed a racial reconciliation between Brit and Boer that was a crucial marker on the path to national white supremacy.[22] With prescience, Hobson argued:

> Let no one deceive himself. This strong deep-rooted general sentiment of inequality cannot be over-ridden by Imperial edict. Any attempt to secure real substantial equality of rights for the natives of South Africa will involve us in hostility with British and Dutch alike, and indeed furnishes the not improbable bond of future union of the now disrupted races which will eventually sever South Africa from the control of Great Britain. (1900, 291)[23]

The Buffalo Pan-American Exposition

As the South African War occupied Great Britain, the United States launched the Buffalo Pan-American Exposition of 1901, which continued the promotion of US imperialism.[24] The very layout, architecture, and

---

[21] The Anti-Slavery Society met in Exeter Hall and the location became shorthand for British reformer conscience.

[22] Clause Eight of the treaty expressly delayed the question of black franchise until after the achievement of responsible government.

[23] Hobson hardly believed in racial equality. For an overview of his deeply paternalist thought, see Long (2005, 71–91).

[24] Robert Rydell argues that US-sponsored World's Fairs from 1876 to 1916 were part of an effort to "manage the world from its own rapidly expanding imperial perspective" (1984, 18). Two detailed overviews were published to accompany the Fair: *The Official Catalogue and Guidebook to the Pan-American Exposition, with Maps of Exposition and Illustrations, Buffalo, N.Y., U.S.A.—May 1st to Nov. 1st, 1901* (1901) and Richard H. Barry's *Snap Shots on the Midway of the Pan-Am Expo* (1901).

color scheme of the exposition suggested an "evolutionary" journey for the spectator that acted as "an allegory of America's rise to the apex of civilization" (Rydell, 1984, 141). The declaration of evolutionary superiority not only relied on racial differentiation, but also decreed that the United States was prepared to be a leader in imperial progressivism.

On the international stage of Paris, the United States used the American Negro Exhibit as evidence of successful race relations and, thus, validation of the US as a progressive imperial power. At first glance, it is astonishing that, at Buffalo, the American Negro Exhibit appeared in truncated form and was tucked far away from the main representations of African peoples on the Midway entertainment section of the exposition.[25] Yet this marginalization of the exhibit shows that, similar to the local conditions in South Africa, the construction of whiteness prevailed, despite the possibilities of subjectivity and rights contained in the discourse of imperial progressivism. National racial reconciliation between North and South in the United States took precedence and minimized reclamations of subjectivity and claims for racial equality, even those like the American Negro Exhibit which had just been used to validate America's beneficent progressivism at the international venue of the Paris Exhibition.

While representations of the ethnographic other were varied at Buffalo, inordinate attention was paid to one of the newest colonial possessions, the Philippines. The Fair lauded the resource-related potential of the islands and depicted the Filipino as a prime candidate for uplift. In the Filipino Village, native Filipinos were displayed along a continuum. While a level of inferiority characterized all these representations, the central consideration—of fitting the Filipino into US progressive imperialism—rescued

---

[25] Recent scholarship demonstrates that some version of the American Negro Exhibit was displayed at Buffalo. The Buffalo and Erie County Library found a scrapbook in its archives about the Pan-American Exposition almost a hundred years after the event. This scrapbook contained a 24-page pamphlet of the "Negro Exhibit" that was displayed in the Manufactures and Liberal Arts building at the exposition. Du Bois was not involved and the evidence is spotty as to whether Thomas Calloway curated the exhibit. It is evident that local African-American women spearheaded the effort to have the American Negro Exhibit at Buffalo and their story is part of a project developed by Drs. Peggy Brooks-Bertram and Barbara A. Seals Nevergold, "Uncrowned Queens," whose website has made several articles available (www.uncrownedcommunitybuilders.com). The official guide to the Exposition does not list the American Negro Exhibit, but lists a photographic display by Atlanta University and exhibitions sponsored by Fisk University, Howard University, the Hampton Normal & Agricultural School, and the Tuskegee Institute. Most certainly these displays were part of the earlier American Negro Exhibit, but no evidence of their content or arrangement remains beyond the listing in the catalogue. See *The Official Catalogue and Guidebook* (1901, 110–111) and Barry (1901). See also Loos, Savigny, and Gurn (2001) and Valint (2011).

the displays from depicting too much backwardness, too much "savagery." At Buffalo, the Filipinos on display projected the benefits of American uplift. An all-Filipino band played the *Star-Spangled Banner* and the local papers claimed that many of the native Filipinos brought to Buffalo cried as the Fair ended (see Rydell, 1984, 151–156). As the United States formally administered colonial areas, its World's Fair followed the standard pattern, projecting colonial peoples as willing subjects for US imperial progressivism.

How different was the display of African peoples. Quite unlike the American Negro Exhibit displayed in the Musée Social, the main representation of African peoples at Buffalo was on the Midway, where exhibits like *Darkest Africa* promised similar representations as that of the *Savage South Africa* shows at the Greater Britain Exhibition. While the *Old Plantation*, directly across the walkway, was projected as less "savage," the continuities between it and *Darkest Africa* were evident. Both exhibitions emphasized fixed characteristics of African people: "savage" in *Darkest Africa* and "cheerful" in *The Old Plantation*. Buffalo, similar to the Greater Britain Exhibition, portrayed African peoples as relatively unchanging ethnographic others.

The stark connotations of *Darkest Africa* are obvious. *The Old Plantation*, in its location near the "savagery" of *Darkest Africa*, directed the eight million attendees at Buffalo to gaze upon the days of contented slavery, where paternalist conditions allowed African peoples to exude their natural characteristics of contentment and cheerfulness.[26] The contented period of slavery, according to the narrative, disappeared as emancipation loosed the threat of the politically empowered yet woefully "savage" black male. The Pan-American Exposition reflected fears over political empowerment and was part of the post-bellum racial reconciliation between North and South.[27] The relegation of African peoples to varying, but static, states of "backwardness" helped to deny inclusion of African Americans and to heal the fracture within the nation's imagined community of whiteness. The Treaty of Vereeniging and the Pan-American Exposition illustrate how the promises of improved race relations embedded in ideologies of imperial progressivism often shattered on nationalist reconciliations of whiteness.

---

[26] Of course, the defenders of slavery also used arguments of progress: slavery rescued the African from savagery, while paternalist guidance allowed the slave to exhibit other natural characteristics such as simple good nature, which, of course would disappear if paternalist ownership slipped. Many scholars have addressed this issue. For a seminal work, see Fredrickson (1971, 256–283).

[27] My arguments here are deeply indebted to Rydell (1984). For more on post-bellum racial reconciliation in the United States, see Blight (2001).

Figure 3.4 War Dance of Cape Lopez Blacks – Darkest Africa, Pan-American Exposition of 1901

Figure 3.5 Three "Culled Gemmen" – Old Plantation, Pan-American Exposition of 1901

These national reconciliations were symptomatic of the disempowerment of non-white subjects and citizens during the construction and maintenance of the global color line and, despite its logic of progress and rhetoric of rights, imperial progressivism was largely in the employ of this construction. Although not catering to the stark perpetuation of the ethnographic other, imperial progressivism positioned peoples of African descent in positions of inferiority on the continuum of racial difference. This positioning safely underwrote open-ended periods of paternalist tutelage that rarely considered even the *potentiality* of racial equality. Thus, despite the Pan-African activism at international forums that demonstrated the subjectivity of peoples of African descent and called for political rights, the display of the harsh hues of the ethnographic remained a staple on the Midway of World's Fairs.

As evidenced by the Pan-African activism detailed in this chapter, however, the deferment of inclusion—the exclusionary practices—did not go unnoticed and often provided the moment where the standard was most exposed.[28] The contradictions of ideational inclusion and practical exclusion helped generate a stream of Pan-African protest that was no longer content with strategies seeking only protections. Instead, Pan-Africanism invoked the weight of subject and citizen into their protest, claiming a host of expansive rights central to valid and meaningful participation in modern society: recognition of a common humanity, equality before the law, freedom of conscience, political participation, and social belonging.[29] This activism contributed to the shift from protests dominated by religiously informed morality to one that repositioned this morality within a more secular, overtly political questioning of the relationship of subjects and citizens to the state.[30]

Without question, however, the perpetuation of the ethnographic other is indicative of the uphill struggle that Pan-African activists faced in their pursuit of rights and equality according to the promise of imperial progressivism.[31] Indeed, the Pan-African Conference had difficulty sustaining an institutional presence. The organizers of the Pan-African Conference started the Pan-African Association to continue its agenda and, while Henry Sylvester Williams traveled to the United States, Jamaica, and

---

[28] For more on this topic, see Roxanne Doty's arguments (1996, esp. 27–51).

[29] On citizenship and its implications in the late nineteenth and early twentieth century, see Hall, McClelland, and Rendell (2000); Cooper, Holt, and Scott (2000); Wallerstein (2003, 650–679).

[30] Reza Afshari uses the term "veritable revolution" to describe the shift away from single-issue moral campaigns such as anti-slavery to the modern notion of human rights which recognizes the existence of multiple and interdependent rights (2007, 6). One crucial measure of this shift is marked by the examination of the relationship between state and citizen.

[31] On the inclusionary and exclusionary nature of liberalism as well as its intimate relationship with imperialism, see Mehta (1999).

South Africa to drum up support for the organization, the association's periodical was never published with consistency and the planned subsequent conferences never materialized.[32] There was thus a significant 19-year lacuna in the formal, institutional aspects of Pan-Africanism until the Du Bois-directed Pan-African Congress of 1919. The context of self-determination in the postwar climate held a different set of possibilities than those offered by turn-of-the-century imperial progressivism. Interwar Pan-Africanism not only found consistent institutional strength, but also developed clear anti-colonial positions that outstripped the possibilities available to turn-of-the-century Pan-Africanists negotiating the terms of imperial progressivism.

While there was no formal institution dedicated to Pan-Africanism after the 1900 conference, many of the actors at the conference participated in a vibrant transatlantic print culture. Beyond Henry Sylvester Williams, W.E.B. Du Bois, Booker T. Washington, and Thomas J. Calloway, Pan-African Conference attendees—such as African Americans Bishop Alexander Walters and musical composer Frederic J. Loudin; West African Mojolo Agbebi; South African John Tengo Jabuvu; Ghana-born, South Africa-residing F.Z.S. Peregrino; and Jamaican J. Robert Love—contributed to a steady exchange of letters and publications. Further, there was a periodical culture in West Africa, South Africa, the Caribbean, England, and the United States that linked peoples of African descent across nation-state boundaries (the papers often ran articles first published by each other).[33] This print culture continued an advocacy that sustained a web of connections between peoples of African descent, regardless of nationality. Thus, despite the long period between the first and second Pan-African conferences, a Pan-African subjectivity expressed through print culture continued to expose the contradictions of imperial progressivism and helped provide a backdrop for the establishment of other institutions struggling against inequality and racism, such as the National Association

---

[32] Up to his death in 1911, Williams remained active as a barrister both in South Africa and England, and served as a local councilor in the Marylebone borough of England in 1906 and 1907 (one of the first black councilors elected in Great Britain). For more on Williams and Pan-Africanism at the turn of the twentieth century, see Sherwood (2011).

[33] The papers of prolific African-American journalist John Bruce represent one of the largest holdings at the Schomburg Center for Research in Black Culture. This collection (which is only partial due to a fire), documents the transatlantic correspondence and also contains articles from a host of black-led publications, including the *West African Record*, *The Jamaica Advocate*, *The South African Spectator*, and the *African Times and Orient Review*. John Edward Bruce Papers, Schomburg Center for Research in Black Culture, Manuscripts, Archives and Rare Book Division, The New York Public Library, Call Number Sc Micro R-905.

for the Advancement of Colored Peoples in the United States in 1909 and the South African Native National Convention in 1912 (which became the African National Congress in 1923).

Human rights scholar Kathryn Sikkink comments that "Virtually any explanation of the rise of human rights must take into account the political power of norms and ideas and the increasingly transnational way in which those ideas are carried and diffused" (Sikkink, 1998, 517). Human rights theorists also argue that the success of advocacy is not only found in its direct influence on practices and behavior, but also is evident in the difference made by advocates in the environment in which all actors operate (Keck and Sikkink,(1998, 25). Certainly, turn-of-the-century Pan-Africanism did not stop imperialism, racialized violence, paternalism, or crass racism. However, it did establish a recognizable transatlantic network that issued a powerful critique that helped keep alive the promise of humanist equality and laid the groundwork for later activism that continued to challenge its deferment.

Works Cited

Afshari, Reza. "On Historiography of Human Rights Reflections on Paul Gordon Lauren's *The Evolution of International Human Rights: Visions Seen.*" *Human Rights Quarterly* 29.1 (2007): 1–67.

Barry, Richard H. *Snap Shots on the Midway of the Pan-Am Expo.* Buffalo, NY: Robert Allan Reid, 1901.

Bederman, Gail. *Manliness and Civilization: A Cultural History of Gender and Race in the United States, 1880–1917.* Chicago, IL: University of Chicago Press, 1996.

Bell, Duncan. "Empire and International Relations in Victorian Political Thought." *The Historical Journal* 49.1 (2006): 281–298.

Bell, Duncan. *The Idea of Greater Britain: Empire and the Future of the World Order, 1860–1900.* Princeton, NJ: Princeton University Press, 2007.

Blight, David. *Race and Reunion: The Civil War in American Memory.* Cambridge, MA: Harvard University Press, 2001.

Brooks-Bertram, Peggy, and Barbara A. Seals Nevergold. "Uncrowned Queens." http://www.uncrownedcommunitybuilders.com. Accessed Jan. 10, 2014.

Bruce, John E. *The Blood Red Record: A Review of the Horrible Lynching and Burning of Negroes by Civilized White Men in the United States.* Albany, NY: The Argus Company, 1901.

Bryce, James. *The Relations of the Advanced and Backward Races of Mankind.* Oxford: Clarendon Press, 1903.

Calloway, Thomas J. "The American Negro Exhibit: At the Paris Exposition." *Colored American,* November 3, 1900: 2–9.

Cooper, Frederick, Thomas C. Holt, and Rebecca J. Scott. *Beyond Slavery: Explorations of Race, Labor, and Citizenship in Postemancipation Societies*. Chapel Hill, NC: University of North Carolina Press, 2000.

Cooper, Frederick and Ann Laura Stoler, eds. *Tensions of Empire: Colonial Cultures in a Bourgeois World*. Berkeley, CA: University of California Press, 1997.

Corbey, Raymond. "Ethnographic Showcases, 1870–1930." *Cultural Anthropology* 8.3 (1993): 338–369.

Darwin, John. "A Third British Empire? The Dominion Idea in Imperial Politics." In *The Oxford History of the British Empire: Volume IV, The Twentieth Century*. Ed. William Roger Louis and Judith M. Brown. Oxford: Oxford University Press, 1999.

Dilke, Charles. *Greater Britain: A Record of Travel in English-Speaking Countries*. London: Macmillan, 1868.

Doty, Roxanne. *Imperial Encounters: The Politics of Representation in North-South Relations*. Minneapolis, MN: University of Minnesota Press, 1996.

Du Bois, W.E.B. *The Conservation of Races*. Washington, DC: American Negro Academy, 1897.

Du Bois, W.E.B. "The American Negro in Paris." *The American Monthly Review of Reviews* (November 1900): 575–577.

Fisher, Rebecka Rutledge. "Cultural Artifacts and the Narrative of History: W.E.B. Du Bois and the Exhibiting of Culture at the 1900 Paris Exposition Universelle." *Modern Fiction Studies* 51.4 (Winter 2005): 741–774.

Fredrickson, George. *The Black Image in the White Mind: The Debate on the Afro-American Character and Destiny, 1817–1914*. New York: Harper and Row, 1971.

Freeden, Michael. *The New Liberalism: An Ideology of Social Reform*. Oxford: Clarendon Press, 1978.

Greenhalgh, Paul. *Ephemeral Vistas: The Expositions Universelles, Great Exhibitions, and World's Fairs, 1851–1939*. Manchester: Manchester University Press, 1988.

Hall, Catherine, Keith McClelland, and Jane Rendell. *Defining the Victorian Nation: Class, Race, and Gender and the Reform Act of 1867*. Cambridge: Cambridge University Press, 2000.

Hobson, J.A. *The War in South Africa: Its Causes and Effects*. London: James Nisbet & Co., 1900.

Hobson, John A. *Imperialism: A Study*. New York: James Pott & Company, 1902.

John Edward Bruce Papers, Schomburg Center for Research in Black Culture, Manuscripts, Archives and Rare Book Division, The New York Public Library, Call Number Sc Micro R-905.

Keck, Margaret, and Kathryn Sikkink. *Activists beyond Borders: Advocacy Networks in International Politics*. Ithaca, NY: Cornell University Press, 1998.

Kelley, Robin D.G. "'But a Local Phase of a World Problem': Black History's Global Vision, 1883–1950." *The Journal of American History* 86.3 (December 1999): 1045–1077.

Kloppenberg, James T. *Uncertain Victory: Social Democracy and Progressivism in European and American Thought, 1870–1920*. New York: Oxford University Press, 1986.

Lake, Marilyn and Henry Reynolds. *Drawing the Global Colour Line: White Men's Countries and the International Challenge of the Racial Equality*. Cambridge: Cambridge University Press, 2008.

Lindfors, Bernth, ed. *Africans on Stage: Studies in Ethnological Show Business*. Bloomington, IN: Indiana University Press, 1999.

Long, David. "Paternalism and the Internationalization of Imperialism: J.A. Hobson on the International Government of the 'Lower Races.'" In *Imperialism and Internationalism in the Discipline of International Relations*. Ed. David Long and Brian C. Schmidt. Albany, NY: State University of New York Press, 2005: 71–91.

Loos, William H., Ami M. Savigny, and Robert M. Gurn. *The Forgotten "Negro Exhibit": African-American Involvement in Buffalo's Pan-American Exposition, 1901*. Buffalo, NY: Buffalo & Erie County Public Library, 2001.

Mehta, Uday. *Liberalism and Empire: A Study in nineteenth-century British Political Thought*. Chicago, IL: University of Chicago Press, 1999.

Munro, Lisa. "Investigating World's Fairs: A Historiography." *Studies in Latin American Popular Culture* 28 (2010): 80–94.

Murray, Daniel. "African American Photographs Assembled for 1900 Paris Exhibition." *Daniel Murray Collection*, Library of Congress. http://www.loc.gov/pictures/collection/anedub/. Accessed Mar. 12, 2018.

The Official Catalogue and Guidebook to the Pan-American Exposition, with Maps of Exposition and Illustrations, Buffalo, N.Y., U.S.A.—May 1st to Nov. 1st, 1901. Buffalo, NY: Charles Ahrhart, 1901.

The Official Catalogue of the Greater Britain Exhibition (London: Spottiswoode & Co., 1899).

Report of the Commissioner-General for the United States to the International Universal Exposition, Paris, 1900 Volume II. Washington, DC: Government Printing Office, 1901.

The Report of the Pan-African Conference. London, 1900.

Rodgers, Daniel T. *Atlantic Crossings: Social Politics in a Progressive Age*. Cambridge, MA: The Belknap Press, 1998.

Rosenberg, Emily, ed. *A World Connecting: 1870–1945*. Cambridge, MA: The Belknap Press, 2012.

Rydell, Robert W. *All the World's a Fair: Visions of Empire at American International Expositions, 1876–1914*. Chicago, IL: University of Chicago Press, 1984.

Rydell, Robert W. *World of Fairs: The Century-of-Progress Expositions*. Chicago, IL: University of Chicago Press, 1993.

Shepard, Ben. *Kitty and the Prince*. Johannesburg and Cape Town: Jonathan Ball, 2003.

Sherwood, Marika. *Origins of Pan-Africanism: Henry Sylvester Williams, Africa, and the African Diaspora*. New York and London: Routledge, 2011.

Sikkink, Kathryn. "Transnational Politics, International Relations Theory, and Human Rights." *PS: Political Science and Politics* 31.3 (September 1998): 517–523.

Smith, Shawn Michelle. *Photography on the Color Line: W.E.B. Du Bois, Race, and Visual Culture*. Durham, NC: Duke University Press, 2004.

The Times, May 9, 1899.

Travis, Miles Everett. "Mixed Messages: Thomas Calloway and the 'American Negro Exhibit' of 1900." Master of Arts thesis, Montana State University, 2004.

Valint, Andrew R. "Fighting for Recognition: The Role African Americans Played in World Fairs." His Master of Arts thesis, Buffalo State University, 2011.

Wallerstein, Immanuel "Citizens All? Citizens Some!" *Comparative Studies in Society and History* 45.4 (2003): 650–679.

Wells, Ida B. *Crusade for Justice: The Autobiography of Ida B. Wells*. Ed. Alfreda M. Duster. Chicago, IL: University of Chicago Press, 1970.

Wright, Gwendolyn. "Building Global Modernisms." *Grey Room* 7 (Spring 2002): 124–134.

4

Black Sojourners in the *Métropole* and in the Homeland: Challenges of Otherness in Calixthe Beyala's *Loukoum: The "Little Prince" of Belleville* and Myriam Warner-Vieyra's *Juletane*

Philip Ojo (Agnes Scott College)

Francophone African narratives such as Calixthe Beyala's *Loukoum: The "Little Prince" of Belleville* (1995)[1] and Myriam Warner-Vieyra's *Juletane* (1987)[2] express and explore the complex experiences of immigrants in the African diaspora. They focus on the problems of learning new cultural codes, on the choice between retaining a native culture or assimilating, and on the conflicts between immigrants and their new host society, particularly those faced by peoples of African descent in the context of postcolonial migration.

Loukoum and *Juletane* function as "narratives" about cross-cultural movements, cultural memories, and individual and collective struggles for integration abroad, and sometimes at home. They serve as a space for criticism and mediation about migration and otherness, and may also be considered as the voices of disenfranchised immigrants of African descent who long for a hybrid space they can call home.

In recent years, with ongoing unrest in many parts of the Middle East, Africa, and Asia, hundreds of thousands of people have migrated to Western countries, fleeing political oppression, religious persecution, violence, and famine, and seeking safety, freedom, a decent living, and a place to call home. However, migration destabilizes identities and communities precisely insofar as it detaches identity from place, though it can also create new nomadic identities and lead to the creolization of global culture (Ahmed, 2003, 1–2).

---

[1] Originally published in French as *Le Petit Prince de Belleville* (1992).
[2] Originally published in French as *Juletane* (1982).

Immigrants arrive at their destination with many uncertainties and encounter numerous challenges. They must find employment and accommodation;[3] adapt to new laws, cultures, and languages; negotiate obstacles to assimilation and integration; endure loneliness and indefinite separation from their families; and sometimes cope with exclusionary behaviors on the part of hostile elements of the host community who claim that immigrants cause huge population surges and put a strain on infrastructure and services.

In France, the preferred destination for citizens of former French colonies,[4] immigrants, particularly Blacks and Arabs, are victims of harassment, cultural *clichés*, and discriminatory views resulting from "the notion that immigrants and their descendants are fundamentally out of place in French society," or for the simple reason that they are "enduringly different from the indigenous majority" (Hargreaves, 1995, 1, 2).

Many immigrants[5] come to realize that despite every effort to negotiate their cultural identity with the dominant society—France, the former colonizer—no matter what they do, they cannot insulate themselves from racial stereotypes and discrimination, interethnic conflict, racial animosity, cultural denigration, and economic marginalization. People of African descent even suffer alienation and rejection when they migrate to other parts of the African diaspora,[6] where they find an insider/outsider dichotomy, an *us* and *them* divide, which constantly generates the question, "Where are you from?" (Hitchcott, 2006a, 73). Difference is indeed the basis of all immigration challenges, as Gloria Anzaldúa posits in her seminal work, *Borderlands/La Frontera* (1999).

Loukoum and *Juletane* are excellent examples of literary treatments of migrant experience in the *Métropole* and at home, of narratives about cross-cultural movements, cultural memories, and individual and collective struggles for integration at home and abroad. They illustrate how literary representations provide a space for criticism and mediation of migration and otherness, and a voice for disenfranchised immigrants who long for a hybrid space they can call home.

---

[3] Newcomers tend to live in immigrant neighborhoods called "Africa," "New Agege," "Little Italy," "Chinatown" or "Little China," "Little India," and "Little Jamaica." This arrangement allows them to share and promote their native culture and national identities.
[4] Mali, Cameroon, Congo (the homelands of the protagonists of Beyala's *Loukoum*), and Guadeloupe (the native land of the protagonist of Myriam Warner-Vieyra's *Juletane*) are former French colonies.
[5] The protagonists in Beyala's *Loukoum* perfectly represent this group.
[6] Myriam Warner-Vieyra's Juletane is an excellent illustration of this experience. A native of Guadeloupe, she relocates to Senegal, her ancestral home.

The Literary Trope of Migration

The literary trope of migration, which suggests both geographical displacement and psychological dislocation, has become a recurrent theme in postcolonial texts that seek to give voice to new relationships between immigrants and locals, suggesting the ways in which immigrants both transform and are transformed by their new country (Ireland and Proulx, 2001, 1–2).

The multifaceted challenges of otherness are articulated with both broad and subtle humor in an increasing number of francophone literary works, including Cameroonian Calixthe Beyala's *Loukoum* and Guadeloupean Myriam Warner-Vieyra's *Juletane*. Both novels focus on the problems of learning new cultural codes, the choice between retaining a native culture and assimilating, and the conflicts between immigrants and their host society, particularly in the context of postcolonial migrations (King, 2004, 809). Although both texts center on immigrant life, engaging with similar challenges of otherness in divergent contexts and dealing extensively with the consequent cultural and psychological effects, *Loukoum* and *Juletane* illustrate the striking complexities and differences between African immigration and the Antillean experience.

Beyala is hailed as one of the most prolific African feminist writers. Although recognized principally for her novels, she has also published essays and short story collections, each focusing on the impact of patriarchy and cultural alienation on African women, and the struggles of navigating the difficult terrain of cultural adjustment and assimilation. Beyala is noted as an exemplary voice of postcolonial francophone literature and she has received several awards (Le Prix Tropique, Le Prix François Mauriac, Le Prix de l'Afrique Littéraire, and Le Grand Prix du Roman de l'Académie française) and achieved international critical acclaim, notwithstanding some allegations of plagiarism.[7]

Beyala's *Loukoum* is an account of immigrant life in Belleville, a Parisian suburb. Through the first-person child narrator, Mamadou Traoré, nicknamed Loukoum, we observe the colorful world of a multicultural diaspora, and the immigrants' need to integrate into French society while still preserving their

---

[7] Beyala's image as a writer has been tarnished by two high-profile allegations of plagiarism, one of which led to her conviction in the High Court of Paris in 1996, the same year she was awarded the prestigious Grand Prix du Roman de l'Académie française for *Les Honneurs perdus*, one of the novels containing material she had allegedly plagiarized (Hitchcott, 2006a). Surprisingly, this conviction did not deter Beyala, who sees plagiarism, consciously or unconsciously borrowing others' ideas, as part of literary creativity. She "may indeed be a plagiarist but, more importantly, she is a player who understands, tests, appropriates and manipulates the institutional limits of tolerance in postcolonial France" (Hitchcott, 2006b, 108).

African roots. The central characters are forced to renegotiate their identities across the constantly shifting border space between Africa and France while attempting to reconcile competing sets of cultural expectations (Hitchcott, 2006a, 66).

Loukoum's father, Abdou Traoré, migrated to France for economic reasons; he was looking for a better life for his family: "I came to this country in the grip of material gain, expelled from my own land by need. I came, we came to this country to save our skin, to buy our children a future" (11, 102). But he discovers that "exclusion is built into the system" (65) and that he must submit to a way of life that robs him of the peace and pleasure of the life he once knew. Abdou's choice of the collective pronoun *we* clearly illustrates the larger presence of immigrants and the painful realities of survival which they must confront in societies refusing to tolerate different cultural habits (Edwin, 2005). Abdou's *we* also indexes the notion of community and communal identity that is an integral part of his worldview, and which is shattered in individualized Western society. His first encounters with Paris are characterized by solitude, competition, and aggression. He learns the order of the day: each to his own, "look out for yourself! Look out for yourself!" (10).

Like his father, Loukoum is aware of the socioeconomic disparity between his family and French bourgeois families. He expresses frustration with his family's marginalization, which he attributes to their poor economic status and their African and immigrant identity. Many African immigrants experience severe financial difficulties; in fact, some have absolutely nothing. They live in poor neighborhoods that lack basic amenities and essential infrastructures (4, 13). This housing arrangement systematizes the exclusion of immigrants from social participation, resulting in a social separation that makes everyone stay in their own district. Even when they achieve economic success, immigrants struggle to integrate into the host community due to their foreignness.

In *Loukoum*, despite their successful jewelry business, M'am and her family are the victims of stereotyping, ethnic alterity, or social inequality because they are so easily identifiable (154–155). As Ireland and Proulx write, "The color of their skin, the spelling of their names, or simply a reference to their neighborhood or address is often sufficient to disqualify [immigrants] in the eyes of an employer" (2001, 11).

As a refuse collector, Loukoum's father fares worse still. As an illiterate, Muslim, first-generation immigrant, he lacks the social capital to participate in French cultural life. The privileges accorded to cultural insiders are therefore unavailable to him, especially because he has resigned himself to never learning the culture of the host nation (Hitchcott, 2006a, 75–83). Abdou is overcome by a sense of loss. It can be measured by his apartment, which has become defamiliarized and strange: "Nothing is called by its name any more. I no longer recognize the geography of the land drawn in MY OWN HOUSE" (91). He is inextricably attached to his native home. More profoundly, Abdou laments the loss of his son to Western education, which he sees as "lend[ing] my son to authorities other than my own—to men and women I do not know but who are qualified to teach, so they tell me. And so the child breaks away from me" (1). Abdou's preference is for Loukoum to be educated with a curriculum entrenched in African culture and values, not the kind of development offered by the French system. The acculturation of Loukoum is so profound that his father's feeling of loss resonates throughout the novel:

> He [Loukoum] has discovered the vocabulary of Paris [...]
> He has acquired other ways of saying hello.
> He knows rituals that throw me.
> He feels repugnance at eating with his hands,
> He imposes other conformities
> He imports tastes, preoccupations.
> He passes from one universe to another without worrying about it.
> He judges ours, feels contempt. (144)

The new Loukoum looks Westernized in every way "for fear that he'll feel lost" or not belong in French society (138); he embodies that hybridization that may provide a redemptory space for migrants.

While *Loukoum*'s protagonists have migrated to France to seek economic opportunities, in *Juletane*, the Antillean protagonist seeks a return to the ancestral homeland of the diaspora, to reconnect with the past. But, as Adele King rightly concludes, "Juletane fail[s] to find what [she] wants in Africa" (1991, 101). She longed to live in the ancestral homeland only to feel unwelcome and is quickly disillusioned: "This homecoming to Africa, the land of my forefathers, I had imagined it in a hundred different ways, and it had become a nightmare" (15). Indeed, the quest turns into a struggle against the prevailing patriarchal system and customs for which she was absolutely unprepared.

Myriam Warner-Vieyra, the author of *Juletane*, is a leading voice of the francophone transatlantic experience, writing about Guadeloupe, France, and Senegal. Her works are powerful renditions of the experiences and psychological traumas of French Antilleans in France and Africa, where they face oppression, isolation, rejection, and disillusionment (Pfaff, 2008, 974).

Warner-Vieyra's *Juletane* relates the displacement and alienation of a young West Indian woman in her search for a sense of place and home. After an initial migration from Guadeloupe to France, Juletane undergoes a second and more painful exile when she marries a West African university graduate named Mamadou. On route to Africa, Juletane learns that her husband already has an African wife and child. This initial shock is followed by others in Africa as Mamadou assumes his role as patriarch, offering Juletane the position of co-wife in a polygamous household. The protagonist, doubly displaced and completely dispossessed, finds herself striving to maintain her equilibrium within the context of a foreign culture. Instead of being welcomed back to the mythical African homeland she had always longed for, she is excluded and isolated from the life of her husband's community. She comes to believe that her only hope to integrate into African life is through motherhood, but is unable to have a child. Considered alien because of her West Indian identity and rendered barren following a traffic accident, Juletane must cope with the stigma attached to her inability to procreate in a patriarchal society. Juletane's profound alienation—stemming from physical, cultural, and linguistic differences—reduces her to silence and foments a violence which ends in tragedy (Proulx, 1997, 698–700).

Juletane's racial identity (a light-skinned Black woman from the West Indies) contributes tremendously to her experience of otherness. In France, she was viewed as an outsider because of her black skin; she is referred to as a beautiful black woman or a cute black girl (80). In Senegal, she is alienated not only because she cannot speak Wolof, the local language, but more importantly because of her skin color and Western personality. She is thus unable to identify with anyone, which for her is equivalent to having no identity: "I have no family, no friends. I even no longer have a name. Here they call me 'the mad woman' [...] a Tubab lady, which equally aggravates me [... Awa] even stripped me of my black identity" (13, 49, 79). Regardless of Juletane's skin color, her identity as Antillean (and therefore French) excludes her from the indigenous space of the Wolof/Senegalese community (52). Evidently, the line separating Juletane from the locals is linguistic, cultural, and ethnic (Said, 1999, 91, 93, 97).

Within eight days of arriving in Africa, Juletane feels completely disconnected from her surroundings, the co-wives, and even her husband Mamadou, who deceitfully brought her into a polygamous relationship and then distanced himself from her (48–49).

As the narrative unfolds, through retrospective interior monologues and journal entries, Juletane "provides the reader with a reconstructible chronology that indicates her spiraling descent into madness" (Fragd, 2002, 492). Her migratory experience turns into a "well of misery [...] living half a life" (5). She begins to experience "a psychological manifestation of (dis)possession and alienation" (492). From this time on, Juletane leads a marginal, increasingly silent and secluded life. Recognizing her "illegitimate" status, because she is a "non-mother," she becomes further detached from those surrounding her, confining herself to a narrow space. Eventually, she exteriorizes her feelings of anger through acts of self-mutilation and destruction (50–54).

The Fault Lines of Culture

Typically, immigrants choose to perform their ethnic identity in one of a number of ways: by maintaining their ethnic difference and thereby remaining forever marginalized; by demonstrating a willingness to integrate completely into the culture of the host country (assimilation); by creating a new identity independent of both the culture of origin and the receiving culture; or by accepting the pluralism of migrant identities, which entails successfully negotiating the hybrid migratory space. Beyala and Warner-Vieyra delve into conflicts of cultures, into the wide difference between French culture and the immigrant culture, and into the immigrants' attitudes towards their home culture and the host culture. Immigrants who are unable to adapt to the new demands of their host culture often retreat into what they see as the safe space of their native tradition, but as the protagonists' experiences in *Loukoum* and *Juletane* reveal, this is a largely unsuccessful means of negotiating migration (Hitchcott, 2006a, 9, 12, 127). To correct cultural imbalance, Shirin Edwin recommends "a reciprocal gesture for cultures to engage in the creation of a genuinely multicultural space [...] where a genuine effort is made to allow other cultural systems to participate without judging their practices." He also points out that this requires an understanding of immigrants' "value systems and then an understanding of their beliefs before eagerly wanting to erase their practices" (2005). Both novels offer cautionary tales; they argue for the importance of such understanding and tolerance.

The Traoré family in *Loukoum* and Mamadou's household in *Juletane* may be tagged as "patriarchal" and the women "marginalized" because of the polygamous set-up, yet it must be understood that this family structure is permitted by Islam, and therefore legitimate for those who practice it, regardless of what other faiths and ideals may think. Polygamy, as Abdou explains, is a sociocultural and political system derived from the need to assure heirs in a community, and it is approved by the Qur'an, the ultimate guide for practicing Muslims. He argues that his actions therefore cannot be described as unlawful, irrational, oppressive, or selfish since they are based on the Islamic code (Edwin, 2005).[8] In *Loukoum*, Abdou absolutely rejects any form of assimilation or hybridization, and the family's conversations

---

[8] For an immigrant like Abdou, to force his faith and traditions on the host community would amount to intrusion. By the same token, Abdou should not be compelled to accept the beliefs and traditions of the host community. As for Juletane, the solution to her terrible experience in Senegal is double-edged: she should have acknowledged local traditions, and the host community should have been more receptive and understanding. In the context of today's global society, the solution would be to create a truly multicultural space that would guarantee freedom of worship and expression of cultural heritage.

almost always have an Islamic flavor: "In the Qur'an, it is written ..." (58), "I have never done anything for anybody, except for Allah when I go to the mosque" (73), "Inch Allah, I said" (93), "The Almighty could hear you and be upset" (173). Abdou is particularly concerned because Loukoum's newly acquired Western attitudes and styles have begun to supplant their native Malian values. Loukoum's transformation clearly favors French culture. Abdou obviously desires a more inclusive French legal system that would acknowledge his African traditions: "it's your legislation that has not integrated my customs" (167), he blames French people and their culture.

The cultural imbalance is so obvious that even Loukoum, who is assimilating French culture, recognizes and opposes attempts to devalue African customs. Reacting to Madame Saddock's indifference to a value system she does not understand or appreciate, and to her consequent effort to instigate a rebellion against Abdou among the Traoré women, Loukoum vehemently condemns her action on the grounds that she is ignorant about marriage in Africa: "[Miss Saddock] has no business sticking her nose in [...] African marriages—she doesn't have a clue what they're all about. She doesn't understand the first thing about the way we live" (80). Loukoum's reaction reflects the constant homesickness that compels immigrants to retain a conscious or subconscious attachment to their native culture. But, as the character of Loukoum also illustrates, this attachment to the ancestral home is often countered by a yearning for a sense of belonging in the current place of residence.[9] This *in-between-ness* is also symptomatic of what Gloria Anzaldúa defines as living in a "borderland," that is, having one foot in two cultures, which implies a rift between a person and their native homeland brought about by separation. In response to the "borderland conflict," many immigrants find themselves in a position of ambivalence *vis-à-vis* the "host" society feeling alternately respect, dislike, or uncertainty (Hitchcott, 2006a, 98–99). The attachment of immigrants to their ancestral homeland, according to Victor Ramraj, "is inversely proportional to the degree individuals and communities are induced to or are willing to assimilate or integrate with their new environment" (1996, 217).

In their search for an identifiable community, Abdou and his son Loukoum adopt two different approaches in negotiating the migratory space, allowing Beyala to explore the complexities of the immigrant's experience more fully. On one hand, Loukoum looks for points of identification with the host culture; his model of home is one in which he is recognized by his peers, but without ever completely abandoning his roots. Although he wants to

---

[9] Caught psychically between two worlds, some attempt to assimilate and integrate, while others withdraw to their native identity (see Ramraj, 1996, 215, 216).

dress like Sylvester Stallone and not like his father, "for fear that he'll feel lost and/or rejected by [his peers]" (137–138), he also describes his pride in going to the mosque wearing a *djellaba* and a *chechia* (native cultural codes) like his father (53).

On the other hand, the conservative Abdou wishes to base his new home life on African values because he feels he has no access to the exclusive imagined community of France; he seeks to reconnect with his traditions and religious values in a culturally different society, and thus experiences his exile as a "poison" that eats away at his flesh (1). The character of Abdou reflects a different social dynamic, that of those who are unable to integrate into the host culture and as a result retreat into ethnic essentialism, either because they cannot feel a real sense of belonging, of community, and comfort with themselves, or because they are strongly committed to preserving and maintaining their native identity (Hoffman, 1999, 39).

In *Loukoum*, Beyala recognizes the common generational nature of different reactions to the immigrant experience. It is thus not surprising that Beyala should use a first-person child narrator instead of letting the adults speak for themselves. Loukoum is a naïve observer who reports without fully understanding what he witnesses, forcing the reader to consider the significance of what is reported. Within the novel, he acts as interpreter for his father, who does not speak the official language of France, but because of Loukoum's relative innocence and inexperience, he is unable to appreciate the fuller significance of his role. It is in such instances that the author allows Abdou to speak for himself. Abdou's explanation to his imaginary French friend best illustrates the contrast between the two generations:

> [Loukoum] has pushed his frontiers away. He has set up his world inside that world of yours, which I cannot penetrate, for his nation, which is yours […], has been formed and protects itself jealously. A one-way street, I can no longer pass through. (156)

According to Nicki Hitchcott, "Abdou is trapped in an invented authenticity that he has created for himself. It is a safe space for a migrant, but one that is ultimately unsustainable" (2006a, 76). Because Abdou refuses to leave behind his homeland and native traditions, which he sees as the only acceptable space, he is unable to adapt to the cultural realities in France.

Narrating Otherness, Critiquing Exclusion

In both *Loukoum* and *Juletane*, the protagonists seek to communicate with others; they wish to be understood; they try to forge social connections to people with whom they can talk with understanding and shared assumptions. Simply put, they long for a space to engage in multicultural communication.

As much as Abdou wants to preserve his religious beliefs and native values, his attitude and rejection of the host culture must not be seen as obstinacy. Abdou longs to be understood and he even tries to explain his differences, beliefs, and habits. He addresses an imaginary French friend with a plea: "no, friend, stop firing words at me that hurt, stop weighing me in your hand like three kilos of lost sunlight. Listen and try to understand" (20). Abdou's efforts to communicate with his imaginary friend are motivated by a desire to express the opposite realities in experiences: "my ideas which are so different" (166). His intentions and actions, including the practice of polygamy and his view of women's status, are based on Islamic law, laid down by God. Abdou therefore fashions a plea for a space that will acknowledge his beliefs instead of wiping them out. The Traoré family seeks what Bhabha calls a dialectic, "the negotiation of contradictory and antagonistic instances" (1994, 25) in a foreign context (Edwin, 2005). Indeed, Abdou's desire is to forge a coexistential space of mutual respect and tolerance.

Abdou's dilemma (*Loukoum*, 10) echoes that of many first-generation African immigrants of Belleville and explains their deep attachment to their African roots. Those who, like M'am's co-wife, Soumana, are unable to translate between European and African cultural models, ultimately fail to survive the migratory experience. When she talks of her impossible dreams of leaving her husband and becoming an actress, Soumana ends up weeping with frustration.[10] Her fate is physical deterioration and, ultimately, death (Hitchcott, 2006a, 86).

Children and young people find it easier to mingle with their peers in the host community, and they also adapt quickly to the local culture. In *Loukoum*, children and a few women negotiate migratory spaces more successfully than men.[11] Loukoum copes with different sets of cultural meanings because he is able to manage and appropriate his generation's enormous wealth—of African, French, and American cultural influences

[10] Soumana wanted to acculturate but she lacked the economic means to gain entry to the cultural space of France.
[11] Like all immigrants, the characters in *Loukoum* fall into three main categories. First, those who are wedded to the ancestral homeland and focus on the preservation of their native religious and cultural beliefs; these are mostly the older generation of men who remain forever marginalized. Second, those who are willing to integrate completely into the fascinating culture of the host country; they opt for a complete immersion into the host community culture, and are mostly children and young men. Finally, those who accept the pluralism of migrant identities, which entails successfully negotiating the hybrid migratory space; these are mostly young men and women (see Hitchcott, 2006, 9, 12, 127; Ramraj, 1996, 217; Ramadan, 1999, 22–24).

(146). He survives the transformative experience of migration because he is able and willing "to play identities, to wear different masks in response to different situations," as Hitchcott puts it (2006a, 131). Loukoum's attitude is typical because the migrant experience is, by definition, a transformative experience, one that is essential for migrant survival. However, Loukoum's strategy is one of strategic appropriation rather than acculturation or assimilation. He puts the past behind him and focuses on the present and the future.[12]

Related to Abdou's efforts to venerate and conserve his ancestral culture is Juletane's nostalgia for an African homeland, though for Juletane, this desire to return "home," *le mal du pays*, is for an imagined version of her ancestral homeland. Juletane is presented as someone who had always longed to see and discover Africa, but her anticipation quickly becomes a source of disappointment, sorrow, and despair because she is ill-prepared for the social realities she must negotiate, as Lulamae Fragd recognizes.[13] Juletane experiences recurring feelings of homelessness, prejudice, intolerance, alienation, and self-hatred when confronted with (African) racism, which makes communion with her forefathers' land difficult (Ramraj, 1996, 223, 226, 227). This is the experience of many immigrants who revisit their ancestral homeland. In many cases, "when immigrants return home to visit family and friends, they feel both that *they do* and that *they don't* belong. […] that this is no longer home for them" (Appiah, 2006, 90–91).

Juletane has difficulty understanding and adapting to Senegalese culture, not only because she was not adequately prepared for the change but, more importantly, because some members of her host family have made life unbearable for her; she has not received the necessary resources and support to adapt (45–48, 65–69, 73–78). Juletane is not only unprepared for the cultural experience but is also unwilling to learn the Wolof/African traditions she had married into; she refuses integration into the African heritage which she has sought to claim as nostalgic attachment. She joins the family neither for the Muslim holiday, Mawlid, nor for the baptism celebration following the birth of Mamadou and Awa's son.

---

[12] Establishing roots and attempting to adjust to the dominant society are not free of conflict, tension, and ambivalence. Those tending towards assimilation are less concerned with sustaining ancestral ties than with coming to terms with their new environment and acquiring a new identity (see Ramraj, 1996, 217, 223). When they have to choose between assimilation and separation, between their immigrant culture and French culture, the temptation of assimilation is very strong, especially for the youth.

[13] Lulamae Fragd points out that "Juletane is faced with an unknown culture and social practices for which she is absolutely unprepared" (2002, 488). In addition to her light skin color and Western mentality, Juletane has no knowledge or understanding of the local traditions, which would have helped to successfully negotiate her place in Senegal.

Thus, her behavior blocks attempts by her co-wife Awa to include her in the community, precluding the possibility of eventually bridging the gap between Antillean and African cultures. "Home: Well, I try to make a place for home," she confesses. "But here—their ways are so strange, so distant from my reality—my learned expectations. They don't treat me like a new daughter. Like 'our' youngest wife. No, I'm still an outsider. Foreigner" (51–52). Juletane, Mamadou, and the members of his household display marked insensitivity to one another and each other's heritage. Juletane rudely ignores Ndeye, refusing to shake her hand when they first meet. Ndeye enrages Juletane by calling her a "Toubabesse" (a White woman), blatantly denying the Antillean woman's African roots (79). Mamadou hurts Juletane deeply by deciding to marry again without consulting either of his first two wives, Awa and Juletane, and by choosing as a third wife a shallow, greedy, vain woman who torments Juletane (Mortimer, 1995, 44).

Juletane is a prisoner of patriarchy. Her barrenness seals her fate, precluding her from attaining a degree of societal acceptance and legitimacy. She turns to madness as refuge and resistance.[14] Alienation, dislocation, and the cultural invisibility of her pain and dehumanization drive Juletane to violent revenge (Mortimer, 1995, 45). Her violence manifests itself in stages. First, her body is the target of her destructive desires. Later, Juletane commits acts of violence against her co-wives and their children (92–93), ostensibly in order to punish her husband who set the stage for her torment (Proulx, 1997, 705). "That slap in the face was the last drop that made my cup of passivity overflow and transformed my patience into a raging torrent," Juletane explains (50) when Ndeye has struck her and destroyed her favorite records, mementoes of her former life. Diagnosed as insane and confined to a psychiatric hospital, Juletane brings back pieces of geographic memory: "a sweet smell … of an emerald island […] Come back to your island" (73). But she finds no comforting image to carry her metaphorically back to the Caribbean. Unable to envisage a new beginning, she dies in the hospital, "alone in a world which she scarcely understood" (58).

Juletane is a double-narration journal involving Juletane as a narrator writing her diary and Hélène, a non-narratee reader who reads the diary after Juletane's death (Ondrus, 2014, 229). Considering the circumstances surrounding the dairy, one can safely say that writing performs several functions in the life of Juletane, who is labeled "foreign" and "mad" by the

---

[14] As Proulx points out, Juletane's experience "illustrate[s] the precarious position of [a woman] who refuse[s] to conform to sanctioned female roles in a patriarchal society" (1997, 699). Juletane's identity as madwoman ("la folle"), an epithet maliciously bestowed upon her by Ndeye, a co-wife, is used by her as a final, self-defeating defense.

natives, and who chooses to live and write within a confined space that she can control: her room, her journal (26–27).

Juletane uses writing to document the disillusionments and abuses she encounters including psychosis (25), cross cultural shock (23), betrayal by her husband (14–15, 22), and ensuing traumatic dreams (38, 60). The diary documents Juletane's agonizing experience in her adopted Senegalese community. She is a victim of the stereotyping imposed on her by virtue of her origin, gender, and barrenness (13, 16): "I am the family scourge, the leper whom they hide and feed for love of Allah, the stranger who Mamadou made the mistake of bringing home" (41). She is also oppressed by Mamadou's insensitivity (Ondrus, 2014, 230).

Once Mamadou casts her aside, Juletane is without a protector and even more vulnerable. In response to her situation, she withdraws physically and psychologically from the sprawling compound of Mamadou's extended family. While she is resigned to the loss of Mamadou's love, she still hopes for some rekindling of his feelings for her. She therefore writes in the futile hope of reuniting with her husband, the intended narratee of her diary; she writes in the hope that he will find her journal one day: "I must finish my journal, it is the only legacy I am leaving to Mamadou. I hope he will read it and will understand how far from my dream he was" (72; Ondrus, 2014, 240).

Denied a listener, Juletane seeks a reader; she desires to communicate with someone, to break out of the self-imposed isolation of her introspective world. The writing process eventually allows her to create an imaginary friend: "Thanks to my diary, I discover that my life is not in pieces" (30). She finds that she can use journal writing to establish the intimacy missing in her life (Mortimer, 1995, 42–43).

Juletane thus views writing as therapeutic and protective: "Writing will shorten my long hours of discouragement, will be something for me to cling to and will give me a friend, a confidante" (5). She continues:

> For years I had wavered between abject depression and raging despair with no one to turn to. It had never occurred to me that putting down my anguish on a blank page could help me to analyze it, to control it and finally, perhaps to bear it or reject it once and for all. (30)

Journal writing comforts Juletane; it becomes a survival strategy and a necessary act of regeneration. With new-found optimism, she writes:

> Since morning I feel calm and serene, even a little happy. Writing does me good, I think, for once, I have something to keep me occupied […] I allow myself to be captivated by the magic of the words […] it is good therapy for my anxieties. Already I feel more secure. […] Today my only certainty is having come to life again. (46–47, 51; Mortimer, 1995, 43)

But writing cannot overcome her vulnerability; Juletane finds that her *tentatives d'évasion* ensnare her rather than set her free. She also finds that she is unable to write herself out of closed space, and that she has become a prisoner: "How ever did I fall into this well of misery[?]" she asks (5). She "questions the writing project, viewing it as an ambiguous endeavour, one that opens the door to self-reflection but risks locking her into an enclosure where morbid thoughts will feed her rage" (Mortimer, 1995, 43): "I wonder if it was a good thing to have started this diary, to be trying to remember a past more filled with sorrows than with joys; to dwell on a present built on troubles, on solitude, despair […]? Stirring up all that, isn't it provoking a sleeping tiger?" (25–26).

Writing subsequently becomes a way for Juletane to realize her goal of getting revenge on all those who cause her heartbreak and agony simply because she is different (Ondrus, 2014, 229). The diary sets the wheels in motion for her acts of murderous revenge and destruction through a series of violent and deadly acts. For instance, she writes about hurting others; she visualizes hurting Ndeye before actually doing so (Ondrus, 2014, 242). She vows to "become more than spiteful" and to make Ndeye "pay very dearly for the two years of insults" she has heaped upon her (50). She uses images to illustrate the force of her feelings about the situation: "I am preparing my vengeance like a very special dish. After I have carefully prepared it, seasoned it, I will savour it slowly, very slowly and carefully. It will be my last meal and my madness will vanish" (62) (Ondrus, 2014, 242).

Juletane's careful documenting of all the abuses resulting from her otherness could be an attempt to achieve catharsis, but there is no evidence of her healing or positive transformation. The violent anger and deadly actions (poisoning her first co-wife's children and disfiguring her second co-wife with boiling oil) are thus difficult to reconcile with the supposedly therapeutic benefits of writing.

However, the embedded non-narratee reader Hélène shows signs of emotional transformation as a result of reading Juletane's saga. Prior to reading Juletane's diary, "The whisky, the cigarettes, the wild parties were a way of arming herself against pity" (56) and Hélène felt "a block of ice around her heart" (79). The act of "read[ing] a true story […] reflect[ing, …] look[ing] back, [and …] question[ing] her usual attitude" transforms her (56). This positive transformation demonstrates the value of writing. Another benefit of this diary is that readers are able to visualize the said abuses, thus permitting close access to Juletane's psyche (Ondrus, 2014, 245, 259).

Expressing Cultural Difference

A major issue related to immigrant life is the inability to communicate effectively in the host country. "An accent is the tell-tale scar left by the unfinished struggle to acquire a new language," writes André Aciman: "An accent marks the lag between two cultures, two languages, the space where you let go of one identity, invent another and end up being more than one person though never quite two" (1999, 11). It is not surprising that language constitutes a central element of the immigrant experience, as different generations are portrayed coming into contact with French language and culture, exploring the relationship between mainstream French and the "peripheral" forms of speech associated with immigrant communities. In order to make these voices heard and to legitimate their presence within the French and francophone world, postcolonial writers create appropriate tools. Considered subversive, this technique entails word play and transformations of standard French, the incorporation of alien words and speech patterns as a way of valorizing immigrant cultures that have long been denigrated. The end product is a composite language whose vitality gives the immigrant voice a new vibrancy (Abu-Haidar, 2001, 83–84, 91).

This innovative writing is put into practice in the two narratives under examination. The authors use a combination of borrowings, standard French, exaggerated characterization, inner dialogue, and omniscient perspective to express the inner thoughts of the protagonists, whose psychology forms the basis of the fiction, and highlight the struggle of immigrants living in the *Métropole* (France) or in the homeland (Senegal).

Beyala, especially, should be praised for the way she uses voice to develop her vibrant characters. French is not the mother tongue of any of the protagonists, but they are forced to operate in French if they are to gain access to French culture. The language of *Loukoum* is marked by a range of registers and tones, switching as it does between the formal and informal and creating a mosaic-like writing style, a hybridized French that allows the author to stage the linguistic interference produced by migration: "Ça a pété *clash*!" (10), "une gosse qu'a pas eu son jouet [...] Elle croque dedans comme ça" (29), "je suis tellement triste à cause que" (39). *Loukoum* is also packed with expletives, slang, and sexually graphic vocabulary. While the language is violent and crude, it is necessarily so to accurately transmit the protagonists' thoughts and experiences. Nicki Hitchcott suggests that "by using the language of migration, Beyala stresses the cultural separation between the immigrant ghetto of Belleville and the surrounding majority ethnic space of France" (2006a, 83).

Warner-Vieyra successfully uses a double-narration journal to expound the agonizing experiences of Juletane in the homeland. This enables readers to better visualize the disillusionments and abuses encountered by the narrator due to her otherness, thus permitting close access to Juletane's psyche. The journal also shows the transformative value of reading as demonstrated by the positive changes experienced by the non-narratee reader, Hélène, after reading Juletane's diary. *Juletane* also uses linguistic borrowings—"his *made-in-France* comfort" (30)—and Africanized French—"Pretty Madame, come see here, come see there; me I will do you good price; me, my tomatoes are nicer" (66) and "your tubab lady" (79). These literary devices enable the author to transfer African phraseology and structures into standard French, thus permitting a faithful expression of the people's lived experience, including colonialization and its historical, sociopolitical, cultural, and linguistic implications for Senegal. By so doing, Warner-Vieyra successfully deals with the disparity between the African material and the medium of expression.

Similarly, in order to ensure that the text reflects a sound vision of Senegal as a multicultural society dominated by Islam, the author intentionally highlights the strong influence of this religion on Senegalese society in several passages. For example, the protagonists' religious affiliations are openly expressed in the following passage even though they are stated in impeccable formal French: "Thank you Lord for this new day" (24); "The Imam [...] held my two hands [...] said some verses of the Qur'an" (46), "I was pleading, sending fervent prayers to the Lord" (72), "for the sake of Allah" (77), and "I heard the voice of the muezzin, calling the faithfuls for the *fajar* prayer" (98).

Conclusion

Loukoum and *Juletane* chronicle the painful realities of survival that immigrants must confront in contemporary societies intolerant of cultural difference. In both novels, the protagonists seek to communicate; they wish to be understood; they long for a space to engage in multicultural communication which can foster understanding, tolerance, respect, and harmony among people of different cultures. While Abdou seeks to communicate by talking to an imaginary friend, Juletane does so through her journal. Abdou and his son Loukoum adopt two different approaches to negotiating the migratory space. While Abdou refuses to leave behind his native traditions and is therefore unable to integrate into the host culture, Loukoum easily assumes other identities and adapts to different situations. As for Juletane, she finds therapy and protection in writing, producing a journal that will ultimately transform her reader, Hélène.

This transformation is an affirmation that communication, and especially reading, writing, and cross-cultural engagement, can bring change; it is indeed the sign that creative texts can have a transformative power, strong enough to overcome the challenges of otherness. Communication can serve as a vehicle for the realization of the dreamed-of global community, a dynamic, expansionist, ethnically polyglot society. This will, however, require adopting "cosmopolitanism which begins with the simple idea that in the human community, as in national communities, we need to develop habits of coexistence [...] of living together (Appiah, 2006, xix).

Works Cited

Abu-Haidar, Farida. "Voices of Change: Interlanguage in Franco-Maghrebi Texts." In *Immigrant Narratives in Contemporary France*. Ed. Susan Ireland and Patrice J. Proulx. Westport, CT: Greenwood Press, 2001: 83–92.

Aciman, André. "Foreword: Permanent Transients." In *Letters Of Transit: Reflections on Exile, Identity, Language, and Loss*. Ed. André Aciman, New York: New Press, 1999: 7–15.

Ahmed, Sara, ed. *Uprootings/Regroundings: Questions of Home and Migration*. Oxford and New York: Berg, 2003.

Anzaldúa, Gloria. *Borderlands/La Frontera: The New Mestiza*. San Francisco, CA: Aunt Lute Books, 1999.

Appiah, K. Anthony. *Cosmopolitanism: Ethics in a World of Strangers*. New York: W.W. Norton, 2006.

Beyala, Calixthe. *Le Petit Prince de Belleville*. Paris: Albin Michel, 1992.

Beyala, Calixthe. *Loukoum, The Little Prince of Belleville*. Trans. Marjolijn de Jaeger. Portsmouth: Heinemann, 1995.

Bhabha, Homi. *The Location of Culture*. London and New York: Routledge, 1994.

Edwin, Shirin. "African Muslims in France: Walking Parallel Bars in Calixthe Beyala's Le Petit prince de Belleville." *Journal of Colonialism and Colonial History* 6.2 (2005). doi: 10.1353/cch.2005.0034

Fragd, Lulamae. "Reading Your Self Home: Myriam Warner-Vieyra's *Juletane*." *CLA Journal* 45.4 (2002): 477–496.

Hargreaves, Alec G. *Immigration, "Race" and Ethnicity in Contemporary France*. London and New York: Taylor & Francis, 1995.

Hitchcott, Nicki. *Calixthe Beyala: Performances of Migration*. Liverpool: Liverpool University Press, 2006a.

Hitchcott, Nicki. "Calixthe Beyala: Prizes, Plagiarism, and 'Authenticity.'" *Research in African Literatures* 37.1 (2006b): 100–109.

Hoffman, Eva. "The New Nomads." In *Letters of Transit: Reflections on Exile, Identity, Language, and Loss*. Ed. André Aciman. New York: New Press, 1999: 39–46.

Ireland, Susan, and Patrice J. Proulx. "Introduction." In *Immigrant Narratives in Contemporary France*. Ed. Susan Ireland and Patrice J. Proulx. Westport, CT: Greenwood Press, 2001: 1–4.

King, Adele. "Two Caribbean Women Go to Africa: Maryse Conde's *Heremakhonon* and Myriam Warner-Vieyra's *Juletane*." *College Literature* 18.3 (1991): 96–105.

King, Adele. "'Postcolonial' African and Caribbean Literature." In *The Cambridge History of African and Caribbean Literature, Volume 2*. Ed. F. Abiola Irele and Simon Gikandi. Cambridge: Cambridge University Press, 2004: 809–823.

Mortimer, Mildred. "The Female Quester in Myriam Warner-Vieyra's *Le Quimboiseur l'avait dit* and *Juletane*." *College Literature* 22.1 (1995): 37–50.

Ondrus, Suzanne Marie. "Writing about Writing: African Women's Epistolary Narratives" PhD diss., University of Connecticut.

Pfaff, Françoise. "Warner-Vieyra, Myriam." In *Encyclopedia of the African Diaspora: Origins, Experiences, and Culture, Volume 3*. Ed. Carole Elizabeth Boyce Davies. Santa Barbara, CA: ABC-CLIO, 2008: 974.

Proulx, Patrice J. "Inscriptions of Silence and Violence in the Antillean Text: Reading Warner-Vieyra's *Juletane* and *Sidonie*." *The French Review* 70.5 (1997): 698–709.

Ramadan, Tariq. *Muslims in France: The Way towards Coexistence*. Leicester: The Islamic Foundation, 1999.

Ramraj, Victor J. "Diasporas and Multiculturalism." In *New National and Post-Colonial Literatures: An Introduction*. Ed. Bruce Alvin King. Oxford: Clarendon Press, 1996: 214–219.

Said, Edward. "No Reconciliation Allowed." In *Letters of Transit: Reflections on Exile, Identity, Language, and Loss*. Ed. André Aciman. New York: New Press, 1999: 87–114.

Warner-Vieyra Myriam. *Juletane*. Trans. Betty Wilson. London: Heinemann, 1987.

PERFORMING IDENTITIES, RECLAIMING THE SELF

5

Staging the Scaffold: Criminal Conversion Narratives of the Late Eighteenth Century

Carsten Junker (Leipzig University)

This essay is about some of the most cynical texts of the eighteenth century, criminal conversion narratives in which enslaved men confess to crimes they allegedly committed and in which they relate their religious conversion while awaiting execution.[1] Criminal conversion narratives—also called "dying speeches," "dying confessions," "criminal narratives," or "confession and conversion narratives"—resemble slave narratives, but their trajectory is different. While slave narratives tell the story of an autobiographical subject who obtains freedom after going through tribulations, dying speeches send their narrators directly to the scaffold to die, while promising a life liberated from sins in the afterworld.[2] Like slave narratives, criminal conversion narratives follow a formulaic script: black narrators recount their experiences of enslavement, in both northern and southern states, and their escapes and journeys throughout what would become the United States, sometimes all the way to the Caribbean and Canada; they relate and confess the crimes they allegedly committed, from stealing food and clothing to raping white women and murdering their masters.[3] As a rule, the narrators then address how they were caught, put into jail, tried in court, found guilty, and sentenced to death. These (auto)biographical accounts are then followed by passages in which the narrators describe their

---

[1] This essay is partly based upon but also reworks ideas from Junker (2016, 268–294).
[2] Robert B. Stepto famously called the narrative pattern of the movement from oppression to freedom and literacy an "ascent narrative" (1979, 167).
[3] As DeLombard notes, "roughly sixty condemned black criminals […] figured prominently in early America's thriving gallows literature tradition" (2012b, 5). Currently, digitized versions of a select number of speeches are easily accessible online via the digitalization project Documenting the American South, a useful database sponsored by the University Library of the University of North Carolina at Chapel Hill. For a discussion of the increasing scholarly significance and archival availability of criminal conversion narratives, also see DeLombard (2012a, 97).

religious conversion, their repentance for the crimes with which they have been charged, and their strong belief in deliverance from their sins through faith. Dying speeches close this way, or conclude with passages written by the white editors and printers who chronicle the events that follow, detailing the execution of the verdict, "death by hanging," from their own perspectives. As ostensibly first-person accounts of the lives of enslaved men, these criminal conversion narratives seem to provide early instances of black life writing that help us recover black speakers' voices. However, these narratives are formulaic enactments of criminal confession and conversion that stage the personae of enslaved black men in ways suited to enact the scripts of white-coded religious and legal discourses.

As Christy Webb notes, dying speeches served their audiences "as both a religious cautionary tale and sensational entertainment" (2004). Relating these texts to the religious, literary, political, and legal discourses of the time allows us to consider how they functioned as cautionary tales, as vignettes of religious and moral instruction, as pieces of leisurely entertainment, and also as instruments of abolitionist campaigning. Rather than imagining that they simply present enslaved men confessing their crimes in remorseful ways, these speeches should be approached with hermeneutic suspicion assessing *who* is staged by *whom*, and to what effect. The veracity and authenticity of the first-person voices of these purportedly autobiographical narratives is questionable.[4] These speeches were published, distributed, and generally transcribed and edited—and very probably authored—by whites; it is therefore necessary to discuss the repercussions of the ways in which the texts stage their black protagonists' narratives of confession and conversion. The hegemonic framework marked by white dominance within which these texts were produced and received presents the appropriate context for a fuller understanding and assessment; social and discursive conditions generated certain notions about the enslaved, notions that ambiguously and ambivalently position the unfree between the poles of slavery and freedom. Dying speeches comply with a dominant discursive framework, performing a two-sided logic of the "subjugation and the constitution of the [black male] subject" (Hartman, 1997, 4) which turns these individuals from enslaved beings into both agential criminals and, potentially, redeemable believers. Dying speeches thus position the

---

[4] DeLombard proposes "Abandoning the pursuit of racial authenticity for a more generative account of black civic presence in print" (2012a, 102); she further maintains that the "published confessions attributed to condemned black criminals are noteworthy less for their authenticity or their dissent than for the ways in which they formalized, publicized, and thus politicized individual black speech (incriminating though it may have been)" (2012b, 31).

enslaved both as dehumanized property and as fellow human beings whose racialized masculinity is conflated with crime. Ultimately, positioning the enslaved as criminals justifies the violence inscribed in the framework of both secular and religious law and helps to secure support for the dominant order of civic society, support based on the putative threat of the enslaved, with security purchased at the expense of their lives.

Crimes, Confession, Conversion

Criminal conversion narratives were published as broadsides or pamphlets. There is little information about how widely they were circulated. In some cases, only one copy is available today (see Hutchins, 2004); in others, broad newspaper coverage of the cases across state boundaries makes it safe to assume that pamphlets were printed in large numbers and reached a wide readership (see Webb, 2004). This form of popular literature was not only read by literate people, but also read aloud to audiences whose members were illiterate.[5] Broadsides with images also signaled their content to illiterate audiences. A careful analysis of four late eighteenth-century dying speeches published in the American colonies and early republic provides a useful case study of the commonalities and divergences within this generic tradition in relation to contemporaneous discourses.

In "The Life, and dying Speech of Arthur, a Negro Man; Who was Executed at Worcester, October 20, 1768. For a Rape committed on the Body of one Deborah Metcalfe," Arthur is repeatedly caught, and repeatedly escapes, surviving by stealing food and clothing.[6] His is a phantasmic and fantastical story about excessive uses of alcohol and sex with women, consensual and non-consensual. While detailed information about the movement of its narrator from Massachusetts to the Caribbean is provided, the description of a white woman's rape is handled evasively: "the Devil put it into my Head to pay a Visit to the Widow Deborah Metcalfe, whom I, in a most inhumane manner, ravished: The Particulars of which are so notorious, that it is needless for me here to relate them" (Arthur, 2004 [1768]). The rape of a white woman, a taboo, is evoked only to leave its

---

[5] For a more detailed discussion concerning the circulation of these broadsides, see Cohen (2006, 18).

[6] During one of his many escapes, Arthur gets involved with a Native American woman with whom he runs away, dressed up in her clothes and passing for a Native American woman himself. This motif of racial passing in gendered drag as a means to escape enslavement is famously used in numerous texts that include, among others, William Wells Brown's sentimentalist abolitionist novel *Clotel; or, The President's Daughter* (1853) and William and Ellen Craft's fugitive narrative *Running a Thousand Miles for Freedom* (1860). See Berthold (1993, 19–20), Weinauer (1996), Sollors (1997, 261).

particulars to the imagination of readers.[7] The narrator explains, but does not regret his actions. He states: "[I] was so unhappy as often to incur the Displeasure of my Mistress, which caused me then to run away: And this was the beginning of my many notorious Crimes, of which I have been guilty" (Arthur, 2004 [1768]). He pays lip service to dominant assumptions about right and wrong, but conceals his feelings: "I was, on the 24th of Sept. last, sentenced to be hanged, which I must confess is but too just a Reward for many notorious Crimes" (Arthur, 2004 [1768]).

In "Dying Confession of Pomp, A Negro Man, Who Was Executed at Ipswich, on the 6th August, 1795, for Murdering Capt. Charles Furbush, of Andover, Taken from the Mouth of the Prisoner, and Penned by Jonathan Plummer," the narrator explains how he managed his master's farm, and was refused free time, even on Sundays. Taking his owner's life is framed and perhaps mitigated by a detailed description of his tormented state of mind. Pomp's legal status is unclear to him, and his master's capitalizing on his labor causes him to feel a continual sense of humiliation that drives him, eventually, to murder:[8] "I told him [a previous owner] that I meant to leave him soon, but he informed me that I was not free. About this time I was seized with convulsion fits which continued to oppress me at times ever after, to the fatal night that I murdered Capt. Furbush" (Pomp and Plummer, 2004 [1795]). Pomp's narrative is undergirded by his sense of equality with the free people around him, and by his sense of entitlement to freedom: "The hopes of being master, husband and owner, on one hand, and the cruel treatment I had received from Furbush on the other, prompted me to wish for his death." Unlike Arthur, whose motivation is explained in terms of unhappiness, Pomp's narrator details his motives in terms of his thwarted ambitions, endowing his narrative with a greater sense of agency.

As with the previous narratives, Edmund Fortis's story is anticipated in the extended title: "The Last Words and Dying Speech of Edmund Fortis, a Negro Man, Who Appeared to Be between Thirty and Forty Years of Age, but Very Ignorant. He Was Executed at Dresden, on Kennebeck River, on Thursday the Twenty-Fifth Day of September, 1794, for a Rape and Murder,

---

[7] Narratives of rape and the rhetoric of sexual violence they employ "do not simply reflect but rather stage and dramatize the historical contradictions by which they are overdetermined" (Sielke, 2002, 5). Work that addresses this discursive overdetermination of white women's rape by black men with reference to and in the wake of the enslavement regime has been framed as the "rape complex" by Cash (1983). See also Hernton (1965) and Spillers (2003).

[8] This corresponds to the legal situation concerning slavery in the Commonwealth of Massachusetts: "Although slavery was legally abolished by the Massachusetts Supreme Court's 1783 interpretation of the state constitution in *Commonwealth v. Jennison*, the practice remained relatively common for a number of years afterwards" (Hutchins, 2004).

Committed on the Body of Pamela Tilton, a Young Girl of about Fourteen Years of Age, Daughter of Mr. Tilton of Vassalborough, in the County of Lincoln." Fortis escapes from a master in Virginia who mistreats him. In England, he signs up for work on a merchant ship from Liverpool—a ship likely involved in the slave trade—and is falsely accused of stealing flour. He eventually returns to the United States via Greenland, settling in Maine, where he marries. "Now my life was dreadful—Drinking, stealing and gaming" (2004 [1795], 5), he notes. The narrative culminates in the rape and murder of a white girl whose corpse he attempts, unsuccessfully, to hide. Fortis's narrative, like that of Pomp, is accompanied by repeated introspective moral and affective assessments of his deeds. After the murder, he writes about himself: "But how shall I describe my feelings on my return home! Oh how dreadful they were!" (2004 [1795], 7).

"Life, Last Words and Dying Speech of Stephen Smith, a Black Man, Who Was Executed at Boston This Day Being Thursday, October 12, 1797 for Burglary" recounts Smith's two forced transportations from Virginia to the West Indies for crimes committed while resisting his master's maltreatment. After a sojourn in Nova Scotia, Canada, Smith eventually lands in Boston, where he is sentenced to death for housebreaking and burning down two houses. Like Arthur's, Smith's account is short and presented in a matter-of-fact way.

While Arthur's and Fortis's narratives exclusively feature their point of view, Pomp's and Smith's narratives are followed by accounts of their executions narrated from the perspective of their editors. Pomp's life is recounted and re-evaluated by Jonathan Plummer. In Smith's case, an anonymous editor provides a detailed description of the execution, presenting Smith's public punishment as a violent spectacle, evoking horror and satisfying the voyeurism of his readers.

Dying speeches mark the moments in which their protagonists recognize their criminal behavior as sinful, and repent. In Arthur's case, it is a priest who prompts feelings of remorse. He concludes his narrative by "gratefully acknowledging the unwearied Pains that was taken by the Rev. Mr. McCarty, to awaken me to a proper Sense of my miserable and wretched Condition," and expressing the hope that his "own sincere Endeavours after true Repentance, will I hope prove the Means of my eternal Well-being" (2004 [1768]). Pomp also becomes a devout Christian in jail. "The Ministers have been kind to me and I believe they are clever people," he remarks. "The Ministers have told me to pray to God, and to the blood of Christ, for a new heart" (2004 [1795]). He follows their advice, stating that he prays between ten and 20 times a day. His prayers lead to a conversion rendered legible on his body in spectacular ways, as his skin color transforms from a darker to a lighter hue:

I [illegible]'d make a very extraordinary priest, and inde[illegible] am turning very fast into one. When I [illegible] here, I was as black as any negro in the country, but now I have scarcely a drop of negro blood left in me, my blood having so far [illegible]ed into the blood of a Minister, that I am a [illegible]y nearly as white as a Mulatto. (2004 [1795])

This extraordinary shift from black to near-white skin serves as an index for the miracle of Pomp's conversion; it symbolically equates physical blackness with the darkness of sin, lightness with religious virtue. Coded in racial terms, this account of his conversion suggests that personal experience is always already implicated in and overdetermined by a symbolic order marked by white hegemony. Religion is part and parcel of this dominance. The transcriber (if not author) and editor of Pomp's narrative, Jonathan Plummer, also presents white supremacy as underwritten by religion. "To crown his ignorance he lost his life by not knowing that murder was a sin" (2004 [1795]), Plummer writes, implying that religious belief could have prevented Pomp from murdering his master. Thus Pomp's subjection to white religious law overwrites another conceivable narrative theme: that of his (potentially morally defensible) resistance to enslavement.

Fortis also undergoes a dramatic spiritual conversion. It takes place over three days, from a Friday, when he envisions that the devil visits him, through to Sunday, when he emerges seeing the light and hearing angels sing. Christy Webb has rightly noted that the narrative "echoes the timeline in Christian belief of Jesus Christ's crucifixion and resurrection and reinforces the [belief in a] transformation made possible through Christ's death" (Webb, 2004). The presentation of Fortis as a Christ figure, as Daniel Cohen has suggested, points readers toward their own potential salvation: "If even such pariahs [as Fortis] could achieve a glorious salvation, surely the humdrum readers of their narratives could aspire to heaven as well" (2006, 79). Paradoxically, however, turning Fortis into a Christ-like figure also distances him from both black and white readers, removing him beyond a sphere of recognizable humanness. The dominant discursive framework of religion can only script the racialized redeemer figure as suprahuman.

In contrast to these embellished narratives of spiritual conversion, the narrator of Smith's account articulates some remorse in a relatively short, convention-ridden passage: "For this Lie of pleading not Guilty, I am ashamed before GOD, whom I have offended, and before Man" (2004 [1797]). There is no explicit moment of religious conversion here, though Smith notes in passing that two ministers had instructed him in religious affairs. He thanks them, and expresses his "hope that GOD will have mercy on me. Now in the 28th Year of my Age I commit my spirit into the

Hands of merciful and just GOD and hope he will receive me for his great mercy's sake." He then goes on to caution his readers against following his example: "I die in peace with all mankind, and beg that all people will take warning by my Awful END" (2004 [1797]).

Authorship and Readership

Such dying speeches, with their discourse of repentant criminality, raise the question of audience. Whom did these criminal conversion narratives serve as manuals of moral and religious instruction, and for whom might they have provided voyeuristic enjoyment? James Weldon Johnson's racially coded notion of a "double audience"—which assumes an audience of "both white and black America" (1928, 477)—provides a useful starting point for a discussion of these questions.[9] Potentially, dying speeches provided vicarious, adventurous journeys and sensational entertainment, presumably for white readers. The accounts of travel offered these readers adventures in far-off horizons; the transgressive behavior of the protagonist offered vicarious experience that was both enthralling and objectionable, marked off by a racial divide. In literary terms, dying speeches are related to picaresque storytelling, to an episodic style of fictionalized narrative that deals with the adventurous journey of a rough and roguish hero of low social standing. The bold courage of the picaresque-style hero could be fascinating and appealing to a black audience as well as to whites. However, in contrast to classic picaresque novels of the time, written in English by authors such as Daniel Defoe, Henry Fielding, Tobias Smollett, or Hugh Henry Brackenridge— novels that were primarily known to educated readers—dying speeches do not offer their audiences comic relief in the sense of proposing the moral or economic triumph of their chief characters, nor do they qualify as critical satire. Rather, the punishment of the racially marked protagonists of these

---

[9] In a 1928 essay titled "The Dilemma of the Negro Author," Johnson discusses the broad recognition black writers were beginning to receive on a large public scale during the 1920s, while noting that the phenomenon of black authorship dates back to the 1770s. Johnson's example is that of the poet Phyllis Wheatley. What is relevant about Johnson's essay for my discussion are his reflections about "double audience" (1928, 477)—the challenges that black writers faced in addressing both white and black audience, the logic being that specific assumptions about different audiences pre-structure authors' writing. What resonates here is W.E.B. Du Bois's concept of double consciousness, as he developed it in his *Souls of Black Folks* (1903). While my point is that dying speeches from the late eighteenth century do not qualify as black-authored texts, as they are overdetermined by the hegemonic interests of white authorship and editorship, I refer to Johnson's concept of "double audience" here because it enables a discussion of the complex dynamics at play in their reception.

criminal conversion narratives provides a narrative closure that consolidates a racially coded existing social order.[10]

Viewed with respect to legal discourse, dying speeches literally created a chasm between free whites and unfree blacks by staging the enforcement of law. These accounts operated as cautionary tales, as Arthur's dying speech signals: "I earnestly desire that this Recital of my Crimes, and the ignominious Death to which my notorious Wickedness has bro't me, may prove a Warning to all Persons who shall become acquainted therewith." Turning to his black audience, the narrator warns: "But in a particular Manner, I would solemnly warn those of my Colour, as they regard their own souls, to avoid Desertion from their Masters, Drunkenness and Lewdness" (2004 [1768]). Thus, unfree blacks who escaped from their plantations or masters' homes are framed as criminals who should expect a death sentence. Arthur's emphatic warning to fellow blacks bespeaks the inescapability of a law that keeps the enslaved in place—more specifically, that reserves for them a status of slave-thing within the bounds of the plantation.

In Stephen Smith's narrative, the warning is addressed to an audience that is not framed in racially distinct terms. It is a clergyman here who urges members of a general public to submit to the law. Declaring the fairness of the trial, the minister cautions readers of the dire consequences of breaking the law. In a cynical passage, the narrator emphasizes the convict's gratitude to the present representatives of law enforcement:

> [Rev.] Dr. THATCHER, at his [the culprit's] request, addressed the numerous croud [sic] which the awful occasion had collected, desired them to be warned by the fate of the Criminal, assured them that he received his Trial fair, forgave all who have ever injured him, and died in peace with the family of Mankind. After a lengthy pause, the Gentlemen of the Clergy having retired, SMITH, addressed himself to Sheriff ALLEN, Mr. HARTSHORN (as jailer) and Mr. LEWIS a Constable, and thanked them for their particular attention and kindness to him. (2004 [1797])

Smith's execution stages the brutal enforcement of the law for both black and white audiences, and does so in ways that affirm the legitimacy of the legal framework and the punishment prescribed for transgression. Confession narratives thus operated as instruments of legal discourse that disciplined the enslaved and the free, and contributed to maintaining the existing social order.

[10] On eighteenth-century picaresque novels in English, see Carter and McRae (1997, 190); Day and Keegan (2009, 60, 204). John Seelye discusses Royall Tyler's *The Algerine Captive* (1797) and Hugh Henry Brackenridge's *Modern Chivalry* (1792–1815) as two of the first North American picaresque novels (1988, 173–175).

In addition to entertaining and cautioning readers, dying speeches can be read as religious tales that serve the purpose of religious instruction and spiritual edification, as vignettes of spiritual uplift. This becomes obvious in passages that relate the religious conversion of the protagonists and express the consolation which they find in their newfound religious faith. The benefits of religious piety were illustrated by painting religious conversion in vivid ways and by offering the promise of redemption. The enslaved were entreated to subject themselves to the regime of religious instruction so that their soul and spirit might be liberated from worldly sins and evils. But treading a path to salvation demanded acceptance of a theological doctrine with inbuilt racial hierarchies. All ministers in the dying speeches are white while black practices of religion are made invisible; black voices are overwritten with a racialized discourse that privileges whiteness as the color of salvation. Pomp's conversion, during which he undergoes phenotypic change and turns white, underlines this point. The speeches pursue a missionary agenda, zealously colonizing the voices of the enslaved.

White readers and listeners who were already devoutly religious received confirmation that their religious exercise was truly redemptive. Their religious empathy for the protagonists of the narratives also became an instrument of the transfiguration of the enslaved from thing to redeemed human being. This assigns white readers discursive agency, putting them in a position of power to redeem the enslaved. For a white audience, dying speeches thus become vehicles for religious self-assurance and self-righteousness—textual enactments of white self-affirmation and self-satisfaction, redeeming white readers, potentially, from a sense of the sinfulness of slavery.

Daniel Cohen relates late eighteenth-century confession and conversion narratives to precursor texts such as New England Puritan execution sermons, pious confession narratives, and spiritual biographies—texts, in other words, that stage theological doctrine, and he contextualizes these narratives within a broad evangelical current that had been gaining force in New England during the 1730s, leading up to the so-called First Great Awakening, "a massive outpouring of evangelical fervor and devotional expression" that lasted for about two decades (Cohen, 2006, 76). As Cohen notes, criminal conversion narratives played a significant part in this religious project because they promoted "a massive upsurge of popular evangelism in New England by the early 1740s" (2006, 59). He argues that ministers were eager to maintain their grip as "prime instigators and architects of early criminal confession and conversion narratives" after the Great Awakening: "In their eagerness to exploit the words of dying men and women for their own pious purposes, New England clergymen helped transform the gallows into a pulpit not only for ministers but for malefactors as well, a forum for literary messages both spiritual and profane" (Cohen, 2006, 59). Ultimately, this led to the secularization of such tracts, as Cohen points out: "by focusing attention on the offenders themselves, the ministers helped cultivate—and legitimate—a biographical interest in condemned criminals that was expressed in increasingly secular terms after the Great Awakening, as printers exercised more initiative and control over their literary output" (2006, 76). The First Great Awakening thus nudged the "shift from ministers to printers as the chief mediators between criminals and readers" (Cohen, 2006, 23). The secularization of the criminal conversion narrative substantially transformed the narrative itself; it "subtly prefigured the rise of sentimental fiction during the late eighteenth century, a new discourse that would also publicize the subjective experiences of the socially powerless" (Cohen, 2006, 79).

Cohen may be correct about the popularization and secularization of this previously religious genre, but by animating the voices of racially marked protagonists like Arthur, Pomp, Smith, and Fortis, and by including them in pamphlets in order to reach a wider audience, neither ministers nor printers gave up their principal narrative authority.[11] Ministers and printers continued to speak in dying speeches, even though large parts are focalized and vocalized through the convicts. This can be conceptualized as narrative ventriloquism.[12] As Jackson points out, "How much of any particular broadside or chapbook purported to be of a criminal's outpouring of himself was the authentic, unaided expression of the criminal who was supposed to have uttered it, rather than the work of a literary ghost, will almost surely never be known" (1989, 56).[13] However, Webb's suggestion that dying speeches such as Fortis's were "probably written with the help of a printer and/or a minister" (2004) underestimates the role played by printers and ministers; they were not merely aids and helpers who assisted enslaved men in bringing their accounts to the world. Pomp's dying speech provides evidence that Jonathan Plummer, his white editor and printer, features as principal executive and author and, more importantly, economic beneficiary.

---

[11] For a useful model that differentiate the term "speaker" in spoken utterances into "animator" (a "talking machine"), author ("someone who has selected the sentiments that are being expressed and the words in which they are encoded"), and principal ("someone whose position is established by the words that are spoken"), see Goffman (1979, 17). Transferred to dying speeches, convicts could be considered animators and imagined authors, while ministers and printers hold the position of principals.

[12] Mita Banerjee introduced the concept of "ethnic ventriloquism" for a reading of canonical nineteenth-century North American literature that focuses on the dynamics and effects of white subjects appropriating the knowledge and unacknowledged authority of ethnically marked speakers. "Ethnic ventriloquism," in Banerjee's words, "represents the strategy of a white subject looking at itself through—presumably—ethnic eyes" (2008, 16).

[13] Jackson speaks of an "announced" authorship in the context of dying speeches (1989, 57).

Plummer interviewed and recorded Pomp's confession and conversion. He was "one of the first authors to try to earn a living with his pen in the years following the American Revolution" (Hutchins, 2004). Plummer acknowledges that there is no authentic material of Pomp's own making; rather, he prides himself in having rewritten the confession, or rather in having over-written the enslaved man's own words: "I ha[illegible] endeavored to preserve the ideas of poor Pomp, in the above speech, though I have taken the liberty to arrange the matter in my own way, [...] to word his thoughts more elegantly [...] than he was able to express them" (2004 [1795], 5). As this shows, we are dealing with the text of a white writer and printer who claims to be speaking for an enslaved man but who appropriates that man's voice for his own purposes, one of which is selling this broadside.

At the bottom of the broadside, Plummer writes that he sells copies for sixpence. He also advertises his services in "various branches of trifling business," offering to write "Love-letters in prose and verse furnished on the shortest notice" (2004 [1795]). This and other broadsides earned money for printers, demonstrating the extent to which dying speeches could be appropriated for secular purposes at this late point in the eighteenth century. Pomp's dying speech points to another level of the commodification of enslaved people's lives beyond their status as dehumanized property.[14]

In addition to their status as entertainment, as cautionary tales, and as vignettes of religious and moral instruction, criminal conversion narratives also served as instruments for abolitionist campaigning. As Hutchins (2004) notes, had Pomp "known the law, he might have contacted a lawyer or abolitionist group rather than attempt, repeatedly and futilely, to escape." It is perhaps more likely that an abolitionist group would have sought out Pomp to turn his case into a crying example, illustrating that his crimes were the results of the apparatus of enslavement. For an audience who read these texts as sensational entertainment, a detailed description of the crimes committed by enslaved men may be considered an indulgence—

---

[14] As if placed under a magnifying glass, questions concerning the overpowering significance of white narrative authority and authorship and editorship can be studied with reference to the debates surrounding *The Confessions of Nat Turner*, a famous confession narrative that succeeds those of Pomp, Fortis, and Smith by another 35 or so years, as it was published in 1831. John Sekora's succinct description of slave narratives as "black messages sealed within a white envelope" (1987, 501) equally applies to Turner's text. It consists of the report of the confession or transcript of an interview that Turner gave to white southern lawyer Thomas Gray after he had been imprisoned for leading the armed uprising that bears his name, as well as Gray's introduction and conclusion. The debate over Turner's/Gray's text extends to the controversies over William Styron's novel of the same title, *The Confessions of Nat Turner* (1967). For a reconstruction of this controversy, see Rushdy (1999, 54–95).

"one man's providence is another's sensation" (Cohen, 2006, 10). But from an abolitionist point of view, the execution of an enslaved person had to be seen as an act of injustice. Convincing readers of the outrageousness of such a verdict was a particularly difficult task, as black male crime was anathema to and counterproductive for an abolitionist agenda. Crime, then, had to be converted from being a potential cause for white anti-black racism into a detestable effect derived from the scandalous conditions of enslavement.

Abolitionists pointed to the dehumanizing conditions in which masters kept their slaves, which directed attention away from the alleged crimes of the enslaved and toward the cruelties that drove the perpetrators to commit their crimes in the first place. Numerous abolitionist texts attest to this shift, decrying the enslavers' moral corruption, their lack of compassion, their lack of good moral judgment, and their willingness to inflict horrific penalties as retribution for minor offenses. Dying speeches relate repeated acts of punishment on the part of the protagonists' masters and indict the slaveholders by revealing how the protagonists' very survival depended on stealing food and clothing. But, more importantly, dying speeches stage access to the perspectives of the enslaved themselves. Because they are written as first-person accounts, they allow for the narrative possibility of focusing explicitly on the effects of enslavement on the enslaved, showing their defenseless exposure to excessive violence, their physical and spiritual suffering, and the denial of their free will.

A prime abolitionist argument concerns the violation of the moral-philosophical and natural rights-based principles of equality and freedom—principles that Pomp is said to deliberately claim for himself. On the whole, however, criminal conversion narratives insist that equality and freedom are realized for the enslaved in the afterlife. By shifting attention to the hereafter, dying speeches validate the redemptive power of religion rather than offering conclusive answers to the question of how these ideals could be realized for the enslaved in the here and now. Dying speeches thus gesture toward Christian religion as a self-referential, self-affirming white practice. And while these accounts, if read as potential abolitionist interventions, point to the criminal behavior of the enslaved as a result of slavery, they also suggest that those who commit crimes must be severely punished. In so doing, they confirm the grip of the law in the hands of white officeholders. They also satisfy the voyeurism of their audiences; they are textual performances of excessive, spectacular violence that keep the enslaved in their place.

In light of the tensions that derive from their multiple purposes, the latent functions of dying speeches requires closer examination, for these speeches define crime in terms of race and gender in particular ways. In staging illegal and sinful acts committed by black men, they anticipate a link between crime and black masculinity and suggest that black men are inherently criminal.[15] The protagonists are dehumanized as criminals and rendered "civil nonentities capable of only criminal agency" (DeLombard, 2012b, 9). These narratives, then, oscillate between potentially humanizing the enslaved by considering them as redeemable subjects, while simultaneously presenting them as pieces of property that can be subjected to violent punishment, condemning them to the sphere of the not-quite-human and preserving civic society as the realm of white power.

Property and Personhood

As criminals whose punishable acts can be redeemed, confession and conversion narratives position the enslaved both as property and persons in relation to whites. This raises the question of the implications that follow from framing the enslaved as both property *and* person in legal discourse. In *Scenes of Subjection*, Saidiya Hartman notes that the enslaved were not subjected to common law, but to slave law; this law constructed them in contradictory ways, both as property and as persons. While one should not ignore "differences, inconsistencies, and contradictions across jurisdictions" (1997, 226), one can note the epistemological implications of general tendencies in legislation: slave law selectively recognized the humanity of the enslaved. This "nullified the captive's ability to [...] act as agent, and, at the same time, acknowledged the intentionality and agency of the slave but only as it assumed the form of criminality" (Hartman, 1997, 80). In other words, the law operated on double standards. On the plantation, the enslaved were framed as property whose free will was not recognized, and they enjoyed no legal protection from white violence; they could be subjected to excessive punishment for acts of resistance. Outside the realm of the plantation, they could be subjected to trial in a court of law, which required regarding them as agents of their own will—as criminals. As Hartman points out, "the enslaved could neither give nor refuse consent [...] yet they were criminally responsible and liable. The slave was recognized as a reasoning subject who possessed intent and rationality solely in the context of criminal liability; ironically, the slave's will was acknowledged only as it was prohibited or punished" (1997, 82).

The paradoxical acknowledgement and rejection of the humanity of the enslaved within legal discourse is complicated further by the politics of empathy invoked within these dying speeches, precursors to the slave

---

[15] Colonial and early national gallows literature was disproportionately devoted to black male malefactors (DeLombard, 2012a, 95).

narrative.[16] Empathy here is also marked by a paradox: it requires white readers to recognize the protagonists as fellow human beings whose suffering they can feel imaginatively as their own. At the same time, empathy is a self-referential feeling that keeps intact the difference between those who feel and those for whom they feel. White readers could feel a sense of abolitionist self-satisfaction, a feeling that promised to be morally empowering for whites, leaving power hierarchies intact.[17]

We could also argue that dying speeches made black men conceivable to white audiences as human beings precisely because they showed that black men could act in exactly the same ways in which white men have always acted. White men murdered and raped black men and women, except that these acts generally took place within the purview of a legal framework that considered the enslaved merely as property; such acts were therefore not recognized as crimes. Nonetheless, dying speeches held up a critical mirror to white audiences; they served as an invitation, and a warning, to rethink the way they used the power with which they were vested.

While these speeches seem to recognize the dehumanizing effects of slavery, they also stage narrative acts that dehumanize the enslaved. Accordingly, dying speeches may more adequately be called *killing speeches*, for they validate the killing of the enslaved according to an inherently unjust secular law while promising them, through death, a more benign heavenly justice. They let the enslaved die, allowing the free to live.[18] Through a conflation of black masculinity with crime, they anticipated assumptions about guilt that still justifies the disproportionately high incarceration of black men today.[19] By staging the scaffold in literal and figurative ways, dying speeches mute black voices and overwrite the agency of black speakers. Thus they suggest the impossibility of the enslaved's participation, as citizens, in the new nation. Ultimately, dying speeches map out narrative trajectories of

---

[16] Jackson has discussed dying speeches as a "possible precursor" to the genre of the "genuine slave narrative," which he situates largely at a period between 1830 and 1860; and while he notes similarities between the genres in narrative form and content, he emphasizes conclusively that the relation between the two is marked by striking differences that pertain to questions of the assumed authenticity of black authorship, the authorization of black narrative voices, and the degree to which there is a direct critique of slavery (1989, 56–57). These genres also diverge in the trajectories of their plotlines: while the autobiographical subjects of slave narratives obtain freedom after many tribulations, dying speeches, in contrast, send their protagonists directly to the scaffold to die in this world, holding a promise of eternal life only in the hereafter.

[17] For an elaboration of this point, see Hartman (1997, 18–21).

[18] I am paraphrasing Michel Foucault here. In his biopolitical discussion of racism, he notes: "The fact that you let more die will allow you to live more" (2004, 255).

[19] For work that sketches a trajectory from plantation slavery to the mass incarceration of black men today, see, for instance, Wacquant (2002), Wilderson (2003), Alexander (2010).

white self-aggrandizement, facilitating white life at the expense of the literal and symbolic death of black lives.

Works Cited

Alexander, Michelle. *The New Jim Crow: Mass Incarceration in the Age of Colorblindness*. New York: New Press, 2010.

Arthur. "The Life, and Dying Speech of Arthur, a Negro Man; Who Was Executed at Worcester, October 20, 1768. For a Rape Committed on the Body of One Deborah Metcalfe. [Boston: S.N., 1768]." *Documenting the American South*. 2004. http://docsouth.unc.edu/neh/arthur/arthur.html. Accessed Nov. 25, 2016.

Banerjee, Mita. *Ethnic Ventriloquism: Literary Minstrelsy in Nineteenth-Century American Literature*. Heidelberg: Winter, 2008.

Berthold, Michael. "Cross-Dressing and Forgetfulness of Self in William Wells Brown's 'Clotel.'" *College Literature* 20.3 (1993): 19–29.

Carter, Ronald, and John McRae, eds. *The Routledge History of Literature in English*. London: Routledge, 1997.

Cash, Wilbur J. *The Mind of the South*. 1941. New York: Knopf, 1983.

Cohen, Daniel A. *Pillars of Salt, Monuments of Grace: New England Crime Literature and the Origins of American Popular Culture, 1674–1860*. Amherst, MA: Univeirty of Massachusetts Press, 2006.

Day, Gary, and Bridget Keegan, eds. *The Eighteenth-Century Literature Handbook*. London: Continuum, 2009.

DeLombard, Jeannine Marie. "Apprehending Early African American Literary History." In *Early African American Print Culture*. Ed. Lara Langer Cohen. Philadelphia, PA: University of Pennsylvania Press, 2012a: 93–106.

DeLombard, Jeannine Marie. *In the Shadow of the Gallows: Race, Crime, and American Civic Identity*. Philadelphia, PA: University of Pennsylvania Press, 2012b.

Fortis, Edmund. "Edmund Fortis, d. 1794: The Last Words and Dying Speech of Edmund Fortis, a Negro Man, Who Appeared to Be between Thirty and Forty Years of Age, but Very Ignorant. He Was Executed at Dresden, on Kennebeck River, on Thursday the Twenty-Fifth Day of September, 1794, for a Rape and Murder, Committed on the Body of Pamela Tilton, a Young Girl of About Fourteen Years of Age, Daughter of Mr. Tilton of Vassalborough, in the County of Lincoln. [Exeter: S.N., 1795]." *Documenting the American South*. 2004. http://docsouth.unc.edu/neh/fortis/fortis.html. Accessed Nov. 25, 2016.

Foucault, Michel. *Society Must Be Defended: Lectures at the Collège de France, 1975–1976*. Trans. David Macey. London: Penguin, 2004.

Goffman, Erving. "Footing." *Semiotica* 25.1–2 (1979): 1–29.

Hartman, Saidiya V. *Scenes of Subjection: Terror, Slavery, and Self-Making in Nineteenth-Century America*. New York: Oxford University Press, 1997.

Hernton, Calvin C. *Sex and Racism in America*. Garden City, NY: Doubleday, 1965.

Hutchins, Zachary. "Summary of 'Dying Confession of Pomp.'" *Documenting the American South*. 2004. http://docsouth.unc.edu/neh/pomp/summary.html. Accessed Nov., 25 2016.

Jackson, Blyden. *A History of Afro-American Literature, Volume I: The Long Beginning, 1746–1895*. Baton Rouge: Lousiana State University Press, 1989.

Johnson, James Weldon. "The Dilemma of the Negro Author." *The American Mercury* 15.60 (1928): 477–481.

Junker, Carsten. *Patterns of Positioning: On the Poetics of Early Abolition*. Heidelberg: Winter, 2016.

Pomp, and Jonathan Plummer. "Dying Confession of Pomp, a Negro Man, Who Was Executed at Ipswich, on the 6th August, 1795, for Murdering Capt. Charles Furbush, of Andover, Taken from the Mouth of the Prisoner, and Penned by Jonathan Plummer, Jun." [Newburyport, Ma: Jonathan Plummer; Blunt and March, 1795]." *Documenting the American South*. 2004. http://docsouth.unc.edu/neh/pomp/pomp.html. Accessed Nov. 25, 2016.

Rushdy, Ashraf H.A. *Neo-Slave Narratives: Studies in the Social Logic of a Literary Form*. New York: Oxford University Press, 1999.

Seelya, John. "Charles Brockden Brown and Early American Fiction." In *Columbia Literary History of the United States*. Ed. Emory Elliott. New York: Columbia University Press, 1988: 168–186.

Sekora, John. "Black Message/White Envelope: Genre, Authenticity, and Authority in the Antebellum Slave Narrative." *Callaloo* 10.3 (1987): 482–515.

Sielke, Sabine. *Reading Rape: The Rhetoric of Sexual Violence in American Literature and Culture, 1790–1990*. Princeton, NJ: Princeton University Press, 2002.

Smith, Stephen. "Life, Last Words and Dying Speech of Stephen Smith, a Black Man, Who Was Executed at Boston This Day Being Thursday, October 12, 1797 for Burglary. [Boston: S.N., 1797]." *Documenting the American South*. 2004. http://docsouth.unc.edu/neh/smithste/smithste.html. Accessed Nov. 25, 2016.

Sollors, Werner. *Neither Black nor White yet Both: Thematic Explorations of Interracial Literature*. New York: Oxford University Press, 1997.

Spillers, Hortense J. "Interstices: A Small Drama of Words." In *Black, White, and in Color: Essays on American Literature and Culture*. Chicago, IL: University of Chicago Press, 2003: 152–175.

Stepto, Robert B. *From Behind the Veil: A Study of Afro-American Narrative*. Urbana, IL: University of Illinois Press, 1979.

Wacquant, Loïc. "From Slavery to Mass Incarceration: Rethinking the 'Race Question' in the US." *New Left Review* 13 (2002): 41–60.

Webb, Christy. "Summary of the Last Words and Dying Speech of Edmund Fortis." *Documenting the American South*. 2004. http://docsouth.unc.edu/neh/fortis/summary.html. Accessed Nov. 25, 2016.

Weinauer, Ellen M. "'A Most Respectable Looking Gentleman': Passing, Possession, and Transgression in 'Running a Thousand Miles for Freedom.'" In *Passing and the Fictions of Identity*. Ed. Elaine K. Ginsberg. Durham, NC: Duke University Press, 1996: 37–56.

Wilderson III, Frank B. "The Prison Slave as Hegemony's (Silent) Scandal." *Social Justice* 30.2 (2003): 18–27.

6

The Plays of Carlton and Barbara Molette: The Transformative Power of African-American Theater[1]

Silvia Pilar Castro-Borrego (Universidad de Málaga)

> All human life is universal, and it is theatre that illuminates and confers upon the universal the ability to speak for all men
> August Wilson

> This should be a theatre of World Spirit, where the spirit can be shown to be the most competent force in the world. Force. Spirit. Feeling.
> Amiri Baraka

Barbara and Carlton Molette were Atlanta-based playwrights, and faculty at Texas Southern University in Houston, Eastern Connecticut State University, and Spelman College. They were members of the Dramatist Guild, and both started their careers as playwrights, teachers, and production designers. They co-authored two books, *Black Theater: Premise and Presentation* (1986) and *Afrocentric Theatre* (2013). The Molettes describe the nature of African-American theater as an expression of culture and as a medium for communicating values. They were part of the "Militant Theater" of the 1970s, which Olga Barrios considered "the most vibrant and prolific decades in Black Theatre," with plays bursting "out like forceful waterfall of red-blood—expression of a long time-held rage and expression of life" (2008, 13).

Rosalee Pritchett (1970), one of the Molettes' earliest major productions, is representative of the conflict and change that occurred in the United States during the mid-1960s and 1970s; it portrays responses to the challenges

---

[1] I would like to express my sincere gratitude to the Spelman College archivist, Taronda Spencer (in memoriam), to Dr. Johnnella E. Butler, and to Randall Burkett, the curator of the African American Marble collection at Emory University in Atlanta. I also wish to acknowledge the support provided by the Spanish Ministry of Science and Research for the writing of this article (FFI2013-47789-C2-1-P). To Barbara Molette (1940–2017) in memoriam.

confronting African Americans at the time, raising issues which are still relevant today. The play discards the integrationist view, claiming that upper-middle-class Blacks who have decided to embrace the tenets and values of the White world, living by its standards, are doomed to failure because White society is not ready for that kind of change and because ignoring their own racial and social position as Blacks will destroy their human agency.[2] *Rosalee Pritchett* was first performed by the Morehouse Spelman Players in 1970, and later staged off-Broadway by the Negro Ensemble Company, together with *Noah's Ark*. Although lacking the bitterness of *Rosalee Pritchett*, *Noah's Ark* (1974) denounces the strategies employed by White America to keep social and economic power inaccessible to Blacks; *Noah's Ark* also explores Black diasporic identity. It was first performed in 1974 by the Morehouse Spelman Players. Both *Rosalee Pritchett* and *Noah's Ark* have all-Black casts and are concerned with both intra-racial and interracial issues of the Black middle class.

The Molettes' later plays are part of what Genevieve Fabre has labeled "The theatre of experience" (1983, 106). *Legacy* (2012), recipient of the Ethel Woodson Award, questions the idea that race is a biological concept; *Kinship* (2011) examines the impact of race, class, and gender on both White and Black characters; *Tee-Shirt History* (2012) looks into the legacy of African-American history as it is perceived by three generations of African Americans. Each of these plays represents a stage in the Molettes' developing creative vision for redirecting Black political and cultural life, but their *œuvre* is more extensive and varied than this might suggest. Among their other plays are *Dr. B.S. Black* (1976) a musical; *Fortunes of the Moor* (1995), which has been presented at the National Theatre of Ghana; and *Prudence* (2005), a historical play inspired by the historical events surrounding Prudence Crandall and the young ladies of color who studied at her academy in 1833–1834. *Prudence* received the Connecticut Commission on Culture and Tourism's Artist Fellowship Award in 2005. In 2013, the Molettes received the National Black Theatre Festival's Living Legend Award.

To understand the Molettes' plays, one must appreciate the extent to which the type of theater they conceive is nourished by the broader cultural perspective of Afrocentricity and its values. Recognizing race as a social construction, and affirming the importance of African agency, the playwrights engage African-American communities and their preoccupations, their shared cultural values, and their distinct cultural and

---

[2] The choice to capitalize the word "Black" referring to people of African descent or their culture, and its counterpart "White," follows the Molettes' stylistic device used to differentiate between people of African descent, the visual sense perception of black, and the negative connotations of the word in Eurocentric culture (2013, 11).

intellectual backgrounds. The Molettes aim to empower Black theater artists to create alternative definitions of success based on the consciousness of their own cultural values, and their cultural identity. By questioning Western rationalism, with its binary thinking, they contend that playwrights should not depend exclusively on box office revenue to measure their success, but rather, they should consider the Black community's support and the positive reception of Black audiences to their work.

The Molettes' Transformative Project

In *Afrocentric Theatre* (2013), the Molettes described their work as "Afrocentric." Theater, they argue, as with any form of art produced by African Americans, is a response to the oppression and racism that exists in North America today. They defend an approach to art based on a set of values which emerges from a solid and well-defined African-American culture. This is what Molefi Asante calls location and African agency, two of the most relevant concerns within the creative process of African Americans (2003, 16). As a result of this conceptualization, the Molettes' work has become central to the contemporary reclamation and re-examination of the purpose and pillars of Black art. In that sense, the Molettes are inheritors of the Black Theater Movement which was a natural outgrowth of both the Civil Rights Movement and the Black Power Movement. The Molettes share with these movements their "avowed objectives of fomenting rebellion against the suppression of the autonomous urge of Black people(s) to define and affirm concepts of existence, essence, and experience as they relate to the reality of being 'black'" (Williams, 1985, 16). According to Amiri Baraka, Black Theater "actually functions to liberate Black people" (qtd in Coleman, 1971, 32–36). The Black Theater Movement also elevated Black consciousness, and eradicated the negative Black image "created by racist-oriented literature and the media, through the creation of a new, more positive Black image" (Williams, 1985, 17). Supporting this idea, Frantz Fanon asserted that Black people felt insignificant and powerless to change their condition of subordination because of their negative self-image (1987, 110). The movement subscribed to the search for a new Black Aesthetic, and its separate symbolism, mythology, critique, and iconology (Neal, 1968, 29).

In this sense, the Molettes are Black nationalists because they support the Black Arts philosophy with their plays, the idea that Black Art "is to be used as a means of effecting the physical, spiritual, psychological, and cultural liberation of Blacks" (Williams, 1985, 18). The Black Aesthetic was about change; it was committed to the liberation of Black people, and it was used as an artistic and creative means to achieve political ends. As Williams points out, the components of the Black Aesthetic can be broken into political, ontological, and cultural categories. This Black Aesthetic called for a radical change of self, freedom, and responsibility, including the affirmation of unique aspects of Black life, such as a Black rhetoric, a style of characteristic diction, syntax, expressions, and mannerisms. The plays and theories of the Molettes have made outstanding contributions to this project. As members of the Atlanta University Center Consortium, Carlton and Barbara Molette helped the independent Black Arts and Black Power organizations through the dynamic Black theater community. They worked with Baldwin Burroughs at the Spelman drama program, the Morehouse-Spelman Players, and the Atlanta University Summer Theater.

The Molettes propose a new acronym describing the contemporary oppression and hegemony of White supremacy in US culture and society: WEPPEO, which stands for "wealthy, elite, powerful persons of European origin." As the Molettes explained, "the WEPPEOs justified the Atlantic slave trade in the framework of Christian morality by creating a system that defined people of African origin as not fully human" (2013, 10). Carlton and Barbara Molette concurred with scholars who argue that African Americans have a solid cultural heritage because "slavery did not destroy all vestiges of African culture among those subjected to its cruelties" (2013, 13). For the Molettes, dramatic creation is an integrative, holistic experience in which different aspects of Black consciousness and figurative representations from myths and folklore converge, becoming a whole where the Black experience springs from historical and spiritual heritage. For them, this is the "vital area of spiritual enlightenment and enrichment that is the theatre" (Wilson, 1997, 502).

Besides teaching, directing, and co-authoring plays, the Molettes did much to uncover the history of African-American theater. Carlton compiled and researched a bibliography of hundreds of plays written by African-American authors over two centuries, dispelling the notion that black drama in the US was a relatively new and underdeveloped tradition. The Molettes' archival work "greatly increased the different and historical sweep of works by black playwrights accessible to African American theaters" (Smethurst, 2010, 182). Barbara not only did this type of scholarly archeology, but she was one of the chief chroniclers of the contemporary Black theater scene in Atlanta for journals outside the city, such as *Black World*. Carlton edited the journal *Encore*, the periodical of the National Association of Dramatic and Speech Arts.[3] They both often returned to Atlanta to act in or direct plays, to work on the National Black Arts Festival, and to help gain support for Atlanta's arts initiatives.

---

[3] The National Association of Dramatic and Speech Arts was an organization of theater workers, scholars, and educators primarily on historically Black campuses founded by Sheppard R. Edmonds in 1936 in the face of Jim Crow discrimination and exclusion.

The body of work created by the Molettes has critiqued and challenged the racism and stereotypes present in American discourses; their work uses culture and history as tools to interpret the collective experience of African Americans. They started writing plays in the midst of the Black freedom movement. Theirs was an emancipatory project, a contribution to "the critique resistance, and reversal of one of the greatest problems of our time, the progressive Europeanization of human consciousness" (Reed qtd in Karenga, 2000, 165). Since their first major production in 1970 with *Rosalee Pritchett*, they have been committed to the multicultural cooperative production of knowledge rather than its Eurocentric authoritative allocation. The Molettes' work treats social problems as life issues. Their plays can be studied as part of what Manning Marable calls a transformative project dedicated to "the collective efforts of Black people neither to integrate not self-segregate but to transform the existing power relationships and the racist institutions of the state, the economy, and society" (2000, 19). Their plays are part of a powerful protest movement that, in the 1970s, demanded the fundamental restructuring of the basic institutions and patterns of ownership within society. With their work, they recall that there must be an active dynamic link between serious scholarship and the concerns of the Black community. These were the tenets of W.E.B. Dubois's life and thought when he engaged in disrupting the binaries inherent in the self/other dichotomy. The Molettes engaged this issue through the construction of agency and the search for wholeness, examining "the ways race and racialization are modified and modulated by intersections of class, ethnicity, gender, and sexuality" (Butler, 2000, 150). They put an emphasis on location, which means, as playwright August Wilson contends, keeping alive all the things that "go in your mythology, your history," that "go into the making of a culture" (2013, 43). Thus, location implies a self-conscious agency and subject position for African Americans. As part of the Black Arts movement of the 1970s and in keeping with the American Negro Theater of the 1930s and 1940s, the Molettes consistently empowered Black theater artists "to create alternative definitions of success, to encourage African agency" (2013, 45) and "to establish a theatre in which African Americans do not have to abandon their cultural heritage in order to create theatre" (2013, 45).

In her study of Black women's theater, Elizabeth Brown-Gillory suggests that Carlton and Barbara Molette's *Rosalee Pritchett* can be classified as a "drama of accusation" or "protest drama" (1988, 20), but the Molettes' plays are representative of the Black Arts Movement which reached its zenith in 1969. As Mance Williams explains, the Movement displayed no interest in "protest" literature or drama, because protest literature implies that "subordinates" are supplicating "superiors" to "undergo a moral appraisal."

Black Art was "about revolt and revolution," as Williams points out. At that time, revolution meant "radical change [...] to win the minds of Black people and to affect them with a new sense of identity and spiritualism" from a political, ontological, and cultural perspective (Williams, 1985, 19–20).

The Earlier Plays

In his study *Black Theatre in the 1960s and 1970s*, Mance Williams argued that protest drama "not only exhorted Black people to stand up for their rights but warned Whites that Blacks would settle for nothing less than their full share of the American Dream" (1985, 112) and Brown-Gillory contends that these plays are often assertive and strong-willed; they hold firm to their right to speak freely and on their own terms (1988, 26). Black actors, directors, and writers started to organize themselves to combat racism and to counteract the problem of racial exclusion within theater. The Black Theater Movement became a source and sustenance for different groups rooted in the Civil Rights Movement, such as the Free Southern Theater and The Negro Ensemble Company (NEC). The NEC was formed officially in 1967 by actor Robert Hooks and paved the way for Black Americans to present a distinct voice that had emerged from a "long and vibrant tradition" (Brown-Gillory, 1988, 1). It has worked to break down walls of racial prejudice through art, becoming the proving ground for some of the country's brightest Black actors, actresses, and playwrights, and an expression of the Black experience in the US.

Rosalee Pritchett easily fit within the NEC's repertoire for the play is a moving comment on the ever-changing social values of Black America. The play proves the absurdity of attempting to gratify pseudo-bourgeois tastes while American society is suffering from a prolonged racial nervous breakdown. *Rosalee Pritchett* is a grim play: none of the characters has learned anything regarding renewal and change by the end; the message seems to be that there has been a massive social paralysis, fixing situations into racially rigid patterns. The Molettes' aim was for the audience to leave this play perturbed and dissatisfied. All its Black characters have suffered a sort of brainwashing, as they have been totally assimilated by White upper-middle-class values.

Rosalee Pritchett is a one-act play in four scenes. The plot does not grow out of characterization, but out of other environmental and experiential forces. The play is informed by the principles of African-American drama, such as creating a sense of community, a feeling of togetherness. *Rosalee Pritchett* turns this into an absence of a sense of community, a strategy that isolates both characters and public, causing estrangement in the Black audience, so that the public identifies neither with the actors nor with the play.

The action of *Rosalee Pritchett* takes place in a southern city during a race riot. Rosalee is an ultra-grand colored lady who meets with three Black friends, Belle, Dorry, and Doll, to play their weekly game of bridge and discuss the current curfew in the downtown ghetto area, which the characters label "vandalism" (Molette and Molette, 1972, 826). Their conversation moves on to their own sense of security in their residential neighborhood and they declare that their middle-class status guarantees their safety, by placing them above the racial violence that takes place in the city. They are concerned about family issues and totally convinced about racial equality in North America. In fact, Rose boasts about joining the "Daughters of the American Revolution" and her son, a medical student who has been invited to join a White fraternity, is expected to marry into a rich White family.

After the game, Rose drives home and is stopped by four National Guardsmen who are patrolling the streets in her neighborhood. Unfortunately, the guards are racist and resent the few Blacks who are successfully integrating, thanks to the efforts of the Civil Rights Movement. One of them, Barron, claims that UN policies are fostering socialism and communism in North America. Another, by the name of Lowe, calls peaceful Blacks "pinkos like Martin Luther Coon [...] a sonofabitch" (Molette and Molette, 1972, 832). They stop Rose's car, accusing her of violating the curfew. She sits straight and hands over her driving license, trusting that the guards will protect her, but they get into the car and beat and rape her. After this, Rose disappears from the rest of the play; she ends up in the hospital suffering from a nervous breakdown, which her friends assume is a case of hysteria. The rest of the play concentrates on how the impact of Rose's sexual assault is stronger when she and her friends refuse to admit it ever happened.

At the end of scene one, the women playing bridge are in whiteface makeup to show their acceptance of the White values imposed on them. These women suffer a total amnesia regarding the racial tension and violence in the US during the 1970s. They exhibit an acute detachment from the values rooted in their African-American cultural and social background. These upper-class Negro women live with the illusion of being White, of being considered equal to Whites, and of being accepted as part of mainstream society. The women suffer from amnesia because they fail to recognize the rape of a Black woman by a gang of powerful White men as a way of putting Blacks down, using sexual violence to control Black womanhood, reducing it to a mere sexual object and toy.

Rose's presence on the stage at the beginning of scene two is isolated in a small pool of light, as she sits on a stool in a padded cell. In a soliloquy, she blames working-class Blacks for the violence in the downtown area.

In scene three, the national guards, fixed in their own Eurocentric values, highlight the relationship between White manhood and violence, and connect this argument with issues concerning the racist attitudes of White manhood in American society during the 1970s. The guards suffer from a terminal case of "Afrophobia," presenting "Afrophobic" behavior and demonstrating that their only way of securing their own identity is by inflicting harm on Blacks: "First nigger that showed his black ass, I'd shoot the shit outta him" (Molette and Molette, 1972, 829). This White violence, the Molettes state, grows out of a general fear of African people and African culture. Evil lies—and in this the Molettes agree with James Baldwin—in the system that instills racist values, not in the individual who reacts to perpetuate and defend them.[4] Thus, the Molettes state that "Black people in America exist in an environment of institutional racism" (1972, 221).

Rosalee's rape by the soldiers, who should have been there to protect her, is not a crime of uncontrollable sexual passion, but one used to vent misogyny and, in this case, racism, and to exert physical, political, and economic control. That the perpetrators of crime here are agents of the law and lawful authority suggests that the root of the rape was a violent physical assertion of White power. The rape scene illustrates how rape has been, and remains, the most lethal weapon used to oppress, suppress, and dehumanize Black women in order to deter their struggles to lead independent lives. Sexual violence and the rape of Black women have been used by the patriarchy to suppress expressions of freedom and sexual freedom. According to Pamela E. Barnett, "rape is violence not only to individual persons, but violence aimed at preserving and perpetuating social domination." Thus we should focus on the issue of "rape's broader cultural meanings and consequences" (2004, xi). In the case of Rose, rape emerges as a narrative strategy tragically undermining the impulse for liberation that characterizes the Civil Rights Movement happening downtown, which is also undermined by the protagonist's refusal to accept the struggle of the rest of the Blacks in the city. Thus, rape "functions as a narrative violence that abrogates transgressive desire and frustrates the utopian political aspirations that underlie such desire" (Barnett, 2004, xii).

As an example of African-American ritual drama, the main stylistic concern of *Rosalee Pritchett* is formalism. Formalism intends to project an ideal form. The actors do not need to pretend to be somebody other than themselves, nor to rely on story content. Emphasizing the minimal development of the play's plot, critic Clayton Riley commented that the ladies in *Rosalee Pritchett* "display all the behavior of *grandes dames* but offer

---

[4] James Baldwin's *Blues for Mr. Charlie* provides, according to the Molettes, "an example of an African American character that chooses to confront the forces that seek to take away his human dignity" (1992, 221).

no statement about that behavior" (1971). However, the significance lies not in what the actresses say, but in how they behave and the emotional impact that this specific behavior has on the audience. Ritual drama is also functional; thus *Rosalee Pritchett* deliberately sought to change the values of African Americans rather than to validate or strengthen existing ones. At the end of the play, the curtain does not fall—there are no curtain calls because nothing is over.

The Shauneille Perry-directed production at St. Marks Playhouse, New York, in 1971 used 300 slides on four different rear-projection screens. For instance, the first scene opens with Rose's speech explaining that she is at the hospital because she has suffered a nervous breakdown. It shows her in very middle-class social venues, including cocktail parties and art gallery events in the company of her White friends, images which are juxtaposed with pictures of the riot and burning buildings. Throughout the play's action, which takes place in the form of flashbacks, Rosalee is sitting in a hospital room on an upstage platform participating in the dialogue and, with pantomime, in the scenes taking place below.

Rosalee Pritchett is a play intended for an African-American audience. Writing for a Black audience is not a simple thing, as Alice Childress remarks, because: "Black audiences are not always waiting with open arms for every word we have to say. Many of them listen with a 'white' ear [...] they want us to say just enough but not too much" (1968, 36). Mance Williams suggests that Black playwrights "should make every attempt to prepare the audience, allowing the collective ethos of the audience to generate the aesthetic criterion, rather than the other way around" (1985, 26). In Black plays, there is a difference in opinion among critics about what the audience needs to be told about the characters. For instance, reviewing *Rosalee Pritchett* for the *Village Voice* in 1971, Arthur Sainer wrote that "the characters are pidgin people, unable to generate their own lives. It's too bad, because the material is potentially rich, the ideas worth exploring. But the exploration doesn't happen" (1971, 59).

During the 1970s Black playwrights were more concerned with intra-racial issues. For instance, in *Rosalee Pritchett* the Molettes actively fight against those Blacks who did not have a sense of an African-American culture, having distanced themselves from lower-class African Americans—activists, writers, and middle-class Blacks—because in trying very hard to achieve the American dream, by moving into upper-class White neighborhoods, and striving to demonstrate to the White world that they were the same, that equality does indeed exist in America, they have lost touch with the roots of Black folk culture.

According to the Molettes, "one such truth that underlies African American character behavior is that Whites, in general, are frequently

The Transformative Power of African-American Theater

Figure 6.1 Rosalee Pritchett (photo by Carlton Molette)

held in contempt by African American people" (1992, 209). Thus, *Rosalee Pritchett*'s inherent contradiction and the hidden powerful message of the play is that if most Blacks have contempt for Whites, why would they want to assimilate and emulate White, Eurocentric culture?

Rosalee Pritchett achieves a positive goal by focusing upon the negative. It offers a negative portrayal of African-American characters in order to lead Black audiences to gain the insight to avoid similar negative circumstances. The audience must be concerned with what happened to cause such a monumental failure. Both Blacks and Whites live in a state of self-deception: Blacks cannot see the racism of American society because they live with the illusion of having been assimilated into it, denying themselves the chance to construct a true identity. The play is successful so long as the audience gains insights into what generated the downfall of the protagonist. The issues addressed by the play are more complex than whether or not the African-American protagonist will prevail at the end. The issues of racism, assimilation, violence, family, and friendship coexist in America with an environment of constant institutional racism, and sometimes its impact is more severe than we recognize at first sight. As Mel Gussow affirmed, "the struggle is not so much against white supremacy as against a more insidious form of racism—the imposition of values by whites on blacks and the acceptance by blacks of those values" (1971). Moreover, the play condemns the notions that Whites are models and Blacks passive receivers. As Alice Childress wrote in her review for *The Spelman Messenger*, *Rosalee Pritchett* is "a play with subject matter firmly rooted in the Black community experience—and Universal in the sense that selfishness, greed and ignorance may be found anywhere" (1979, 43).

Noah's Ark, a play in two acts, offers a more futuristic, Orwellian view of North American society. This dystopic play introduces a society where information is manipulated by a "big brother" (Molette and Molette, 1981, 185) who practices massive vigilance, social and political repression, and promotes institutional racism. The play uses symbolism to convey its major themes as it foresees a future "flood" of increased suppression of civil liberties and personal freedom. Noah Thompson, the eponymous hero, is building a wooden box to ship his son to the Caribbean, where there is a resistance camp working to liberate American Blacks from White oppression. The play denounces US colonial interventionism in Africa steal the natural resources increasingly needed by the US because white Americans, who are the only ones with unlimited access to them, engage in excessive consumption.

In *Noah's Ark*, the government controls supply and demand through the use of consumer "C cards," limiting the personal freedom of Blacks by determining what they can and cannot buy. "C cards" ensure that people who earn less money cannot spend it on "frivolities," but only on those things the government considers essential.[5] People are searched by the police after shopping, to make sure they do not "steal" anything. By implication, the play raises the question of the nature of a Black American response to an overt appropriation of African resources. Each Black family is allowed only a small portion of the wealth and natural resources of the country. In this way, the US government limits Black men and women's potential access to wealth and power at the same time as it engages in warfare in Africa, Asia, the Philippines, and the Caribbean in order to gain control of the world's natural resources and thus maintain its power.

Noah, a college professor in his forties; his brother Adam, a priest; and their wives Gladys and Ruth discuss the unfair situation of US Blacks and explain the situation to Esther, a Nigerian economist visiting the country. Noah, assertive and strong-willed, tries to explain the unconstitutionality of the fiscal measure to Valery, his former student, and now a college professor in the Midwest, who pays them a visit. Valery contends that "consumer cards are the best thing that could happen to poor (Black) people [...] who have to buy food for their families instead of throwing [their money] away" because they are "fiscally irresponsible" and "need to be controlled" (Molette and Molette, 1981, 185). The debate ends up with Noah claiming "the last vestige of freedom" he has left by defending Valery's right to speak her mind, even if he strongly disagrees with what she says. In act one scene two, we learn that the government is going to open "neighborhood centers" in order to control Black people, who from now on are not going to be able to withdraw their money from the bank, so Noah has bought gold and silver coins with his savings. They all know about these measures because his son, Danny, runs an illegal radio station, without a license or an assigned frequency.

Act two starts with Gladys and Ruth denouncing the situation of Black mothers who are driven to quit their jobs and to rely on welfare because their consumer cards are of a higher category, but not high enough for them to pay for private housing and daycare. Gladys and Ruth miss the old days, when Black people earned US dollars and enjoyed more freedom and greater democratic rights. When the armed officials start taking Black boys from

---

[5] In fact, this is the case today with EBT cards and WIC subsidies. EBT (electronic benefit transfer) cards are issued by the government for food and cash benefits. This electronic system allows a recipient to authorize transfer of their government benefits from a federal account to a retailer account to pay for products received. EBT is used in all 50 states, the District of Columbia, Puerto Rico, the Virgin Islands, and Guam. EBT was first implemented in June 2004. The WIC (women, infants, and children) food subsidies program developed out of the need to dispose of farm production deemed to be surplus under commodity price support programs. Although they make political sense, they do not make economic sense. Farm policies that increase commodity prices harm the low-income families whom food subsidy programs are supposed to help.

his son's school without prior notice, Noah has the revolutionary idea of sending Danny out of the country in a wooden box. He takes this drastic decision when he realizes that he will not be able to obtain a visa for his son to leave the country. Young Black college students are being drafted to fight overseas in Africa if they don't get a B average in school. Danny will be among them. Noah instills in his son the idea that the first responsibility of Blacks has always been survival. The characters of *Noah's Ark*, unlike those in *Rosalee Pritchett*, fully identify with the continued oppression of most Blacks in the US. They actively fight institutionalized forms of racism, calling for alternative ways of resisting and bonding.

Noah's box recalls the biblical boat, and it becomes a symbol of resistance, as it stands for the opportunities which Blacks might have in the future, and an alternative physical (geographical) location where they can act with freedom, and be recognized as proactive, full human beings. The box also recalls the symbolism of Moses in the bulrush cradle that saved him as an infant. The strong symbolism of Noah's Ark, and the floods present in the Bible—and in the consciousness of Christian, White, Western culture—are used to denounce the lack of opportunities that Blacks have in American society. The ark or box will help Black Americans to preserve their moral and cultural values "locked" within that will take them into the future.

The three-scene play is skillfully written and it meets the functionality that links this type of theater to the values of African-American minstrel performances that continued well into the 1950s. The goals and functions of these Black performances were none other than to ridicule, through the use of comic irony, the White slave owner. This type of African-American theater, which remains largely unknown and undocumented in American theater history, was a "significant factor in the mental health and physical survival of African American people within the slave experience and beyond" (Molette and Molette, 2013, 78). *Noah's Ark* employs comic irony when brothers Noah and Adam joke about their will to build as many boxes as they possibly can to ship out young Black men escaping from an environment of systematic oppression. The boys will be shipped away as "art pieces" belonging to the Black church.

Noah's Ark does not end in bitterness like *Rosalee Pritchett*, where all the characters are paralyzed by the false belief that they have been fully integrated in US mainstream society. On the contrary, it contains colorful insights both historical and cultural into Black community life. In this way the play achieves a celebratory tone, combining comic irony and the use of double meaning. For instance, when Danny complains at a White restaurant that the chicken is "half-raw" because it has been only partially pan fried in lard, he signifies the two policemen who are in the restaurant when he exclaims, "Lard! Woman, the only thing lard is good for is keeping pigs warm in the winter time!" (Molette and Molette, 1981, 196). In this way, linguistic imagery becomes functional because it allows the young Black man to use language as a weapon to "encourage and strengthen the capacity to retain self-control in the face of insult and abuse" (Molette and Molette, 2013, 183). Rhetorical skill is a well-defined survival mechanism for African Americans that employs the word games known as "The dozens" and is used by traditional Afrocentric heroes such as the signifying monkey. Besides this, the historical references of the play engage the way Noah ships away his son with the actual shipping of Henry "Box" Brown, a slave from Virginia who in 1849 was sent to Philadelphia inside a wooden crate three feet long, two feet wide, and two-and-a-half feet deep by White abolitionists.

The Later Plays and the Theater of Cultural Revivalism

In *Legacy* (2012), a two-act play set in southern Georgia in 1974, both White and Black characters are forced to reassess the meaning of their troubled past and the racial consciousness they have imbibed through exposure to southern traditions. *Legacy* was staged in Atlanta by the Black Theater Network under the direction of Larry Ruth and by the Working Title Playwrights directed by Andrea Frye in 2013. The play departs from the premise that the southern landscape and southern Whites become enemies of Black people.

Amanda is the play's White protagonist; it is important to her to maintain the comfort of a good reputation offered by her status in the southern "aristocracy." She is the "grand old lady" who might not be a real racist, just someone who does not accept her past and the heritage shaping her emotions. She has lived most of her life in a self-deceiving state, considering herself above Blacks and most Whites in Overton. It is not until the arrival of her niece that she is able to confront her past, and to finally understand the meaning of its legacy. She has a difficult time accepting the fact that Justine, her beloved European niece, is Black.

The real twist of the play comes in scene nine of act two, when Amanda reveals her lifelong secret: back in 1945, when she attended Agnes Scott College in Atlanta, she had dated a Black man. Not only this, but she had passed for Black whenever she had visited him at Fisk University, where he was studying medicine. At last, Amanda is forced by circumstances to face not only reality in the present, but also the legacy of her emotional past. She must acknowledge her own hypocrisy in rejecting her sister's marriage to a Black man, when she herself had in fact been in love with another. She must come to terms with her own cowardly behavior, which she had called "honor," in not facing up to the prejudice of the South and in giving up, as her sister Camille had done, those "honorable" southern values, a legacy of slavery. Instead, Amanda installed herself in the comfort that White privilege, high class, and family heritage had afforded her, thus betraying her personal past.

Amanda's niece, Justine, functions as a foil; through her presence, Amanda grows in humanity, discarding the prejudice and lies that have ruled most of her adult life. Fearless, she now resolves to re-establish her connection with her diasporic kin in France, embracing a new interracial family, and seeking cultural definition through communication and community building, even if this entails losing her privileged status at home. Justine carries both the legacy of her African father—who refused to visit Georgia in the mid-1950s because the South, in his view, was not a safe place for a Black man—and the legacy of her mother, a member of elite White southern society.

When Justine talks to her aunt, she learns that her maternal great-great-great-grandfather had owned slaves, and that the West African village of her paternal grandfather had been decimated by the slavers. She must face a legacy of violence and denied privilege on her Black side, and the legacy of oppression exerted by her White forebears. Justine is totally comfortable with her Black identity, and aware, living in Paris, of being part of the African Diaspora. However, while visiting her aunt in Georgia, she becomes painfully aware of the issues related to racial difference and class difference which directly affect her.

Gertrude, Amanda's best friend, reminds her that the only place in the US where Blacks were integrated was in sports—football. She uses this argument to warn Amanda that her niece will never be accepted by the local high society because of her Black skin. Amanda will have to drop some of her firm beliefs and views of the South in order to make room for her niece. Justine is seen as a threat to the values of the old South, which is rooted in the myth of "racial purity." The hypocritical behavior of local politicians and neighbors is revealed when only Gertrude attends Amanda's party.

Amanda's Black domestic attendants discuss how the concept of race has changed over time, adding another perspective to the issue of interracial personal politics. As CJ points out, the fact that there are Black families in the South who are passing as White makes a nonsense of the myth of racial purity. Although her aunt's house does not, at first, pose any direct physical threat, Justine learns, in her outings with CJ, that Blacks have to be aware of the unwritten rules that pertain south of the Mason-Dixon line, and need to read every situation correctly. At the tractor pull, CJ points out "the redneck zone" that they cannot enter. This is but one strong remnant of segregation, the "separate but equal" that in 1974 is interpreted by Blacks as "a matter of respect. We respect their space and they respect ours" (Molette and Molette, *Legacy*, unpublished manuscript written in 2012, 64). Later, however, on the night of the party, White supremacists throw a Molotov cocktail at Amanda's porch. This shows Justine the ugliness of southern territory, with its legacy of slavery, recalling the fear of the South felt by Justine's father. The violence of the White supremacists echoes the ways in which, according to Harris, "southern territory came to be identified with torture and death" (2009, 5). Justine does not allow fear to conquer her, nor to control her life. Both Justine and CJ violate this rule repeatedly, as well as another unwritten rule of the old South, that "colored servants are [only] allowed to enter through the front door of the white house when they are carrying something" (Molette and Molette, *Legacy*, 19). As the niece of homeowner Amanda, Justine breaks this rule. She urges CJ to follow her example because she has trouble "adjusting to southern traditions" (Molette and Molette, *Legacy*, 25). She asks him to use the front door when he returns to pick her up. His answer is full of concern about the negative consequences this might have for his family: "please ask your aunt Amanda if she's going to fire my sister if I use the front door" (Molette and Molette, *Legacy*, 26).

Gossett points out in her review that *Legacy* poses a key question: can southern tradition be embraced without paying homage to the time that it reflects? In the play, Georgians face the dilemma of how to be progressive while celebrating southern tradition. This becomes all the more problematic because the traditions and manners of the south "ultimately reflect the days of slavery" (Gossett, 2013). Though written in 2012, *Legacy* repeats many of the themes raised in *Rosalee Pritchett*, a play written in the 1970s. Both plays deal with issues of class within the Black community which continue to be part of the contemporary struggle of racial discourse. As Carlton Molette points out, the people who were actively fighting against it in the 1970s have now become part of the problem.[6] Both plays explore legacies of the past, and discuss how African Americans deal with racial awareness and consciousness, questioning whether the conception of race is a biological concept or a cultural one. As August Wilson remarks, the ideas of self-determination, self-respect, and self-defense that governed the life of many African Americans in the 1960s are valid and self-urging today. African-American playwrights feel that the need to alter their relationship to society and to alter shared expectations as a racial group is more urgent today than it was in the 1960s and 1970s.

---

[6] Unpublished interview with Carlton and Barbara Molette conducted at Spelman College in June 2012.

The Ten-Minute Plays

The heroes of the Molettes' ten-minute plays display an impulse for survival, human dignity, and respect for their community. The characters are invested with comic heroism, defining themselves through their witty language and the linguistic imagery they use. *Tee-Shirt History* (2011) is one of this group; other examples are *Kinship* (2012), *Out of Time* (2012), produced at the Turtle Shell Theater's "Eight Minute Madness Festival" on West 43rd Street, New York in 2011, and *Move the Car*, which opened May 31, 2012 at the Warehouse Performing Arts Center in North Carolina as part of an evening called "Car Craze." *Tee-Shirt History* opened as a contribution to "the local" on July 11, 2012 in Atlanta's Essential Theater.

Tee-Shirt History is concerned with the intra-racial issues of the Black community. It features two heroic figures. Cooksey, an elderly Black gentleman, stands for community dignity. The younger Rasheed, who is on his own search for a better future, helped by his wit and spark, learns to trust the wisdom and knowledge of the older generation. The play demonstrates young peoples' ignorance about Black history. Rasheed is a Black man in his late twenties who aspires to own his own business. He sells tee-shirts in Atlanta near the entrance to Piedmont Park, where an event commemorating Martin Luther King's birthday is about to begin. The tee-shirts are printed with Dr. King's famous phrases, but the quotations are incorrect. Even though the sentence indicates that Rasheed has made a mistake, he is at the same time making a political statement by changing the famous phrases. One reads, "I HAD a dream." Cooksey, a former participant in the Civil Rights Movement, tries to reason with Rasheed about the wrongness of his business endeavor. Rasheed consistently confuses Dr. King and Malcolm X, which exasperates the elder Cooksey. The play also references Booker T. Washington and his support for Black business in Atlanta.

As Cooksey states, there was a time when Black businessmen helped one another with small loans so that they could launch their businesses. The play critiques the lack of solidarity among Blacks in the US, due, among other factors, to class issues. By remarking on how integration has destroyed many Black owned business, the play focuses on how little progress has been made. A Black police officer refuses to allow Rasheed to sell anything, claiming that it is illegal. Cooksey claims that it is the officer's responsibility to help young Blacks by overlooking laws based on racial prejudice; in other words, he calls for civil disobedience. The legitimacy of the law is brought into question, and the play ends with Cooksey offering help to young Rasheed, not only with a first-hand history lesson, but also by contributing financially to his enterprise. *Tee-Shirt History* demonstrates that a knowledge of history from an Afrocentric perspective helps younger Blacks to counteract racism and prejudice at a personal level.

The Molettes' most recent plays continued to be part of the Black intellectual tradition; they take an Afrocentric perspective, falling within the paradigm of the "Theater of Experience" which "offers blacks an image of themselves that disputes the validity of images offered by the white world" (Fabre, 1983, 107). This type of theater seeks to integrate all aspects of Black life and to show how Black life interacts with the White world. It is committed to the search for a Neo-African or Africanist Theater.

Embracing and Disseminating African-American Culture and Values through Afrocentric Theater

As Paul Carter Harrison contends, "theatre is an arena where the destiny of Blacks can be staged; it is a privileged environment where art can save the ethos of a people" (qtd in Fabre, 1983, 201). For dramatists like Carter Harrison and the Molettes, culture involves all levels of experience: language and idiom, behavior and thought processes, strategies for survival, narrative and popular legends, even the characteristics which the collective imagination gives to heroes of the community. For these dramatists, theater should revalidate the spirituality of Black America, revive the collective race memory by retaining a remembrance of slavery, and reinstate an African vision of the world. Theater such as this endows the Black community with autonomy and renewable strength and claims Black experience as part of the cosmos; it is in this fundamental relationship that Blacks must find the arms for their resistance. Their intuitive knowledge of the world helps them to confront elements that threaten group cohesion and universal harmony (Fabre, 1983, 202–203). African-American theater becomes a potent political tool. Both Harrison and the Molettes propose a drama that takes its organizing principles from African philosophy. Afrocentric aesthetic standards are rooted in Afrocentric cosmology, which the authors claim as the birthright of African-American theater.

Afrocentric theater calls for community bonding that is realized through *nommo*, or word power. According to Molefi Asante, the concept of *nommo* (the term comes from a Dogon creation myth) reflects African society's search for harmony and wholeness through the spoken word (1998, 97–107). The force and integrity of the drama is realizable, according to Lewis Nkosi, only in its performance (1965, 111). It is through *nommo*, the power of the word, according to Jahnheinz Jahn (1961, 127), that the human being becomes a *muntu*, a being endowed with spirituality, with intelligence and soul. In *The Magara Principle* (1994), Jahn suggests that a person's spiritual well-being and happiness depend on connecting the living with their ancestors, since *muntu* includes the living, the dead, and the gods; *muntu* is an active force that causes and maintains all things in relation (1961, 18). Theater also bears a historical relationship to time, because "in dramatic discourse the past becomes a syntagmatic element of the total history of Afro-Americans, which is decoded, recognized, and separated into units" (Fabre, 1983, 217). Theater provides a space "where people can be confronted by their history" and have the power to reshape and reenergize the past.

In writing about "the most problematic part of the country historically for black self-realization and fulfillment" (Harris, 2009, 17), the Molettes take on a task which is difficult for Black writers: "the capacity of imagining without stereotype southern landscape and white southern character" (Harris, 2009, 18). Their insightful and powerful dialogues encourage us to question a belief system based in the ideology of White supremacy and its attendant stereotypes. Their plays move us to better appreciate alternative cultural perspectives. As representatives and inheritors of the Black intellectual tradition and the Black Arts Movement, the Molettes' plays offer harsh criticism of the ideas and behavior of those Blacks who deny the existence of a solid African-American culture, and they propose ways to celebrate Black heritage and culture. Their collective body of work is a clarion call for self-definition and agency; they use Afrocentric theater as a powerful tool for seeking healing and wholeness, illuminating the struggle that still continues, altering the intellectual and moral consciousness of Black Americans.

Works Cited

Asante, Molefi Kete. *The Afrocentric Idea*. Philadelphia, PA: Temple University Press, 1988.

Asante, Molefi Kete. *Erasing Racism. The Survival of the American Nation*. Amherst, NY: Prometheus, 2003.

Barnett, Pamela E. *Dangerous Desire: Literature of Sexual Freedom and Violence since the Sixties*. New York: Routledge, 2004.

Barrios, Olga. *The Black Theatre Movement in The United States and in South Africa*. Valencia: BJC, Universitat València, 2008.

Brown-Gillory, Elizabeth. *Their Place on the Stage: Black Women Playwrights in America*. New York: Greenwood Press, 1988.

Butler, Johnnella E. "African American Studies and the 'Warring Ideals': The Color Line Meets the Borderlands." In *Dispatches from the Ebony Tower*. Ed. Manning Marable. New York: Columbia University Press, 2000: 141–152.

Childress, Alice. "Rosalee Pritchett." *The Spelman Messenger* (1979): 41–43.

Coleman, Michael. "What is Black Theatre? An Interview with Imamu Amiri Baraka." *Black World* 20 (1971): 32–36.

Fabre, Geneviève. *Drumbeats Masks and Metaphor: Contemporary Afro-American Theatre*. Trans. Melvin Dixon. Cambridge, MA: Harvard University Press, 1983.
Fanon, Frantz. *Black Skin, White Masks*. New York: Grove Press, 1978.
Gossett, Neely. "Dramaturg Neely Gossett on Barbara and Carlton Molette's LEGACY." www.workingtitleblog.com/2013/09/17/dramaturg-neely-gossett-on-barbara-carlton-molettes-legacy. Accessed Jan. 12, 2016.
Gussow, Mel. "Theater: Condemning an Insidious Form of Racism." *New York Times*. Jan. 22, 1971.
Harris, Trudier. *The Scary Mason Dixon Line: African American Writers and the South*. Baton Rouge, LA: Louisiana State University, 2009.
Janhainz, Jahn. *African Culture and the Western World*. New York: Grove Press, 1961.
Karenga, Maulana. "Black Studies: A Critical Reassessment." In *Dispatches from the Ebony Tower*. Ed. Manning Marable. New York: Columbia University Press, 2000: 162–170.
Marable, Manning. "Introduction: Black Studies and the Racial Mountain." In *Dispatches from the Ebony Tower*. Ed. Manning Marable. New York: Columbia University Press, 2000: 1–28.
Molette, Barbara J. "Black Women Playwrights: They Speak: Who Listens?" *Black World* 25 (1976): 28–34.
Molette, Carlton. "The Way to Viable Theater? Afro-American Ritual Drama." *Black World* 22 (1973): 4–12.
Molette, Carlton W., and Barbara J. Molette. *Rosalee Pritchett*. In *Black Writers of America: A Comprehensive Anthology*. Ed. Richard Barksdale and Keneth Kinnamon. New York: MacMillan, 1972: 824–835.
Molette, Carlton W., and Barbara J. Molette. *Noah's Ark*. In *Center Stage: An Anthology of 21 Contemporary Black-American Plays*. Ed. Eileen Joyce Ostrow. Oakland, CA: Sea Urchin, 1981: 179–196.
Molette, Carlton W., and Barbara J. Molette. *Black Theatre: Premise and Presentation*. Bristol, IN: Wyndham Hall Press, 1992.
Molette, Carlton W., and Barbara J. Molette. *Afrocentric Theatre*. Bloomington, IN: Xlibris, 2013.
Molette, Carlton W., and Barbara J. Molette. *Legacy*. Unpublished manuscript.
Molette, Carlton W., and Barbara J. Molette. *Tee-Shirt History*. Unpublished manuscript.
Neal, Larry. "The Black Arts Movement." *Tulane Drama Review* 12 (1968): 29–39.
Nkosi, Lewis. *Home and Exile*. London: Longmans, Green and Company, 1965.
Reed, Ishmael, *Multi-America: Essays on Cultural Wars and Cultural Peace*. New York: Viking, 1997.
Riley, Clayton. "My Quarrels Notwithstanding, I Liked Them." [Review of *Rosalee Pritchett*]. *The New York Times*. Feb. 7, 1971.

Sainer, Arthur. "Bogged Down and Busy, Busy, Busy." *The Village Voice.* Jan. 28, 1971: 59.

Smethurst, James. "Black Arts Movement in Atlanta." In *Neighborhood Rebels: Black Power at the Local Level.* Ed. J. Peniel. New York: Palgrave, 2010: 173–190.

Williams, Mance. *Black Theatre in the 1960s and 1970s: A Historical-Critical Analysis of the Movement.* Westport, CT: Greenwood Press, 1985.

Wilson, August. "The Ground on Which I Stand." *Callaloo* 20.3 (1997): 493–503.

MOVED TO ACT:
CIVIL RIGHTS ACTIVISM
IN THE US AND BEYOND

7

"Together We Can Build a Nation of Love and Integration": The 1965 North Shore Summer Project for Fair Housing in Chicago's Northern Suburbs

Mary Barr (Kentucky State University)

"We live here, and we must speak up. We stand here today to say we no longer, by silence, condone the evil system of segregation perpetuated by realtors such as Quinlan and Tyson."[1] This defiant pronouncement was not made in Alabama, Georgia, or Mississippi, the familiar sites of Jim Crow. It was made in a Chicago suburb in 1965 at the height of a movement that confronted such discrimination as just as racist as that perpetrated in the Deep South. Activists in several northern cities, including Chicago, Detroit, and Philadelphia, took to the streets during the mid-1960s to pressure state legislatures and city councils to pass open housing laws.[2] When, in 1966, Martin Luther King, Jr. brought his Southern Christian Leadership Conference (SCLC) north to desegregate Chicago's neighborhoods, several organizations had already been fighting vigorously to eliminate housing discrimination. Prominent among these was the Housing Opportunity Program (HOP) established by the American Friends Service Committee (AFSC), a Quaker civil rights organization founded in 1917. Through its director William Moyer, a professional organizer, the HOP came to the forefront of the 1965 North Shore Summer Project, an open housing campaign that challenged discriminatory practices in the suburbs lining the lakeshore north of Chicago. The Summer Project stated its goal on student recruitment flyers: "To have the North Shore real estate industry adopt nondiscriminatory policies and practices."[3] To achieve this goal, it sought

---

[1] North Shore Summer Project Staff, "Quinlan and Tyson Continues its Discriminatory Practices," n.d.
[2] For a broad overview of open housing campaigns in the North see Sugrue (2009), esp. chapters 7 and 12; Meyer (1999).
[3] North Shore Summer Project Staff, "What About Chicago's North Shore?" n.d.

"to overcome fear with love, to meet emotionalism with logic, to counteract rumor with fact" (see Mabley, 1965).

Affluent and middle-aged white women spearheaded the Summer Project with help from local college students home for school break and black homebuyers wanting to move to the suburbs. Together they hoped to convince exclusive north shore communities to admit black residents. While King's Chicago housing campaign is well known, the North Shore Summer Project has been largely ignored.[4] Reflecting on the Project a few years after it ended, political scientists Michael Barkun and James Levine wrote: "It seems safe to predict that historians of the future will pass over this group" (1967, 21). They were partly right. William Moyer and his co-authors did not even mention it in *Doing Democracy: The MAP Model for Organizing Social Movements* (2001).

The North Shore Summer Project: Background and Organization

The North Shore Summer Project developed from existing AFSC efforts to combat unfair housing practices. The Project was heavily influenced by the non-violent philosophy of Martin Luther King, Jr. and the AFSC's Quaker foundations. Strategies and tactics, however, including a rally that featured King, seemed to appease residents more than challenge them. For example, opinion polls and demonstrations, which took the form of vigils where protestors stood silently and gave out leaflets to explain their grievances, were employed to educate and persuade homeowners, not inconvenience them. Project members fought an uphill battle; some residents wanted change, but most were quite comfortable with things the way they were. Ultimately, the Project failed to integrate Chicago's northern suburbs where, in the twenty-first century, less than 1 percent of the population, excluding Evanston and Skokie, is African American. Despite this enduring dismal statistic and the North Shore Summer Project's failure to change housing policies, it did leave a worthwhile legacy. The Project succeeded in drawing attention to closed housing issues. Additionally, by the end of the summer, many actively involved white residents had intensified their commitment to civil rights.

During the Great Migration, beginning around 1915 and continuing into the 1960s, African Americans learned that the North practiced its own style of racism, one that was deeply entrenched in the structures and systems of discriminatory housing policies, resulting in sharply defined black and white neighborhoods. Segregated residential areas in the North kept housing

---

[4] In Ralph (1993, 100), for example, the North Shore Summer Project is only briefly examined.

separate and unequal, essentially doing the work of Jim Crow (see Sugrue, 2009). Housing was arguably the single most important factor in determining access to good schools, well-paid jobs, and recreational space. On Chicago's Southside, a seven-mile strip known as "the black belt" was the only place African Americans could live until that ghetto spread west (see Spear, 1967). Wealthy suburbs lining Lake Michigan to the north were mostly off limits. Nonetheless, black enclaves were allowed to exist on the fringes of the suburbs, acting as labor pools that ensured the availability of black workers. In *Sundown Towns: A Hidden Dimension of American Racism* (2005), sociologist James W. Lowen explains that most of America's first suburbs (built along railways and streetcar lines) made room for servants and workers, including independent African-American households. Close proximity was advantageous; commuting from the city was too expensive and it was difficult, according to historian Kenneth Jackson, for servants to arrive in time to warm the house and fix breakfast (qtd in Lowen, 2005, 122–123). It was thus a matter of mutual convenience for black servants to live in communities adjacent to their white employers but, as Lowen also notes, the Great Migration struck many suburbanites as a threat of invasion of their neighborhoods. In response, they acted quickly to exclude minorities (Lowen, 2005, 273).

Developers protected suburban communities from an influx of minorities by adding racial and ethnic clauses to deeds, restricting property to white Christians. Homeowners banded together to form neighborhood associations and to establish racial covenants regulating sales and rentals. Owner occupancy was an index of stability and civic pride. Zoning laws prohibited the construction of apartment buildings and low-income housing. High-rise apartment buildings were discouraged because they were considered unsightly and detrimental to single-family-home neighborhoods. Since such multiple-unit housing was what renters, who generally had lower incomes, could afford, the absence of the high-rise apartments effectively kept them out of the suburbs.

Real estate agents acted as the first line of defense in the community politics of segregation. The Evanston-North Shore Board of Realtors (ENSBR), to which virtually all brokers operating on the North Shore belonged, played a key role in effectively backing housing discrimination. The board controlled its members' policies through a written constitution, a central office, regular meetings, and a monthly newsletter. With its far-reaching power, ENSBR effectively kept homes out of the reach of minority buyers: by employing a multiple listing service for member agencies; by refusing to list homes for sale on a nondiscriminatory basis; and by declining to help black home seekers. Statistical data illustrate the results of these discriminatory practices. The Board listed over 2,000 homes for sale in 1964, yet only five black families moved to the North Shore that year. Moreover, HOP records indicate that there were 20,000 qualified black families in Chicago who wanted to buy homes, while only 0.025% of that total had been helped by North Shore agents in recent years.[5] The realtors relied on a conservative rhetoric of individual rights to defend their policies. Arguing that "nobody wants to sell to Negros," "the community isn't ready for it," and "the owner has the right to sell to persons of his choice," realtors repeated their claim to be acting as agents for their clients and thus powerless to change the situation despite their recognition that equal service and treatment for all home seekers was morally right. Emphasizing voluntary action, they wanted solutions that appealed to hearts and minds, and claimed that integration was best accomplished "calmly." Matters of conscience were not, they claimed, within their purview: "We don't understand the harassment of the real estate man. He cannot bring brotherly love if the majority of the people don't want it."[6]

It was the ENSBR, as the mouthpiece for area realtors, which eventually replied to the Summer Project organizers' questions, charges, and demands (Barkun and Levine, 1967, 26). In its early stages, organizers made an effort to understand the real estate agents' position through a series of interviews with them. During these discussions some realtors projected blame on their professional organization while others held homeowners responsible. Most agents said that if the ENSBR issued a clear policy directive, they would follow it, but they were unwilling to do anything without a directive. Some agents said that a mandate from the community would be necessary before they would review their practices. This gave white residents the authority to decide if, and when, realtors would do the right thing. Because brokers projected blame for their actions on residents, the North Shore Summer Project organizers concluded that agents might adopt nondiscriminatory policies, but were afraid to make changes without reassurances from residents. Local residents were not ready to give such a mandate.

An almost insurmountable obstacle confronting the Project was the pervasive apathy of most suburban residents with regard to racial discrimination. Residents didn't see a relationship between the racial composition of their suburbs and the turmoil in distant urban ghettos, where inadequate housing, high unemployment, discrimination, poor schools, and poverty were rife. Because of residential segregation, most whites didn't interact with black people in a meaningful way; their perceptions were shaped in large part by distorted portrayals in the mass media. Media reports focusing on the Civil Rights Movement in the South may also have influenced northerners' complacency. It was within this context that the North Shore Summer Project

---

[5] North Shore Summer Project Staff, "Prospectus," n.d.
[6] "Evanston Real Estate Brokers' Council Adopts Policy Against 'Forced Housing,'" *Evanston Review*, May 27, 1965, 19.

took shape. Advocates from the North Shore had already been active in a fair-housing network established by the HOP and HOME, Inc., a listing service for minority home buyers. They were now poised for greater activism.

The steering committee set up to launch the North Shore Summer Project determined that the real estate industry had not kept abreast of changing national patterns in equal rights. Local fair housing advocates knew of people, like themselves, on the North Shore who would welcome any qualified buyer as a neighbor and, through the HOP, African-American buyers who could afford and wanted to buy houses on the North Shore. Project leaders concluded that housing discrimination stemmed more from misunderstanding than from prejudice and bigotry. This dictated the group's strategy to gently educate North Shore communities. They believed that both education and persuasion would expose the fundamental contradiction between liberal discourse and suburban realities.

The Summer Project targeted 13 lakeshore suburbs north of Chicago, including Evanston, Glencoe, Wilmette, Kenilworth, Winnetka, Highland Park, Skokie, Lincolnwood, Morton Grove, Glenview, Northfield, Northbrook, and Deerfield. At the time, it was the region's largest effort to combat housing discrimination. With the exception of Evanston and Glencoe, these communities were "whites only." Evanston had the largest African-American population, followed by Glencoe, but black residents were isolated geographically in both suburbs. According to the Summer Project's general information sheet, numbers were minimal in the other targeted suburbs: "There were seven black families living in Skokie; two in Highland Park; and the lily-white communities of Lake Forest and Kenilworth were home to one Negro family each."[7] There were no African Americans living in Winnetka, where the project's main headquarters would be located.

The Summer Project had unusual resources for a protest group. Financing came from the wealthy North Shore. Area housing groups accepted contributions and generated revenue by selling buttons and bumper stickers at rented project offices. Offices, referred to as "Freedom Centers," were furnished with supplies, including mimeograph machines. Members were highly educated and able to offer professional advice and support; a freelance journalist helped the group to write its public narrative. Members' husbands also provided services; an executive at a major broadcasting company acted as a consultant on media relations; and a candidate for Congress gave local leaders political advice.

The Project was well thought out and tightly organized. Field offices were easily identifiable. They were located in rented storefronts and had

---

[7] North Shore Summer Project Staff, "General Information For North Shore Summer Project," n.d.

large banners hanging outside that read, "North Shore Summer Project Freedom Center (town name) Headquarters."[8] The project's chief sponsor, the AFSC, provided staff services. William Moyer, who headed the HOP, was named executive director. A professional organizer, he assumed the bulk of logistical chores. Other responsibilities were divided among ten subcommittees. Representatives from the subcommittees formed an executive board that assumed overall responsibility for the project. Although there was leadership at the top, the strategy of grassroots organization demanded that residents participate and direct activities at the local level. Town chairmen were named and Freedom Centers were opened in each of the participating suburbs. Local housewives, student volunteers, and black home seekers were key players in the movement. It is difficult to estimate the true size of the Summer Project, but there were about 400–500 active adult members and 100 students (Barkun and Levine, 1967, 24). Women were an integral part of the Summer Project, but the visible leadership was often male. Women acted as town chairs and did much of the day-to-day work, but even as the Summer Project empowered women, it held rigid views of the roles that they could and could not play. In organizational records and newspaper articles, female members were identified by their husband's names.

Sponsorship for the Summer Project involved civic, social, and religious organizations in every North Shore community. Much of the program's success was owed to support from churches and synagogues, which were an integral part of North Shore life. Reverend Buckner Coe headed the clergy committee, responsible for organizing religious institutions. Kay Coe, his wife, helped to draft the plan for the Summer Project. Before joining the project, she had worked for years on open housing through involvement with HOME, Inc. Mrs. Coe would serve as secretary of the steering committee and as chair of the Wilmette group. She arranged for her husband's church, the First Congregational Church in Wilmette, to be used as a meeting space. Nicknamed Brown's Chapel—a reference to the Selma, Alabama church from which voters' rights marches were organized—this is where the North Shore Summer Project's early and formative meetings were held. As the knowing reference suggests, the organizers were acutely aware of what was happening in the southern Civil Rights Movement.

Reverend Coe worked closely with Moyer, the head of the HOP, successfully enlisting the support of 140 clergymen, 40 of whom took active roles. He came from a long line (five generations) of activist ministers. His uncle, Allan Knight Chalmers, chaired the Scottsboro Boys defense committee in the 1930s and had been president of the NAACP legal

---

[8] North Shore Summer Project Staff, "A Statement of Purpose," n.d.

and educational fund in the 1940s.[9] In March 1965, Coe joined other white clergymen and answered King's plea to come to Selma. It was at the "real" Brown's Church in Selma, surrounded by King, John Lewis, and C.T. Vivian, that Coe decided, "he had to do something at home. Something direct."[10]

Reverend Emory G. Davis, of Bethel AME Church in Evanston, served as chairman of the steering committee and worked with Moyer to develop the nonviolent strategy. Davis delivered weekly sermons to a congregation of more than 400 people. His "Altar Call" column was published in the *Chicago Defender* and 35 other newspapers nationwide. "Realtors like to think of themselves as religious, law-abiding, respectable citizens. But the god they worship is money. They should go to the bank on Sunday instead of to church," he was quoted as saying.[11] Davis worked from a Freedom Center located in the Evanston Council of Churches.

Sally Olds chaired the public relations committee charged with building a relationship with local and national media outlets. She wrote and distributed press releases, called press conferences, handled inquiries from reporters, and publicized events. The way realtors and community members interpreted the North Shore Project was vital to its overall success. Weekly suburban newspapers provided coverage, but with the exception of one *New York Times* article, the national media failed to report it (Wehrwein, 1965, 12). Since the national media was also the northern media, editors may have lost some of their enthusiasm for pointing out the region's flaws. It can also be said that housing segregation did not make for compelling television. The daily metropolitan news did not pay much attention either, revealing the role the media played in discounting northern struggles.

Jean Mitten, from Evanston, headed the personnel committee; charged with recruiting student volunteers, she sent informational flyers to colleges and universities. Jean Cleland, a resident of Wilmette, oversaw the maintenance committee assigned to housing, feeding, and transporting student volunteers. Organizers hoped to recruit an equal number of white and black college students, believing it was "important to have persons in its project representing a wide variety of religions, nationalities, and races."[12] According to the organization's prospectus, and in reference to

---

[9] The Scottsboro Boys were nine young black men charged with rape, wrongfully convicted, and sentenced to death in Scottsboro, Alabama in 1931.
[10] Carol Kleiman, "Profile-Buckner Coe," *North Shore Summer Project Newsletter*, I.6, Sept. 14, 1965, 4.
[11] Carol Kleiman, "A Look at Rev. Davis," *North Shore Summer Project Newsletter*, I.4, Aug. 6, 1965, 4.
[12] North Shore Summer Project Staff, "Student Participant Application Form," n.d.

Mississippi activists, volunteers would need to dig deep to summon "the same courage, stamina and guts that enabled COFO [Council of Federated Organizations] workers not to give up last summer when the going got rough."[13] Student volunteers were given a ten-dollar weekly stipend (Routliffe, 2013). Some from outside the area received room and board from North Shore residents.

Applicants gave lengthy answers to the following essay questions: (1) Give your reasons for wanting to participate in the North Shore Summer Project and (2) What methods would you use in relieving tensions and building understanding in personal and group relations? The latter connected to the group's overall strategy to keep things calm. Finally, students confirmed availability for the entire eight-week period. Student applicants were asked to describe their educational background, including awards and scholarships, and to list their office skills, such as typing, shorthand, and mimeographing. The program also exploited other skills: summer events counted on their musical talents. Red Cross training may have been viewed favorably too. Although violence wasn't expected in the peaceful suburbs, the AFSC took out an insurance policy for all students in case of illness, accident, or death.

Student volunteers were carefully vetted to meet high standards of maturity, responsibility, and commitment. Students would bear a heavy responsibility for the program's success and would have to cope with a variety of difficult and important situations. The personnel committee relied on reference letters in its selection process. Personality, ability to get along with others, and emotional stability were extremely important. To conduct interviews, students had to be intelligent and articulate. They also had to be trusted to follow through and get things done.[14] After careful review, a shortlist of applicants received in-person interviews. Preference was given to (1) students attending colleges on the North Shore, (2) students living on the North Shore who had gone away to college, and (3) black students from Chicago.

Of the approximately 100 students who participated in the North Shore Summer Project, between 50 and 70 were full-time. The rest worked on weekends and evenings. Almost all of the students were from the North Shore, either residents or in college there—bearing out the position that "this is a local problem with local people working to solve it."[15] With

---

[13] North Shore Summer Project Staff, "Prospectus of the North Shore Summer Project," n.d., 3.
[14] Jean A. Mitten, "Form Letter Addressed to Student Reference Writers," n.d.
[15] American Friends Service Committee, "Report to the Field Foundation on Chicago Metropolitan Area Housing Opportunity Program," October 1965, 3.

the exception of a few mature high school students, most were enrolled in college. The majority of the volunteers were white upper-middle-class college students for whom money was not a concern. Relatively privileged and imbued with idealistic American values, these students believed in equality and were shocked to find out that it didn't exist. The vast majority attended colleges in the Midwest, almost all in the Chicago area. The second highest number of recruits came from educational institutions located in the northeast. Only five students attending colleges in the South were selected, including one applicant from the University of Mississippi. A few students from northern colleges had enrolled in exchange programs with southern institutions. Several of the volunteers came from historically black colleges and universities. Recruiting black students was difficult, however. Volunteers had to be able to forego summer jobs. Black students did not live in the area and had the extra expense of commuting from Chicago if they did not lodge with a North Shore family.

Academically, student volunteers were high achievers and some already had experience protesting in the South. JoAnn Ugolani, a white student from Highland Park had marched in Selma; she said that she was eager to bring the Civil Rights Movement home (Samuels, 2002). June Carter, a black student from Chicago, was also among the volunteers chosen. Both girls had attended Mundelein College in Chicago. Carter then graduated *cum laude* from Loyola University and had been awarded a Woodrow Wilson Fellowship for graduate work in history at the University of Chicago. Grace Meigs Damman was among the few high school students recruited. She had recently graduated from Sidwell Friends, a prestigious Quaker-affiliated school near Washington, DC, and planned to matriculate at Smith College in the fall of 1965.

Like many of the volunteers, Rick Momeyer had previous experience in the southern movement. In 1962, he left Alleghany College in Ohio to spend his sophomore year as an exchange student at Fisk University in Nashville. While at Fisk, he met "concerned, enthusiastic, and dedicated" students. Momeyer was only in Nashville for ten days before he was arrested and jailed for breaking a Jim Crow law by sitting with an integrated group at a lunch counter. That same year, he met John Lewis and Bernard Lafayette, who later directed the AFSC Urban Affairs Program in Chicago and was an executive member of North Shore Summer Project.[16] Momeyer was a graduate student at the University of Chicago when he started working on the Summer Project. He and his new wife became co-directors of student activities. They acted as advisors, counselors, and listeners to more than

---

[16] John Lewis and Bernard Lafayette were members of the Nashville Student Movement and instrumental in the founding of SNCC.

100 young people. "Students got an awful lot of education," Momeyer said, "It comes as something of a shock to learn the fears, defenses and prejudices of your own neighbors. You also learn a lot about yourself."[17] A year earlier, he had participated in the Mississippi Freedom Summer Project. He remembers hearing about the murder of James Chaney, Andrew Goodman, and Michael Schwerner from Bob Moses. It was a "reality check," recalled Momeyer. Everyone was scared but the volunteers turned fear into motivation and decided to fight harder.[18]

The Mississippi Freedom Summer Project and the North Shore Summer Project

Volunteers with experience from the Mississippi Freedom Summer Project knew how to apply the tactics and ideologies they'd learned in Mississippi to the northern context.[19] Those who had spent time in Mississippi, or who had marched in Montgomery and Selma, had attended marches and rallies, registered voters, conducted teach-ins, learned the techniques of nonviolent direct action, and listened to civil rights giants like Martin Luther King, Jr., Bob Moses, James Forman, and Fannie Lou Hamer. Mississippi had been described as a "closed society"; "The same could be said about white neighborhoods in the North that excluded Negro families."[20] Organizers stated: "Now it is time to do something about our own hometown."[21] William Moyer, the executive director of the North Shore Summer Project, consciously borrowed the name of the Mississippi Freedom Summer Project in an attempt to transfer glamour to the quiet, tree-shaded suburban streets (Barkum and Levine, 1967, 23).

The tactical and ideological imprint of the Mississippi Freedom Summer Project was everywhere evident in North Shore Summer Project's agenda. Local community decision-making efforts reflected the SNCC's consensual style and brand of participatory democracy; all participants had the right to speak and vote during meetings. As on the Mississippi Freedom Summer Project, student volunteers provided manpower for the North Shore project; they used educational and persuasive techniques and activities that had

---

[17] Carol Kleiman, "Profile – Ric and Sue Momeyer," *North Shore Summer Project Newsletter*, Aug. 20, 1965.
[18] Oral History Interview, Freedom Summer AV Collection, Miami University Libraries, Oct. 10, 2009.
[19] Moyer spent time in Mississippi and must have known some of the northern volunteers because he was listed as a reference on at least one application. See McAdam (1988, 159).
[20] North Shore Summer Project Staff, "What About Chicago's North Shore?" n.d.
[21] North Shore Summer Project Staff, "A Statement of Purpose," n.d.

proved effective in civil rights struggles across the country. The Project was designed to dramatize the issue of the closed community in the North in much the same way that Mississippi's closed society in the South had been illuminated. Bringing diversity to the northern suburbs demanded that the Project publicly dramatize the fact that black citizens were being denied the right to choose where they wanted to live in Chicago's North Shore. To do this, they needed to "register" white sellers willing to sell their houses on a nondiscriminatory basis. They had to publicly demand that the real estate system serve all citizens. And they had to work with black families who wanted to live in the North Shore neighborhoods of their choice.[22]

Organizers made every effort to associate the Project with the national black freedom struggle, but it was difficult to make resistance based on apathy as clearly visible—or as publicly interesting—as resistance which utilized overt violence against those petitioning for their rights. Concerned about bad publicity, government officials were willing to work with the activist leaders, a collaborative arrangement exemplified in the relationship which the movement built with the police. In contrast to southern forces, local police departments protected project activities. According to Michael Barkun and James Levine, "Throughout the summer, the law enforcement apparatus was consistently geared to cooperation with the Project, so that the communities' image could be left untarnished in the eyes of the outside world" (1967, 34). It was probably because of this calculation that when Martin Luther King, Jr. came to Winnetka, traffic and crowds were controlled efficiently and effectively. While local communities worked hard to give the project visibility, this basic difference had implications even more marked than did the similarities between the two projects. Highland Park residents promoted the Project by entering a float in the Fourth of July parade. A station wagon pulled a three-dimensional facsimile of the project's symbol, an equal bar enclosed by the outline of a house. Behind the float were three convertibles—red, white, and blue—carrying some 25 student volunteers. A slogan on one of the convertibles read: "In your heart you know it's right." The submission was well received by people attending the celebration.[23]

"Negroes Want to Live Next Door so they Can 'Marry Our Daughters'"

Local fair housing committees prepared for the summer well in advance. They constructed lists of houses for sale in their areas, including homeowner's names, addresses, and telephone numbers, and plotted them on maps.

---

[22] North Shore Summer Project Staff, "What About Chicago's North Shore?" n.d.
[23] "Community Notes," *North Shore Summer Project Newsletter*, 1.5, Aug. 20, 1965, 4.

Volunteers compiled lists of residents and organizations that agreed to support their efforts. Local committees planned public educational meetings and a speaker series. Once the Project got underway, they sponsored demonstrations, including daily silent vigils. Throughout the summer, they continued negotiating with realtors with whom they were now familiar.

The interfaith religious ceremony, held on June 29, 1965 to launch the project's headquarters in Winnetka, included a rabbi and ministers affiliated with various Christian denominations. The ceremony began with a brief prayer that ended "We, therefore, dedicate this Freedom Center in the name of all that is good and just and right and honorable in the sight of Almighty God."[24] Following the opening address, ministers rallied the crowd using call and response, a form of verbal interaction that had black southern roots. Five days later, student volunteers arrived to attend a week-long orientation.

From June 25 through July 4, student volunteers were schooled on race and housing on the North Shore. Orientation packets contained articles on local real estate practices and terminology. The president of the ENSBR was invited to speak to students. Volunteers also attended workshops on the history and methods of nonviolence. AFSC staff provided training in nonviolent protest. The day after the volunteers arrived, Dora Williams, ostensibly a typical North Shore matron, hosted a reception at her home in Winnetka to introduce community volunteers to students.[25] Lerone Bennett Jr., senior editor at Chicago-based *Ebony Magazine* and author of *Before the Mayflower: A History of the Negro in America* (1970), addressed the volunteers invited to Williams's reception.

Students spent the next eight weeks interviewing white homeowners about their willingness to participate in an open market. Beginning on July 5, they followed a daily routine that was highly structured. They arrived at Freedom Centers by 9:00 a.m. each morning to receive lists of families selling homes through the Evanston-North Shore Board of Realtors. Student canvassers then visited sellers in pairs. They had been schooled in good manners and etiquette. Jean Mitten, student recruitment chair, made sure that canvassers arrived in daylight, had credentials and badges, and were dressed nicely—"no dirty sweatshirts and jeans."[26] Mitten instructed students to be polite, to use friendly persuasion to get answers, and to leave gracefully if faced with resistance. When volunteers arrived on doorsteps, they introduced themselves by name, explained that they were North Shore Summer Project fieldworkers, and then conducted their interviews.

---

[24] North Shore Summer Project Staff, Dedicatory Ceremony Program, June 20, 1965.
[25] The reception was held on June 26, 1965.
[26] "Summer Project Seeks 70 Student Interviewers," *Evanston Review*, May 27, 1965, 11.

They used a questionnaire designed by graduate students enrolled in Professor Victor Rosenblum's summer seminar at Northwestern University.[27] The same graduate students also helped train Summer Project volunteers in interviewing techniques. Student volunteers were instructed not to veer from the well-designed questionnaire. Northwestern affiliates, including political science doctoral students Michael Barkun and James Levine, also helped tabulate the results.

Homeowners received letters about the project before it started. Students began each interview by asking residents if they had any questions about the letter. Then they asked, "Will you show your home to any buyer your realtor brings regardless of the buyer's race, color, creed, or national origin?" If homeowners answered "Yes," they were asked to sign pledge cards (eventually shown to brokers and African-American buyers) and petitions. Homeowners who answered "No" were asked to explain their decision. Students gave a scripted response: "If we overcome this (these) objection(s) will you show your home to any buyer regardless of the buyer's race, color, creed or national origin?"

Drawing from information in their orientation packs, students were well versed and ready to rebut any number of excuses homeowners might offer. If a resident expressed concern about plummeting property values, they were able to cite findings from *Property Values and Race* (1960) by Luigi Laurenti, who had concluded that when non-whites entered a previously all-white neighborhood consisting primarily of single-family homes, prices of residential property in the area would probably not decline and may very well rise. If homeowners produced a property deed stating that their home had to be sold to Christian Caucasians, students reminded them of the 1948 Supreme Court decision in *Shelley v. Kraemer*, which held that courts could not enforce racial covenants. If homeowners feared that a sale to one black family would open the floodgates to other minorities, students explained that North Shore property was too expensive for blockbusting to be a real possibility, that rapid block-by-block change and neighborhood transition happened in relatively low-income areas usually adjacent to large black ghettos. Finally, if the interviewee suggested that African Americans were inferior, and therefore would not make good neighbors, volunteers noted that there had been at least five great African civilizations, beginning in 1046 BC.

A number of students commented on the hostility they faced. One student volunteer reported that during an interview conducted in southeast

---

[27] It is unclear exactly what the arrangements were between the Summer Project and Northwestern University, but on May 12, 1965, representatives approached the Law and Social Sciences program asking for assistance.

Evanston, a woman became "very emotional." She stood behind her screen door and scolded him: "Negroes want to live next door so they can 'marry our daughters.'"[28] An irate letter to the editor of a local newspaper was also representative of a segment of the community that opposed integration: "I (and my neighbors) do not want another Fillmore [San Francisco] district in our community. Wherever Negroes move, the neighborhood soon deteriorates into a crime-ridden slum resembling that infamous district."[29]

Some property owners were more discreet. They said they were opposed to an open market, projecting blame on racist neighbors. Students tested these claims by interviewing 1,560 community members who were *not* moving. These residents were asked a series of questions, the final and most significant of which was, "Suppose a Negro family moved next-door to you—what would you do?" A small minority (9.4%) said they would sell their home or move; a greater percentage of respondents (22.5%) indicated that they would accept, even welcome, their new neighbors; 28.7% of those interviewed, however, remained neutral, saying they would do nothing at all, revealing the community's apathy.[30] The data collected by students would be compiled into a report and released to the public in August through the media.

Publicly Dramatizing the Housing Problem

Silent vigils and a speaker series were used as conduits to transmit the outcomes of the surveys and to elicit action for transformation. Every day, beginning on July 9, for close to two months, daily vigils were held between 10:00 a.m. and 2:00 p.m. at real estate offices not adhering to fair housing standards. Vigils introduced a spiritual element to the protest by invoking introspection and self-examination on the part of its participants. The role of a vigil in a nonviolent movement was to awaken the consciousness of a people in a community to a serious problem. Northern white liberals were susceptible to protest because they valued their identity as upholders of race neutrality. Standing vigil required volunteers to draw on discipline they had learned in workshops on nonviolence. They stood silently and weren't allowed to smoke or talk. Instead they passed out leaflets. One such flyer, titled "North Shore Summer Project: A Public Witness," read: "The people you see before you are participants in a vigil,

---

[28] "'Neighbors Would Object,' Respond Whites to Selling to Negro," *Evanston Review*, Jul. 29, 1965, 14.
[29] See Barkun and Levine (1967): 30. By the late 1950s, San Francisco's Fillmore district was filled with minority renters because white homeowners had fled for the suburbs.
[30] North Shore Summer Project Staff, Summary Report, Aug. 29, 1965.

a period of watchfulness. We announce publicly, and to ourselves, our own responsibility for segregated housing. WE ALSO ANNOUNCE WE CAN NO LONGER COOPERATE WITH SUCH A SYSTEM."[31]

For the most part, these gatherings did publicize the extent of housing discrimination and generated action to combat it. Those luminaries who headlined the meetings, such as the Reverend C.T. Vivian, John Hope Franklin, and Martin Luther King, Jr., contributed to the realization of these goals. The rally that featured King was the Project's logistical *tour de force*. Fortuitously, the civil rights leader, who was then president of the SCLC, was in Chicago as part of his ten-day people-to-people tour of northern cities. Demonstrating a strong emphasis on labor and economic challenges, King's tour signaled an increasing focus on the urban ghettos of the north and on his insistence that the struggle be extended to give greater prominence to northern challenges to equal civil rights. King's appearance drew a record-breaking crowd that police estimated to be between 10,000 and 15,000 strong. Not even the appearance of a group of American Nazi Party members wearing swastikas could detract from the significance of the event. Because of the local attention it received, King's appearance enabled the Summer Project to associate itself with the national Civil Rights Movement in a way that it had not achieved previously. Dr. King's charismatic appeal proved to be a very effective way to reach the community. The crowd included hundreds of civil rights sympathizers from Chicago, but the vast majority were local residents. "The King rally had a predominantly Negro cast and an integrated audience," Barkun and Levine noted: "In contrast to most project activities, this was *not* white people pontificating to other white people about the plight of Negroes. The physical presence of the 'oppressed group' dramatized the message expounded by the speakers" (1967, 31). In a typically inspiring speech, King talked about America's schizophrenic personality, ending with an admonition that vindicated the work of the North Shore Summer Project: "Racism in housing will not be removed until there is an assault on the structures of power that profit from it. What may be profitable to a realtor is not profitable to a city."[32]

As the King rally exemplified, the Summer Project and government agencies worked well together. Project leaders knew that they had to establish a good rapport with the local governments of the suburbs in order to ensure effective use of the data. It was only toward the end that the Project began to alienate politicians. Officials, concerned with the community's

---

[31] North Shore Summer Project Staff, "A Public Witness," n.d.

[32] "Dr. King, Rev. Davis Ask Equality, American Dream at Winnetka Rally," *Evanston Review*, Jul. 29, 1965, 92.

image, had consistently cooperated with the Project but as it became more successful in broadcasting its unflattering message, it started to lose governmental support. Tensions between the Project and local government began to emerge when organizers made plans for the final march and rally to be held on August 29, and were denied a permit by the Evanston City Council. Reverend Coe defended the Project: "We have abided by legal and peaceful limits during the entire summer and were quite surprised to find we are now considered insurrectionists."[33] For the first time, project coordinators threatened to take legal action: "The right of free assembly is constitutionally guaranteed. We find it hard to believe that Evanston would attempt to deny such rights and require us to seek remedial steps."[34] "The deeper the attack on entrenched practices and institutions," Barkun and Levine argue, "the less assistance an attacking organization can expect from suburban political leaders, who were selected *on the condition* that they conserve traditional values and minimize cleavages within the community" (1967, 34). Reluctantly, permission for the rally was granted.

The final march was a vibrant event that affirmed the determination of the North Shore Summer Project even as it came to an end. Some demonstrators carried signs reading "Equal housing"; others' signs read "uhuru," the Swahili word for "freedom," which had been used as a slogan in the East African independence movement. Reverend Davis addressed the crowd: "The North Shore Summer Project ends. But the civil rights movement is on the North Shore to stay. We've proved we can march at home as well as in Selma." John Lewis, president of SNCC, was another featured speaker at the rally. There is nothing wrong with being an agitator, he said, "if you're agitating for the right thing."[35] The crowd sang civil rights songs such as "Black and White Together": "Together we can build a nation / of love and integration." The rally ended with the crowd holding hands and singing "We Shall Overcome."

Organizers used this event to present a ten-page report reflecting the outcomes of eight weeks of intensive research. At a press conference after the march, organizers and volunteers continued to distribute the report. Reverend Davis personally presented the report to Louis A. Pfaff, president of the Evanston-North Shore Board of Realtors. The report concluded that realtors, not North Shore residents, were primarily responsible for racist housing discrimination: "The realtor has obviously conducted his business according to his own fears and prejudices, not according to the unknown wishes of the seller."[36]

---

[33] "Summer Project Denied Rally OK," *Evanston Review*, Aug. 19, 1965, 1.
[34] "Summer Project Rally OK'd," *Evanston Review*, Aug. 26, 1965, 1.
[35] "Rally, Report End Summer Project," *Evanston Review*, Sept. 2, 1965, 83.
[36] North Shore Summer Project Staff, Summary Report, Aug. 29, 1965.

Conclusion: "There Is No Jerusalem on Lake Michigan"

The North Shore Summer Project was much less dramatic in its impact than the Mississippi Freedom Summer Project, but that is only to be expected. They responded to very different social and political dynamics. The frustration induced by fighting a status quo of complacency is visible in the assessment of the volunteers. Organizers, protesters, and volunteers began to ponder the effectiveness of the Summer Project even during its short life. Midway through the summer, student volunteers doubted that the data they collected so meticulously would make a difference and began to register their disappointment that the movement was not militant enough. The students' concerns were exacerbated by a generation gap between older AFSC members and youthful volunteers. The students, who were more idealistic than their older counterparts, were much more willing to blame the homeowners as much as realtors for discriminatory housing policies based on racism. The age difference between interviewers and respondents also created communication barriers, affecting both data and more visceral responses. Indeed, students viewed some pledges to desist from racial discrimination in selling or resting property as merely perfunctory.

The Summer Project was also weakened by the lack of black involvement. It struggled to recruit black middle-class couples to be the first to buy houses in white neighborhoods. African-American families did not necessarily want to live where they were not welcome. As a result, the movement was about white people trying to convince other whites that black people should be free to buy any house they wanted. With the majority of African Americans living in the inner city, there were neither enough black buyers to exert pressure on realtors nor enough black students to be prominently represented in the movement. A largely white target audience struggled to identify with the largely African-American housing problem. Prosperous homeowners, who had never encountered racial marginalization in housing, were somewhat detached from the distinctive race-based problem faced by African-American tenants and potential house owners. Consequently, as the students correctly feared, the data exposing racist housing discrimination could not be transformative if a large segment of the people needed to act was out of touch.

Despite such weaknesses, all was not lost. The North Shore Summer Project did succeed in drawing attention to the issue of closed housing, bringing awareness of the racist implications of a housing problem to thousands of suburban residents. Hundreds of whites were actively involved, and whether genuinely committed or not, over 12,000 people signed a petition asking brokers to serve all home seekers equally:

We, the undersigned North Shore residents, believe that all peoples should have equal access to all housing in all communities without regard to race, color, creed or national origin. This is the American ideal. We believe in the American ideal. Therefore, we ask that real estate brokers serve all customers alike, and that all listings, including multiple listings, be shown and sold without regard to race, color, creed or national origin.[37]

The movement also had an important impact on the personal growth of individuals who performed its work. For some members, the North Shore Summer Project was a transformative experience, a personal journey of commitment to racial justice.[38] Project member Sally Olds noted that as a result of their experience, white liberals were transformed into white activists. In the wake of the North Shore Summer Project, For Real Estate Equality (FREE), an Evanston project, sought to involve more African Americans from that community's black west side, where student volunteers had been well-received. It worked to collaborate with residents for future planning and to ensure long-term effectiveness. The group's programming schedule included workshops on nonviolent action and educational talks given by leaders of the SCLC and SNCC; these yielded tangible results. FREE gave practical assistance, including some financial support, to African Americans who could not find or afford housing. The alliance between the SCLC and AFSC, formed from collaborations in the North Shore Summer Project, supported Martin Luther King, Jr's Chicago Freedom Movement one year after the North Shore Summer Project ended. Encouraged by the commitment he witnessed at the height of the Project, King came back to urge a continuation of the struggle. A year after the end of the Project, on August 5, 1966, protesters marched against racism and held a rally in Marquette Park, on Chicago's southwest side, despite a hostile counter-demonstration by an estimated 4,000 whites.

Brief as it was and tenuous as its direct impact on segregation on the North Shore proved to be, the North Shore Summer Project did leave an important legacy. The day after his visit to the North Shore, Martin Luther King, Jr. offered a balanced, if tentative affirmation to a Chicago audience: "There is no Jerusalem on Lake Michigan, but I must also say that [...] she [...] is no Sodom doomed to an imminent destruction."[39] At least in part, the city owed its status as "no Sodom doomed for destruction" to the North Shore Summer Project.

---

[37] Sally Olds, "News Release," Aug. 19, 1965.
[38] Student volunteers exemplified Karl Marx's maxim that people cannot change the world without changing themselves in the process. See Bloom (1987, 7).
[39] "Dr. King Confronts Chicago and the North," *The National Observer*, Aug. 2, 1965.

Works Cited

American Friends Service Committee, "Report to the Field Foundation on Chicago Metropolitan Area Housing Opportunity Program," October 1965, 3.

Barkun, Michael, and James Levine. "Protest in Suburbia: Case Study of a Direct-Action Movement." *Syracuse Law Review* 21 (1967): 21–44.

Bennett, Lerone Jr. *Before the Mayflower: A History of the Negro in America.* New York: Penguin Books, 1970.

Bloom, Jack M. *Class, Race, and the Civil Rights Movement.* Bloomington, IN: Indiana University Press, 1987.

"Community Notes," *North Shore Summer Project Newsletter*, 1.5, Aug. 20, 1965, 4.

"Evanston Real Estate Brokers' Council Adopts Policy Against 'Forced Housing,'" *Evanston Review*, May 27, 1965, 19.

"Dr. King, Rev. Davis Ask Equality, American Dream at Winnetka Rally," *Evanston Review*, Jul. 29, 1965, 92.

"Dr. King Confronts Chicago and the North," *The National Observer*, Aug. 2, 1965.

Kleiman, Carol. "Profile-Buckner Coe," *North Shore Summer Project Newsletter*, I.6, Sept. 14, 1965, 4.

Kleiman, Carol. "A Look at Rev. Davis," *North Shore Summer Project Newsletter*, I.4, Aug. 6, 1965, 4.

Kleiman, Carol. "Profile - Ric and Sue Momeyer," *North Shore Summer Project Newsletter*, Aug. 20, 1965.

Laurenti, Luigi. *Property Values and Race.* Berkeley, CA: University of California Press, 1960.

Lowen, James W. *Sundown Towns: A Hidden Dimension of American Racism.* New York: The New Press, 2005.

Mabley, Jack. "Can Love Win over Fear on North Shore?" *Chicago's American*, Friday May 14, 1965.

McAdam, Doug. *Freedom Summer.* New York: Oxford University Press, 1988.

Meyer, Stephen Grant. *As Long as they Don't Move Next Door: Segregation and Racial Conflict in American Neighborhoods.* Lanham, MD: Rowman and Littlefield Publishers, 1999.

Mitten, Jean A. "Form Letter Addressed to Student Reference Writers," n.d.

Moyer, Bill, JoAnn McAllister, Mary Lou Finley, and Steven Soifer, *Doing Democracy: The MAP Model for Organizing Social Movements.* British Columbia: New Society Publishers, 2001.

"'Neighbors Would Object,' Respond Whites to Selling to Negro," *Evanston Review*, Jul. 29, 1965, 14.

North Shore Summer Project Staff, "A Public Witness," n.d.

North Shore Summer Project Staff, "A Statement of Purpose," n.d.

North Shore Summer Project Staff, "General Information For North Shore Summer Project," n.d.

North Shore Summer Project Staff, "Prospectus of the North Shore Summer Project," n.d., 3.
North Shore Summer Project Staff, "Quinlan and Tyson Continues its Discriminatory Practices," n.d.
North Shore Summer Project Staff, "Student Participant Application Form," n.d.
North Shore Summer Project Staff, Summary Report, Aug. 29, 1965.
North Shore Summer Project Staff, "What About Chicago's North Shore?" n.d.
Olds, Sally. "News Release," Aug. 19, 1965.
Oral History Interview. Freedom Summer AV Collection, Miami University Libraries. Oct. 10, 2009.
"Rally, Report End Summer Project," *Evanston Review*, Sept. 2, 1965, 83.
Ralph, James R. Jr. *Northern Protest: Martin Luther King, Jr., Chicago and the Civil Rights Movement.* Cambridge, MA: Harvard University Press, 1993.
Routliffe, Kathy. "Jean Cleland Helped Open Housing on North Shore." *Wilmette Life*, Nov. 4, 2013.
Samuels, Rich. "Civil Rights on the North Shore: Bringing the Movement Home." WTTW Newscast. Jan. 2002. http://www.richsamuels.com/nbcmm/vault/2001cs_nscr.html. Accessed Jan. 20, 2016.
Spear, Allan H. *Black Chicago: The Making of a Negro Ghetto*. Chicago, IL: University of Chicago Press, 1967.
Sugrue, Thomas. *Sweet Land of Liberty: The Forgotten Struggle for Civil Rights in the North*. New York: Random House, 2009.
"Summer Project Denied Rally OK," *Evanston Review*, Aug. 19, 1965, 1.
"Summer Project Rally OK'd," *Evanston Review*, Aug. 26, 1965, 1.
"Summer Project Seeks 70 Student Interviewers," *Evanston Review*, May 27, 1965, 11.
Wehrwein, Austin C. "Dr. King Attends Winnetka Rally: Wealthy Suburb of Chicago Fails to Halt Address." *New York Times*, Jul. 26, 1965: 12.

8

Redrawing Borders of Belonging in a Narrow Nation: Afro-Chilean Activism in the Hinterlands of Afro-Latin America

Sara Busdiecker (Spelman College)

"Negra, ándate a tu país, vienes a puro prostituirte!" These words—"Black, go back to your country, you come here just to prostitute yourself!"— were part of a string of insults directed at Gloria María Grueso Mina, an Afro-Colombian woman residing in Chile. According to her, two women approached her on a street in the northern Chilean city of Arica on November 17, 2013 and, unprovoked, yelled racist invectives at her and shoved her, apparently intent on compelling Grueso Mina to move herself and her car from the spot where she had been waiting. Her accosters, she later realized, were Carmen Ocaya Grandon and her daughter Lissette Sierra Grandon, the latter an elected city council member in Arica (Lumbanga de Arica, 2013).

Incidents such as this, in which individuals of African descent are subject to verbal and physical aggression simply for the color of their skin, are hardly unique to Chile. When combined with disparities in education, income, health, and housing observable between African descendants and majority *mestizo* (mixed Indian and European ancestry) populations throughout Latin America, it is no wonder that Afro-Latin Americans are moved to act, in the form of identity based collective organizing and activism, in pursuit of equality (Hernández, 2013; Mullings, 2009; Rahier, 2012). In Chile, hostility of the sort faced by Grueso Mina had reportedly been on the rise at the beginning of the twenty-first century, not only for blacks but also for others perceived as "not Chilean" in some way. This rise corresponds with what has been described as "the most important migratory influx of the last forty years," originating primarily from other Latin American and Caribbean countries (United Nations, 2013). Despite the unfortunate familiarity of Grueso Mina's experience, it was nevertheless an opportunity to draw public attention not only to racism, but also to the very real presence of African descendants in present-day Chile. The latter might seem of lesser significance than the act of racism itself were it not for the fact that the presence of African descendants in this particular nation is regularly overlooked and even denied outright in both official and popular representations of the country.[1]

The exchange between Grueso Mina and Sierra Grandon was reported in various media outlets, though Sierra Grandon denied that the exchange ever took place. Grueso Mina wrote a letter to the head of the Arica City Council reporting the incident and requesting assistance. A month later, several local organizations also directed a letter to the council, circulating it publicly as well, denouncing the lack of response to Grueso Mina's original communication and to what had occurred, stating that "silence is part of the 'structural racism' maintained by public institutions for more than two centuries" ("Chile: Silencio," 2013). Further, their letter indicated that, in accordance with the recommendations of local, national, regional, and international human rights institutions, incidents such as this should at the very least be investigated to determine if racism and xenophobia were in fact involved. Chile's anti-discrimination law, known as the Ley Zamudio, was passed in 2012 to offer legal recourse in the event of acts of discrimination. The letter accused the city council of an ethical and moral dereliction of duty for not addressing, or even discussing in its meetings, the accusation of abuse of power by one of its members.

Among the six organizations supporting Grueso Mina and calling for action through the letter, three were Afro-Chilean groups based in or near Arica—Organización Lumbanga, Organización de Mujeres Afrodescendientes Hijas de Azapa, and Asociación de Organizaciones y Comunidades Afrochilenas Azapa Territorio Ancestral. The others included two for Colombians residing in Chile, and one for immigrants in general. While Gloria María Grueso Mina is Afro-Colombian, at the time of the incident she had lived in Chile for 30 years, was married to a Chilean, had three Afro-Chilean children, and was a member of an Afro-Chilean organization. Unlike María Grueso Mina, most members of the Afro organizations responsible for the letter were Chilean by birth and traced their ancestry to African descendants present in Chile's northern region for several generations. Before 2000, none of these Afro-Chilean organizations existed; now, they are just three of an ever-increasing number of such groups unified

---

[1] While I employ the term "Afro-Chilean" in this essay, the more common term used by members of the population itself is *afrodescendiente*, "Afro-descendant." An explanation for their choice will be offered later in the essay. My own use of "Afro-Chilean" is intended for the purpose of distinguishing those Afro/African descendants with historical roots in what is now Chile from African descendants with roots elsewhere in Latin America.

around African descent. Individually and collectively, these groups have come to be the public face and voice of a population present, but virtually invisible, for over 400 years.

The discussion that follows examines the historical and contemporary roots of Afro-Chilean invisibility and the nature and trajectory of collective organizing that has emerged only since the early 2000s among Afro-Chileans to counter that invisibility.[2] Chile's African-descendant population occupies multiple margins—hinterlands—that shape its particular collective experience, identity, and struggle. During exploratory fieldwork carried out in and around Arica over the course of June 2010, I observed the extent to which the early stages of the Afro-Chilean struggle for inclusion in the nation relied, and continues to rely, on notions of descent above and before notions of race, color, blackness, or even ethnicity or culture—ideas and realities that feature prominently in the collective organizing of Afro descendants elsewhere. The phenotypic and cultural reality of a majority of the Afro-Chilean population seems a likely explanation for the primacy of discourse around descent and recovery. While many African-descendant populations in the diaspora have faced the challenge of social and political invisibility, the invisibility faced by Afro-Chileans is compounded by the hue of their skin and the loss of distinct cultural expressions. The pale-hued bodies of many of Chile's contemporary self-identified African descendants are often read as phenotypically indistinguishable from the Chilean majority; their cultural identity, until the onset of collective organizing, was similarly read, and even lived, as indistinguishable. Regardless of whether or not Afro-Chilean activism is, in fact, markedly different from the activism practiced by Afro descendants elsewhere, the fact that there is a desire and need for it in this forgotten corner of the global African diaspora, and that it has appeared systematically and publicly only since the turn of the twenty-first century, highlights the temporally and spatially enduring nature of struggles for equality in the African diaspora.

---

[2] This chapter reflects the preliminary steps of what I intend to be an ongoing ethnographic project on emergent grassroots organizing among Afro-Chileans. These preliminary steps include ethnographic fieldwork carried out in Arica and Valle de Azapa in June 2010 along with tracking of the popular press and social media related to Afro-Chileans from the early 2000s onward. The fieldwork emphasized interviews with individual Chileans who self-identify as Afro-descendant and participant observation in meetings and events involving different Afro-Chilean groups in Arica and Valle de Azapa. In order to protect the anonymity of those interviewed, names are not used in connection with quotes, and some information from the interviews is paraphrased or otherwise integrated into the text alongside analysis informed by published sources. Interviews were conducted in Spanish; all translations are my own.

Belonging in a Narrow Nation

Chile is a "narrow nation" not only in terms of the slender expanse of land contained within its political borders (217 miles at its widest point), but also in terms of who its citizenry is popularly imagined to be. Much like neighboring Argentina to the east, and Argentina's northern neighbor Uruguay, Chile is perceived to be one of Latin America's white nations (Sater, 1974). This is both a racial whiteness, associated with European phenotypic characteristics, and a social whiteness, associated with European cultural practices and beliefs. The description in the *Lonely Planet* travel guide offers a good example of this view of the country: "Most Chileans are mestizos, although many can still claim purely European descent. In much of the country, social class is still a greater issue than race" (Bernhardson, 1993, 33). In a national context such as this, with a narrow conception of who belongs, dark-skinned individuals like Gloria María Grueso Mina become perpetual outsiders; blackness and African descent have no natural place in the nation, but are instead associated with foreignness, leading to admonishments of the sort directed at Grueso Mina—"go back to your country."

According to the 2002 national census, 4.6% of Chile's 15,116,435 inhabitants were registered as belonging to one of eight officially recognized indigenous ethnic groups (Comisión Nacional, 2003).[3] The Mapuche represent the vast majority, 87.3%, of the indigenous population. It is they who tend to dominate, and therefore define, discussions of diversity and discrimination in the country, when such discussions take place. The vast majority, 95.4%, of the national population is not considered ethnic (i.e., indigenous) and is assumed to fall into the categories of *mestizo* or white, which are not included on the census. Notably, Chile's *mestizo* is reported to be more white than indigenous, according to recent DNA sampling of the population described in the national popular press (Donoso, 2011).[4] Claims that race is a biological reality that can be identified through DNA or through other biological or

---

[3] Results from the more recent 2012 census were challenged because apparently 10% of the population was left out of the process.

[4] A genetic study carried out by Francisco Lizcano of the Universidad Autónomo de México calculated that of the 95.4% of the population that is not "ethnic" (i.e., indigenous), 52% is white/European and 44% is *mestizo*. A separate study by the Universidad de Chile calculated the breakdown to be 30% European-descendant and 65% *mestizo* (mixed indigenous and European) descent, further asserting that European descent is predominant in the mixture of these *mestizos* (Donoso, 2011). Of course, DNA is not the same as the lived experience, connection to heritage, and identification of those from whom the DNA comes. The point, therefore, of including these statistics is to demonstrate that the narrative of Chile as a white/*mestizo* nation emerges from contested scientific discourse as well as from historical and political discourse and popular culture.

physical markers is contested within the scientific community (Yudell et al., 2016). Consequently, rather than these statistics being *proof* that Chile is primarily white, they are instead but one example of the sociopolitical forces, both contemporary and historical, propelling the *perception* that Chile is primarily white. The census, after all, has not counted African descendants as a separate category since 1940. At that time, blacks and mulattos were reported to number 1,000 and 3,000 respectively (Garrison, 2003). With no official data on how many African descendants there are now, this part of the population has suffered statistical erasure. There has *not*, however, been an *actual* erasure of people identifying as African descendant, something that became clear with the formation, beginning in the year 2001, of multiple organizations based around shared African descent. The activities and demands of these groups have pushed the borders of belonging in Chile, challenging traditional expectations of who Chileans are and, by extension, what it means to be Chilean.

In the Hinterlands of Afro-Latin America

In *Afro-Latin America: 1800–2000*, historian George Reid Andrews defines "Afro-Latin America" as those nations in the Spanish and Portuguese speaking Americas whose populations of African descent meet a "threshold of significance" (2004, 4). That threshold, he suggests, is at least 5–10% of a nation's population. He explains: "This seems to be the level at which 'blackness' becomes a visible element in systems of social stratification and inequality, and at which African-based culture—patterns of sociability and group expression—becomes a visible part of national life" (2004, 4). With this as his criterion, his otherwise geographically and temporally wide-ranging book is silent on certain locations in Latin America. Based on the content and geographical focus of the ever-expanding field of Afro-Latin studies, Andrews is not the only one paying particular attention to nations that meet or exceed that percentage.[5] Chile is *not* one of those nations.

The demographics at the center of Andrews's criterion are rooted in colonial-era slavery and its legacy. He explains that the "heartlands of Afro-Latin America" historically were highly developed centers of

---

[5] Among those making this same observation are Wade (2006), who points to a bias toward Brazil in the literature, and Gudmundson and Wolfe (2010), who point to Mexico and Central American nations as among the overlooked in both scholarly and popular terms relative to the islands of the Caribbean, the United States, and Brazil. It must be noted that, *Afro-Latin America: 1800–2000* aside, Andrews does explore elsewhere the histories of African descendants in locations falling near or below that "threshold of significance," including in *The Afro-Argentines of Buenos Aires, 1800–1900* (1980) and *Blackness in the White Nation: A History of Afro-Uruguay* (2010).

plantation-based export production to which large numbers of enslaved Africans were imported, places like Brazil, Venezuela, Cuba, and Puerto Rico. These locations, where the descendants of these imported enslaved Africans have stayed, remain the heartlands of Afro-Latin America today. Demographic estimates of Afro-Latin America at the turn of the nineteenth, twentieth, and twenty-first centuries show that by 1900 Chile was relegated to what could be called the "hinterlands of Afro-Latin America" by virtue of its exceedingly small African-descendant presence.[6] In the absence of a comprehensive census, sources attempting to acknowledge an African-descendant presence today estimate it to stand at no more than 1–2% of the national population, if that. Rather than being a reason for exclusion from serious scholarship on Afro-Latin America, this low percentage makes a study of the Chilean population all the more compelling. Not only has this extreme minority sustained itself in the face of extensive phenotypic and cultural invisibility or extinction, but it generated multiple identity-based organizations that, in ten short years, made inroads into gaining state and popular recognition of African descendants as a real collectivity and an important part of the nation.

Arguably, Afro-Chileans occupy multiple hinterlands beyond the merely demographic, and just as demographics have implications, so too do other kinds of hinterlands for the particular experiences and challenges faced by the unknown number of African descendants inhabiting Chile. Afro-Chileans occupy the *geographic* and *sociopolitical* hinterlands of Afro-Latin America as well as those of their nation.[7] The place they occupy in scholarship (whether local or international) might also be described as a hinterland. Afro-Latin American studies has expanded exponentially in recent years (as noted by Dixon, 2012; Andrews, 2009; Wade, 2006). Over the past 20 years, amidst an increasing number of monographs, edited volumes, journals, professional organizations, and conferences dedicated specifically to Afro-Latin America, a diversification in subject matter and geographic focus is observable, which includes a move away from slavery and from the

---

[6] Andrews opens *Afro-Latin America* with three maps, credited to William Nelson, illustrating the estimated percentage of blacks and mulattos in Latin American nations as of 1800, 1900, and 2000.

[7] "Hinterland" is not to be confused with "borderland" as it has been used elsewhere (e.g., Gloria Anzaldúa, 1987) with a concern for boundary crossing, cultural and racial mixing, or contested space. Instead, I mean to invoke an outer margin that is geographic, physical, and sociopolitical. While both the phenotype and cultural identity of many Afro-Chileans could easily be described in terms of *mestizo*-ness, it would be the homogenous *mestizo*-ness shared by the larger nation. With their focus on claiming African descent, on being *afrodescendientes*, and reclaiming the traditions of earlier generations of ancestors, notions of mixed-ness or a unique *mestizo*-ness have not taken hold in the discourse of the Afro-Chilean organizations.

locations of Brazil, Colombia, and the Caribbean which have garnered the lion's share of attention in the past (Andrews, 2009). All this contributes to progress toward a decentering of the United States in scholarship on blackness and the African diaspora. It seems a fitting shift in light of the fact that a majority—85%—of Africans transported through the transatlantic slave trade arrived in the Caribbean and Latin America (Curtin, 1972) meaning that "the heart of the New World African diaspora lies not north of the border, in the United States, but South" (Andrews, 2004, 3). Amidst the growing attention being paid to Afro-Latin America, Chile remains but a footnote, seldom if ever mentioned in scholarship, with the exception of a limited number of historical investigations into colonial-era slavery (see Mellafe, 1984; Flusche and Korth, 1983). The intervention made here intends to respond to that void, but also to try to explain which factors of the Chilean situation led to that void in the first place.

A brief accounting of how blacks originally came to inhabit what is now Chile suggests that the process of rendering this population marginal and invisible began long ago. The first blacks to arrive did so in the company of the Spaniard Diego de Almagro who, in 1536, set out to explore and conquer the southern portion of the Andes. He was accompanied by an army of 100 blacks and a far larger number of Indians. When de Almagro failed, his compatriot Pedro de Valdivia returned in 1541 to make another attempt, again in the company of enslaved Africans. Blacks continued to enter the territory, initially passing through Panama or Cartagena and stopping in Callao on the coast of Peru, and later arriving via an overland route from Buenos Aires. Under slavery, they were used to supplement the indigenous labor force, working in agriculture, mining, construction, domestic service, and as cowboys. Because Chile was a remote colony, and not a particularly wealthy one, the effort and cost of importing slaves was prohibitive and consequently slavery never became the significant institution it was elsewhere in the Americas. One estimate suggests that only 0.01% of the entire transatlantic slave trade was Chilean, situating the area at the margins of the transatlantic slave trade. Chile declared independence from Spain in 1810, and in 1823 it became the first Spanish American republic to abolish slavery (Mellafe, 1984).[8]

It was at that point that Chile's African descendants were erased from the nation's historical record, seemingly vanishing into the general population upon their emancipation. If and when blacks are mentioned in relation to Chile—at least prior to the inception of Afro-Chilean organizing in 2001—

---

[8] Chile's then 4,000 enslaved blacks were freed that year without restriction, joining an already existing population of free persons of color that, almost 50 years earlier, likely numbered between 13,000 and 15,000 (Klein and Vinson, 1986).

the standard narrative asserts that slavery was never a significant institution there, ended early, and that the small number of blacks who were present blended into the dominant population through miscegenation or died out due to alcoholism, disease, and climate (Francisco Encina qtd in Sater, 1974). Such a minimizing or dismissive narrative is a challenge in itself, and not just because it hides the very real contributions made by enslaved and free blacks to building the colony and then the nation. It also discounts the inherently exploitative and unequal circumstances under which they did so. It implies that blacks were never numerous enough to be of consequence or to inspire systematic discrimination once free.

Afro-Chileans occupy the geographic and sociopolitical hinterlands of Afro-Latin America in addition to the obvious demographic margins.[9] Chile offers an example similar in many ways to that of neighboring Bolivia in this regard. Neither conforms to the socioeconomic expectations of the origins and subsequent development of a plantation system in the Americas. While most African-descendant populations in Latin America confronted increasingly mixed (i.e., mulatto/*mestizo*) societies post-emancipation, Bolivia had an overwhelmingly indigenous one and Chile an overwhelmingly white/European-influenced one. This has had implications for the identity formation of both Afro-Bolivians and Afro-Chileans and has led to different forms of activism in the two countries.

In the Hinterlands of the Nation

Despite their absence from census records since 1940, a concentrated Afro presence can be found in present-day Chile if one looks, quite literally, to the physical margin of the nation; that is, to its northern border. It is in the city of Arica and the neighboring Valle de Azapa and Valle de Lluta that Afro-Chilean activism was born and has flourished.

Arica is a port city of approximately 195,000 inhabitants located 11 miles south of the Peruvian border, making it the northernmost city of this long and narrow nation. Valle de Azapa and Valle de Lluta are rural areas stretching southeast and northeast from the outer limits of the city. With this border zone as the center of the Afro-Chilean population and its organizing efforts, it is necessary to introduce the term *afro-ariqueño* (Afro-Arican) here, which is used locally in addition to *afrodescendiente*. This location-specific label reveals that the emerging image of what it means to be

---

[9] I argue elsewhere that despite the global reach of the African diaspora, there are nevertheless certain locations and circumstances outside of the African continent in which people of African descent are perceived as *particularly* "out of place" physically, culturally, socially, and historically relative to other locations and circumstances (Busdiecker, 2009).

African-descendant in Chile is actually based on realities in this particular place. The nearby border plays a significant role in those realities.

As several locals were quick to point out to me, Arica is closer to the capital of Bolivia than it is to the capital of Chile. La Paz is an eight-hour bus trip from Arica while Santiago, Chile's capital city, is about 24 hours away by bus. This distance from the political, economic, and population center of the country means that all of Arica's inhabitants (not just Afro-descendants) reside at the periphery of their nation.[10] With regard to this location, one local activist with whom I spoke at length observed that most Afro-Latin American organizing starts in urban centers or capital cities, making what is happening in Arica unusual. What he was describing, as he discussed the formation of various groups, was the creation of a "center" at what was otherwise an edge.

The historically contested nature of the Chile-Peru border is implicated in the identity formation of all locals. After the War of the Pacific (1879–1883),[11] Chile and Peru signed a treaty; it stipulated that Chile would administer the provinces of Tacna and Arica for ten years. After that, a plebiscite would allow the area's inhabitants to decide their nationality. That plebiscite never occurred. In 1929, it was decided that the area would be divided between the two countries, with Arica belonging to Chile and Tacna to Peru. A process of *chilenización* (Chilenization) took place in the area that involved the aggressive promotion of Chilean national identity through the press, schools, and churches, and through the forced removal of non-Chileans (Skuban, 2007). Afro-descendants who resided in the region, cultivating cotton and sugarcane and producing olives and olive oil, were among those forced over the border into Peru. Their presence and contributions to the local economy and culture were erased from the landscape and narrative of the nation. However, some Afro-descendants managed to remain in the region or returned to claim lands left behind.

Neither Chile nor Peru tells the story of this group.[12] Their ancestors originally arrived as Africans, were Peruvian during slavery, and alternately Peruvian and Chilean at different times post-emancipation (see Sater, 1974). The eventual nationality of *any* descendant of the transatlantic slave trade is a product of chance, the result of where slave traders transported their captives. This arbitrariness of citizenship is perhaps heightened for the

---

[10] The local population includes *mestizos*, Aymara Indians, and immigrants from neighboring nations.
[11] The War of the Pacific involved a struggle between Chile, Bolivia, and Peru over disputed territory along the Pacific coast rich in valuable mineral resources, including sodium nitrate.
[12] This account was similarly told by at least five individuals, in separate interviews, as they explained their family history in the region.

African descendants in Chile because the contested border between Chile and Peru was decided so recently; many families still preserve a living memory of being Peruvian. The unfailing use of the terms *afrodescendiente* and *afroariqueño* for self-reference, as opposed to *afrochileno*, may be a reflection of their relationship, tenuous in manifold ways, to the nation; the choice of the former links them to the larger African diaspora (*afrodescendiente* being the most inclusive term and increasingly popular among activists throughout Afro-Latin America) and the latter to a very localized sphere of belonging, avoiding the nation entirely.[13]

Another sociopolitical force implicated in the identity of Afro-Chileans and Chileans in general is the notion of *la raza chilena* (the Chilean race). The idea dates back to the early 1900s and to the work of Chilean physician Nicolas Palacios, who asserted in *La Raza Chilena* (1904) that Chileans belonged to a unique and superior race. While *mestizaje* (racial mixture) is a process and ideology found throughout Latin America, its manifestation in Chile, following Palacio's claims, was distinct. He proposed that Chileans were a unique mix of Spaniards and valiant Araucanian Indians. The Spaniards who colonized Chile were not just *any* Spaniards, but rather of predominantly *Germanic* bloodlines descended from the Visigoths. Because of this mix, Palacios said that Chileans should *not* be considered Latin like inhabitants of other nations in Latin America; instead, Chileans were a *superior race*. This positive characterization was embraced by the population and a mindset based on the notion lingers to the present day, where it is reflected in, among other things, a downplaying of any internal diversity in the Chilean national population and the idea of Chilean identity as essentially white. Contributing to a racially and culturally whiter nation were immigration policies, focused on northern Europe, that operated before, during, and after the height of *la raza chilena* discourse (see Rout, 1976). The *raza chilena*, then, contributed to a *narrow image* of *who* is Chilean or who *belongs* to Chile; it does not allow for consideration of blacks, blackness, or African descent.

Motivation for Action

"No one ever talked about being Afro [...] People might have guessed about their origins and history, but you couldn't talk about those things. Everyone was [just] Chilean." These were the words of an Afro-Chilean woman in her forties, recalling her childhood in Valle de Azapa during an interview. She went on to explain that at school they never learned about

---

[13] *Morenos de Azapa* is another local term, though more common prior to collective organizing efforts. *Moreno* is a general term for those with a brown skin tone.

the history of slavery in Chile, much less about a black presence in Chile post-emancipation. Hers was a story of silences. Such historical, social, and statistical silences, erasures, and invisibility are only a part of the reality faced by Afro-Chileans. The experience of Gloria María Grueso Mina, described at the outset, is evidence of a different, more overtly aggressive exclusion from the nation.

In an interview, a self-identified *activista afrodescendiente* (Afro-descendant activist) in his thirties recounted to me an incident in which his identity was questioned when crossing the border back into Chile from Peru. A border official doubted he was really Chilean because he appeared "too dark to be Chilean." The insinuation was that he was a Peruvian trying to pass as a Chilean, but *not* that he was a black or Afro-descendant foreigner. Peruvians are expected to be darker skinned—more *moreno*, brown-skinned—than Chileans because of the prominent indigenous population in that country. This same individual, who was viewed as perhaps too *moreno* to be Chilean, went on to describe how in Chile he is often perceived as too *mestizo* to be Afro-descendant. He acknowledges that aside from sometimes being viewed as a bit browner, he "looks like any other *mestizo* Chilean" and, he readily admits, his straight black hair definitely does not help to convince anyone otherwise. When he first started presenting himself as an Afro-descendant activist, he was met with skepticism so often that he took to carrying a photo of his black grandmother in his wallet to give people proof of his ancestry.

Herein lies one of the unique challenges to Afro-Chilean activists and activism—the challenge of rallying behind African descent while inhabiting bodies perceived as white or *mestizo*. Afro-Latin populations across the region encompass a great deal of diversity and that diversity includes the presence of racially mixed individuals. In Chile, the extent of that mixing is great and one can see the impact of slave-era demographics, *la raza chilena*, *chilenización*, immigration policy, pervasive silence, and aggression on the very bodies of *afrodescendientes*. It is for this reason that *descent* appears primary—over "race," color, and blackness—in uniting the population. Reclaiming ancestry, including the history and customs of one's predecessors, offers a means to establish the reality of collective identity in the absence of visible "proof of difference" on the body.[14]

The invisibility of African descent on the body, while important to the Afro-Chilean experience, is not shared by all. Prominent activist Marta Salgado Henriquez has communicated a different sort of personal experience in public speaking engagements, newspaper articles, and in her own writing, as well as in an interview with me. She opens a 2010 essay with the following assessment of her experience:

---

[14] I seldom heard the term *negro* (black) used, even casually, during fieldwork.

For many years I had to struggle because of being different. My hair, my color of skin, made me look different from people in my city and, of course, the rest of my social environment, my school, the community in which I lived. Over the course of my life, I endured the mocking laughter of those who called me "negra," as if my color was something bad or something that wasn't normal for people, [all this] right up to now when I am among the group considered senior citizens. (2010, 225)

Salgado is one of the founders of the country's first Afro-Chilean organization, Oro Negro, formed in 2001. The original objectives of the group are typical of the many organizations that followed: to achieve political and social recognition of Afro-descendants in Chile; to recover and disseminate Afro-descendant history and culture; to see to the education and training of Afro-descendants so that they can participate in various professions; to protect Afro-descendants from discrimination in education, health, housing, and employment.

Redrawing Borders of Belonging

The 2001 formation of Oro Negro came late to the field; in the rest of Afro-Latin America, the early 1990s saw a sharp rise in collective organizing and grassroots social movements (Dixon and Burdick, 2012). Marta Salgado cites her participation, and that of a few other Afro-Chileans, in the Regional Conference of the Americas held in Santiago in late 2000, as the impetus for the formation of Oro Negro. The conference in Santiago was one of many events held around the world in preparation for the September 2001 World Conference against Racism, Racial Discrimination, Xenophobia and Related Intolerance held in Durban, South Africa. Salgado recalls being met with surprise from other attendees, including Afro-descendants from other Latin American countries, who were unaware of an Afro-descendant presence in Chile.

Additional groups were formed soon after Oro Negro, drawing their membership from Chile's northern region. Organización Lumbanga was founded in 2003 and has since, along with Oro Negro, attracted the most public attention. Other groups include Comparsa Tumba Carnaval and Agrupación Arica Negra. A group for elders was formalized in 2010, Agrupación de Adulto Mayor Julia Corvacho. Two groups dedicated to women were also formed, Colectivo de Mujeres Luanda and Agrupación Mujeres Afrodescendientes Rurales Hijas de Azapa. Oro Negro itself divided into an NGO and a dance group, Comparsa Oro Negro. Attempts at umbrella entities intended to promote greater communication and coordination between different Afro-descendant organizations, as well as a unified voice before the public and state, have included the Alianza

Afrochilena, the Confranternidad de Familias y Agrupaciones Afroariqueñas, and the Asociación de Organizaciones y Comunidades Afrochilenas Azapa Territorio Ancestral.[15]

While the preceding list is not necessarily exhaustive, it does point to considerable activity and efforts at community building among Afro-descendants in the area. Considering the limited size of the population, its geographic concentration, and the fact that such organizational life only started in 2001, the number of organizations is impressive. Participants explain that the groups differ somewhat in terms of their focus, some emphasizing music and dance or culture more broadly, and others emphasizing education and politics. Additionally, some draw their membership from rural areas while others draw primarily from within the city limits of Arica. Some allow non-Afros to join, others do not. Interpersonal differences were also hinted at as an explanation for the apparent rapid proliferation of groups.

What all the organizations have in common is the goal of valuing and promoting Afro-descendant identity. To that end, these groups have been responsible for researching the history of people of Afro descent. They have collected oral histories from elders, culminating in the local publication of two books by two prominent activists, *Lumbanga: Memorias Orales de la Cultura Afrochilena* (*Lumbanga: Oral Memories of Afro-Chilean Culture*) by Cristian Baez Lazcano and *Afrochilenos: Una Historia Oculta* (*Afro-Chileans: A Hidden History*) by Marta Salgado Henriquez. These groups have organized workshops about history, music and dance, culinary traditions, instrument construction, and traditional crafts as well as seminars and conferences on various themes, all as a means to educate both Afro-descendants and others.

Music and dance have been particularly important in engaging public attention, with various groups participating in local folk parades and other performances. A closer look at what is danced provides insight into the cultural loss and re-creation experienced by the population. At one group's rehearsals, I watched as choreography was created using the motions involved in harvesting olives. No dance with these motions existed or had been passed down to this generation; in the absence of preserved dances (the *tumba carnaval* being an exception),[16] the group used an activity important to their history to create something representative of their identity. The music played was subject to

---

[15] The municipal government of Arica formed an Oficina de Desarrollo Afrodescendiente (Office of Afro-descendant Development) in 2010, a sign, in part, of the impact of civil society efforts on government. The office explains its purpose as "breaking the barriers of structural racism, rendering the Afro-descendant community visible, in accordance with [...] the Durban Declaration and Plan of Action" (Municipio de Arica, 2010).

[16] *Tumba carnaval* refers to a dance performed by African descendants in Arica during carnival. Oral history suggests that it dates back several generations. Accompanied by the rhythm of drums, dancers attempt to push each other with the movement of their hips.

a similar process of invention. I observed, for instance, two skillful percussionists search the internet, looking for Afro-Latin sounds to inspire their own rhythms; they were searching, they explained to each other, for something that "sounded African" to be combined with a "Chilean sound or rhythm" to create something uniquely their own. These efforts at developing informed moves and sounds were contrasted, by those belonging to that particular group, to less rigorous creations on the part of other groups. As one activist explained it, other groups, in the absence of any investigation or information, would "Africanize everything and produce something that has nothing to do with anything particularly Chilean or *afro-ariqueño*." However, whatever is performed likely helps display an element of shared expressive culture that is distinct from that of other non-Afro-descendant Chileans.

The Patrimonial Slave Route, a local branch of UNESCO's larger Slave Route Project, is another important venture. It was publicly inaugurated in 2009 and represents the efforts of the Ministry of National Assets in conjunction with various Afro-descendant groups who had been working on it for two years prior. It is a touristic and cultural route comprised of 12 locations across Arica, Valle de Azapa, and Valle de Lluta. These include a small museum of Afro-Chilean history, a plaza in what was once a black neighborhood (known as Lumbanga) during the colonial period, and a church in which enslaved blacks were once baptized. This route inserts Afro-descendant history and an undeniable Afro-descendant presence into the physical landscape, thereby publicly claiming/reclaiming the spaces which Afro-Chileans and their ancestors have moved through. The route has seen various degrees of use and upkeep; it remains to be seen if its full educational and economic potential will be realized.

Two major long-term political efforts include formally petitioning for legal recognition of Afro-Chileans as an ethnic group and for their subsequent inclusion as a group in the national census. There has been extensive activity around these demands, particularly on the part of the Alianza Afrochilena, including public demonstrations (marches and performances), letters, and meetings involving government and census officials. Despite coverage in the news media and, most significantly, grassroots realization of a pilot census of Afros in the northern region in 2009, Afro-descendants were ultimately denied ethnic status and not included in the 2012 census. This, according to activists, is one of the greatest hurdles, "because if you are not there [in the official statistics] you don't exist," and if you do not exist, then securing collective rights and protections, political representation, formal inclusion in public policy, development projects and school curricula, and the systematic tracking of disparities and discrimination are formal impossibilities. "You cannot be dealt with as a group," explained an activist, "if you do not officially exist as a group." In 2013, the Instituto Nacional de Estadística

(INE) announced that, for the first time, it would survey around 5,000 homes in the urban and rural areas of Arica and Parinacota in order to capture a representative profile of the Afro-descendant population and its housing, education, and income realities. This was a direct response to the years of petitions and proposals for statistical inclusion generated by the Afro-descendant population itself.[17] The survey resulted in a count of 8,415 self-identified African descendants from 5,700 households canvassed in the northern region between August and November of 2013 (Bertin, 2014). Despite this long-awaited act of recognition and official statistical proof of presence, the 2017 national census, once again, did not give respondents the opportunity to identify as African descendants and so no data on the population was officially collected at a national level.

Reconfiguring the Heartland

The emergence of Afro-Chilean organizations from civil society, beginning in the early 2000s, marked a collective and organized attempt to achieve visibility and equality for this long-overlooked population. The varied activities of these groups have, taken as a whole, contributed to a gradual shifting in the landscape of Chilean identity and perhaps even Afro-Latin identity. The activities of these groups have challenged and redrawn multiple borders of belonging. Recovering the history of Afro-descendants in the area has meant redefining to whom Chile "belongs" and who "belongs" to Chile. A presence of over 400 years' duration means that Afro-descendants have contributed to the nation for as long as those of Spanish descent: "The black is part of the *raza chilena*, not the romantic, pseudoscientific myth, but the real *raza*; those who lived, worked, and struggled to free and build Chile" (Sater, 1976, 38). While the pale-hued bodies of many of Chile's Afro-descendants have made their relationship to blackness a seemingly tenuous one, their efforts at cultural recovery represent a collective declaration that African descent belongs to them regardless and that they belong to the larger African diaspora community in Latin America and across the globe, even if that larger community never knew they existed. It would appear that Chile's Afro-descendants have simultaneously challenged the whiteness of Chile and what the blackness of Afro-Latin America looks like and how it is lived. While the pursuit of official state recognition of

---

[17] Similar petitioning and proposals are observable among African-descendant populations elsewhere in Latin America. They received attention in the wake of the 2001 adoption of the Durban Declaration and Program of Action, which included among its policies and practices for states a call for statistical data collection and disaggregation of groups vulnerable to racism and xenophobia.

the population continues, a degree of popular recognition has already been achieved. Afro-Chileans, through their own collective efforts, are moving beyond the statistical, geographic, and ethno-racial hinterlands to which they have been relegated for centuries, redrawing the borders of belonging in the Chilean nation as well as within Afro-Latin America.

Works Cited

Andrews, George Reid. *Afro-Latin America, 1800–2000*. Oxford: Oxford University Press, 2004.

Andrews, George Reid. "Afro-Latin America: Five Questions." *Latin American and Caribbean Ethnic Studies* 4.2 (2009): 191–210.

Anzaldúa, Gloria. *Borderlands / La Frontera: The New Mestiza*. San Francisco: Aunt Lute Books, 1987.

Baez Lazcano, Cristian. *Lumbanga: Memorias Orales de la Cultura Afrochilena*. Arica, Chile: Herco Editores S.A., 2010.

Bernhardson, Wayne. *Lonely Planet Chile and Easter Island*. Berkeley, CA: Lonely Planet Publishers, 1993.

Bertin, Ximena. "Censo revela 8.415 afrochilenos viven en Arica." *La Tercera*. Feb. 15, 2014.

Busdiecker, Sara. "Where Blackness Resides: Afro-Bolivians and the Spatializing and Racializing of the African Diaspora." *Radical History Review* 103 (2009): 105–116.

"Chile: Silencio del Concejo profundiza el racismo ante abuso de poder de una concejala Ariqueña." *Legado Afro: Portal de Noticias Afrolatino y Caribeño*. Dec. 19, 2013. http://legadoafro.bligoo.com.uy/chile-silencio-del-concejo-profundiza-el-racismo-ante-abuso-de-poder-de-una-concejala-ariquena. Accessed Jan. 26, 2014.

Comisión Nacional del XVII Censo de Población y VI de Vivienda. *Censo 2002: Síntesis de Resultados*. Santiago, Chile: Empresa Periodística La Nación S.A., 2003.

Curtin, Philip. *The Atlantic Slave Trade: A Census*. Madison, WI: University of Wisconsin Press, 1972.

Dixon, Kwami, and John Burdick, eds. *Comparative Perspectives on Afro-Latin America*. Gainesville, FL: University Press of Florida, 2012.

Donoso, Fernando. "El ADN genético de los chilenos." *Revista Enfoque*. Sept. 21, 2011.

Flusche, Della M., and Eugene H. Korth. *Forgotten Females: Women of African and Indian Descent in Colonial Chile, 1535–1800*. Detroit, MI: Blaine Ethridge Books, 1983.

Garrison, Rob. "Chile." In *Africana: The Encyclopedia of the African and African American Experience*. Ed. Kwame Anthony Appiah and Henry Louis Gates. Oxford: Oxford University Press, 2005: 57–61.

Gudmundson, Lowell, and Justin Wolfe. "Introduction." In *Blacks and Blackness in Central America: Between Race and Place*. Ed. Lowell Gudmundson and Justin Wolfe. Durham, NC: Duke University Press, 2010: 1–24.

Hernández, Tanya Katerí. *Racial Subordination in Latin America: The Role of the State, Customary Law, and the New Civil Rights Response*. Cambridge: Cambridge University Press, 2013.

Klein, Herbert, and Ben Vinson III. *African Slavery in Latin America and the Caribbean*. Oxford: Oxford University Press, 1986.

Lumbanga de Arica. "Acto de Racismo y Xenofobia en Chile hacia Mujer Afrodescendiente por parte de Concejala Municipal." *YouTube*. Nov. 28, 2013. https://www.youtube.com/watch?v=bPiJUuıbIoA. Accessed Jan. 29, 2014.

Mellafe, Rolando. *La Introducción de la Esclavitud Negra en Chile: Tráfico y Rutas*. Santiago, Chile: Editorial Universitaria, 1984.

Mullings, Leith, ed. *New Social Movements in the African Diaspora: Challenging Global Apartheid*. New York: Palgrave MacMillan, 2009.

Municipio de Arica. September 2010. https://www.muniarica.cl/index.php. Accessed Sep. 15, 2010.

Rahier, Jean Muteba, ed. *Black Social Movements in Latin America: From Monocultural Mestizaje to Multiculturalism*. New York: Palgrave MacMillan, 2012.

Rout, Leslie B. *The African Experience in Spanish America*. Cambridge: Cambridge University Press, 1976.

Salgado Henriquez, Marta. "El legado africano en Chile." In *Conocimiento desde Adentro: Los afrosudamericanos hablan de sus pueblos y sus historias Volumen I*. Ed. Sheila Walker. La Paz: Fundación PIEB, 2010: 223–270.

Salgado Henriquez, Marta. *Afrochilenos: Una Historia Oculta*. Arica, Chile: Herco Editores S.A., 2013.

Sater, William F. "The Black Experience in Chile." In *Slavery and Race Relations in Latin America*. Ed. Robert Brent Toplin. Westport, CT: Greenwood Press, 1974: 13–50.

Skuban, William E. *Lines in the Sand: Nationalism and Identity on the Peruvian-Chilean Frontier*. Albuquerque: University of New Mexico Press, 2007.

United Nations Office of the High Commissioner for Human Rights. "Committee on the Elimination of Racial Discrimination considers the Report of Chile." 2013. Aug. 14, 2013. http://www.ohchr.org/EN/NewsEvents/Pages/DisplayNews.aspx?NewsID=13629&LangID=E. Accessed Jan. 29, 2014.

Wade, Peter. "Afro-Latin Studies: Reflections on the Field." *Latin American and Caribbean Ethnic Studies* 1.1 (2006): 105–124.

Yudell, Michael, Dorothy Roberts, Rob DeSalle, and Sarah Tishkoff. "Taking Race out of Human Genetics." *Science* 351 (2016): 564–565.

9

Lowcountry, High Demands: The Struggle for Quality Education in Charleston, South Carolina

Jon Hale (University of South Carolina)
and Clerc Cooper (Tulane University)

South Carolina played a prominent role in shaping the nature of public education in the United States. It also laid the framework for the conservative counterrevolution in the 1940s, and ultimately, for the New Right of the 1960s and '70s. The history of the long struggle for quality education in the state included policies of segregation, equalization, and desegregation that reflected and shaped legislative recalcitrance and malfeasance at the federal level. It was not until 1963 that school desegregation legally began in South Carolina. The Palmetto State lagged behind all but Mississippi, which opened its public schools to a small handful of African-American students in the fall of 1964, more than ten years after the *Brown v. Board of Education* (1954) decision declared that segregation was inherently inequitable and, therefore, unconstitutional. Too often the history of desegregation begins with the massive resistance by states like Mississippi and South Carolina, states that refused to desegregate and which employed legal maneuvers to maintain a segregated system. This focus pulls attention away from sustained grassroots organization and activism at the local level, which was focused on making the public school system live up to its promise of equality for all students.

Public education dates back to Reconstruction, when it embodied the desire of formerly enslaved communities to acquire literacy, which was equated with freedom. Focusing on the history of desegregation in South Carolina generates productive insights into how desegregation unfolded across the country, and how local actors defined "desegregation" in the context of the larger struggle. It also illustrates the nuanced experiences of attending desegregated schools. The perspective of those who experienced the desegregation of white schools at first-hand suggests that the struggle for desegregation occurred not only in the courtrooms that have been enshrined as the milestones that led to desegregation, but also in the classrooms which young people courageously desegregated on their own. At the beginning of the twenty-first century, more than half a century after the historic *Brown v. Board of Education* (1954) decision, the struggle for quality education continues.

Equalization and the Struggle for a Quality Education in the Lowcountry

By the Second World War, over 60 years after the end of Reconstruction, the NAACP equalization campaign visibly and directly challenged social injustices within the public education system. In Charleston, the struggle for equal salaries for teachers was at the forefront of the Civil Rights Movement (Tushnet, 2004, 70–81).[1] In June of 1940, the Supreme Court refused to review a teacher salary equalization case, *Alston v. City School Board of City of Norfolk*, letting the lower court's decision stand, which ruled that the salaries of black and white teachers must be equal between equally qualified teachers. With the *Alston* decision in mind, the South Carolina General Assembly voted in 1941 to raise all teacher salaries according to a merit system in an attempt to meet the demand for equalization. Bolstered by the legislative move, the all-black Palmetto State Teacher's Association (PSTA) in South Carolina supported the ongoing efforts of the NAACP to equalize salaries, much to the chagrin of state officials (Charron, 2009, 154–156; Potts, 1978, 61–68). In defiance, local school districts refused to renew the contracts of those involved with the equalization campaign, such as J.T.W. Mims, principal of Bell Street High School and president of the Palmetto State Teachers Association (PSTA) from 1942–1944, and J.R. McCain, PSTA president between 1946 and 1948 (Potts, 1978, 66–67).[2] Educators continued to press their demands despite sanctioned resistance. On November 10, 1943, NAACP lawyers filed for *Duvall v. J.F. Seignous et al.* The trial on February 14, 1944 took only 15 minutes. Judge J. Waties Waring brought the *Alston* case to the school board lawyers' attention and ruled in favor of the plaintiffs.[3]

Although the NAACP originally pursued an equalization strategy, the organization eventually embraced the more radical move to desegregate schools. As states came on board with equalization policies, the NAACP pushed forward by advocating for full equality under the law. In 1944, black

---

[1] This strategy was adopted across the South. See Bolton (2005, 33–60).
[2] The reaction of white educational policymakers contradicts the prevailing thesis that black teachers were not active in the Civil Rights Movement.
[3] As a result of the *Duvall* decision, the South Carolina General Assembly put in place a procedure for teachers like Duvall to file a salary complaint. See Charron (2009, 164–165); "Court Orders" (1944).

students applied for admission to South Carolina's colleges, including 32 seniors from the Avery Normal Institute who submitted applications for admission to the College of Charleston (Baker, 2006, 66; Drago, 1990, 230–231). In 1946, John H. Wrighten applied for admission to the University of South Carolina Law School. After being denied, he sued the Board of Trustees of the University of South Carolina. The court's ruling established the foundation for the state's policy of equalization (Jenkins, 2009, 30–31).[4] The state invested in a new law school at South Carolina State University in Orangeburg, allocating $200,000 for a building and $30,000 for a law library. When prompted with inquiries about the high costs, the Dean of the University's law school explained, "Gentlemen, well I'll tell you, the price of prejudice is very high."[5]

South Carolina played a critical role in the history of the nationally and internationally celebrated *Brown v. Board of Education* (1954) decision. The *Briggs v. Elliot* (1952) case, which originated in Clarendon County, was one of the five lawsuits that were combined under the *Brown* case. The *Briggs* case began in 1948, when Reverend Joseph A. DeLaine and local parents filed suit for adequate transportation to the local segregated school their children attended. In 1950, with the support of the NAACP, the plaintiffs refiled their case, surpassing transportation and asking for equal educational opportunities in Clarendon County. Thurgood Marshall, the lead NAACP attorney in the *Brown* case and protégé of Charleston Hamilton Houston, the legal architect of the NAACP assault on segregation, argued this case in Charleston, where Judge Waties Waring in a dissenting opinion ruled that "segregation is per se inequality" (Waring qtd in Yarbrough, 1987, 196, emphasis original; see also Burton, Burton, and Appleford, 2008, 191; Baker, 2006, 87–107). Though the NAACP lost the case and South Carolina continued to equalize its public school system to avoid desegregation, local activism supported a swelling grassroots movement that sustained the push for a quality education and established a legal precedent in the monumental *Brown v. Board of Education* (1954) decision.

Avoiding Desegregation in South Carolina and the Blueprint for the New Right

In the post-war period, local activists and the NAACP forced South Carolina to adopt new strategies to avoid desegregation. The plans reflected a regional move across the South and began to lay the foundations for the rise of the New Right and the Republican Party, which supplanted

---

[4] Wrighten also applied to the College of Charleston in July 1943. See Baker, 2006, 66.
[5] August T. Graydon, interview with Walter Edgar, July 10, 1991 (Edgar, 2012, 165).

the traditional power of the Democrats. In Mississippi and Virginia, for instance, state government implemented plans that avoided desegregation through an abandonment of public education, a strategy that continued to shape conservative politics. Governor Byrnes, who held office between 1951 and 1955, articulated this at the national level. Politically, he continued to push for protection to enable states to act of their own accord, supporting the political faction that developed after Strom Thurmund and the Dixiecrats in 1948.[6] Following their lead, Byrnes advocated a position of states' rights and the right of state delegates to vote in direct opposition to the national Democratic Party.[7] This laid the groundwork for the historic shift of white Southern and segregationist politicians to voting with the Republican Party, beginning with Barry Goldwater in 1964. Education became a critical battleground in the historic reconfiguration of conservative politics in the American South.

Forewarned by the attempts to desegregate the state's institutions of higher learning in *McLaurin v. Oklahoma* (1950), in which the University of Oklahoma was ordered to admit Charles McLaurin into a graduate program, and *Sweatt v. Painter* (1950), in which the state of Texas was ordered to admit the plaintiff to the state law school or to build a separate law school for African Americans, the state of South Carolina chose to avoid desegregation with strong legal measures. Rather than prepare for the inevitable order to desegregate, South Carolina legislators reasoned that equalizing schools would preclude an order to desegregate. Legislators therefore embarked on a comprehensive equalization scheme, striving to uphold the "separate but equal" provision and maintain a constitutionally justifiable, yet still segregated school system (Dobrasko, 2005, 12–20; Baker, 2006, 93–95). In 1951, Governor Byrnes encouraged the South Carolina General Assembly to consolidate the school districts, eliminating the dual black and white systems, but maintaining separate schools. In Charleston County, for example, the 21 school districts were consolidated into eight. The governor also supported legislation to establish a three-cent sales tax to help equalize black and white schools, the first sales tax in the Palmetto State. He created the Education Finance Commission to disburse the revenue from the state sales tax to the school districts. The funds were to be distributed at

---

[6] The Dixiecrats put forward Strom Thurmond as a presidential candidate in 1948, who garnered less than 3% of the popular vote. Though defeated, this laid the groundwork for the shift toward a solidly Republican South by the 1970s. For a full history on the Dixiecrats and the rise of the New Right, see Crespino (2007); Crespino (2012); Lassiter and Crespino (2010).

[7] For a full biography on Strom Thurmond, see Crespino (2012, 61–69); "Statement of Governor James F. Byrnes, July 22, 1952," James F. Byrnes Papers, Series 7, Box 12, Folders 1–13, Strom Thurmond Institute archives, Clemson University.

a rate of 15 dollars per pupil (calculated based on daily average attendance) per year for a period of 20 years.[8]

Legislative attempts to equalize schools constituted a calculated strategy to construct a legally defensible facade of racial equality in education. As a result of the Byrnes Plan, $124,329,394 went to public education between 1951 and 1956, which funded new buildings, resources, and transportation statewide. Although African Americans comprised only about 40% of South Carolina's school pupils, almost two-thirds of that money went to black schools (Dobrasko, 2005, 14; Baker, 2006, 99–104). In peninsular Charleston, the school district provided six schools for black students and developed plans to expand existing schools and build new ones. Burke High School, which served the entire eighth through twelfth grade population of Charleston School District 20, received half a million dollars to improve its facilities and to build five more buildings for the 1954–1955 school year (Baker, 2006, 103). Soon after, plans emerged for a new school for blacks at the foot of the Cooper River Bridge, near the newly expanded America Street Housing Project (Smyth, 1991, 107). The $625,000 East Bay Street Negro Elementary School opened in February of 1955, which was reported to be "nearly identical to Memminger Elementary School," a school serving peninsular Charleston's white population, "in construction, equipment, and quality of finish" ("City's Newest School," 1955). Two years later, school officials opened the Columbus Street School for African-American students. Additionally, the city transferred Courtenay Elementary from whites' hands to black control in 1958 (Dobrasko, 2005, 33). Local school construction was the last attempt to invest in public schools in order to maintain segregation (Smyth, 1991, 107; Dobrasko, 2005, 14; Baker, 2006, 99–104).

The feigned attempts at equalization were merely superficial, however, and officials quickly exhausted the money allocated for the campaign. At the conclusion of 1956, the Charleston County School District (CCSD) had already used all of the money it would receive from the Education Finance Commission until 1960. Therefore, Charleston superintendent Robert Gaines suggested a bond election to raise the $1.1 million required to further equalize schools. Gaines realized, however, that the only way a bond election would be voted in by the populace was if it supported both black and white schools. Therefore, the bond he proposed allocated $300,000 for improvements to High School of Charleston, Rivers, and James Simons Elementary as well as $800,000 for improvements to Burke, Archer Elementary, and Simonton

---

[8] School districts could receive the money they needed to equalize schools up front, allowing them to begin "establishing and maintaining adequate physical facilities." See Dobrasko (2006, 11–13).

Elementary. He believed that "If we show evidence of moving ahead rapidly on these projects, the Negro population will be satisfied. If we do not, we will quite possibly be faced with an integration suit" (Baker, 2006, 125, 203). Black Charlestonians, led by the efforts of the local NAACP, protested the bond election and defeated it. J. Arthur Brown, the president of the NAACP, led the opposition, believing it was "high time" that the school board begin to comply with the *Brown* decision (Baker, 2006, 125).

The local *News and Courier* was not hesitant to take a stance on desegregation, joining the state in its vehement opposition to desegregation. In September of 1956, the paper proclaimed that "South Carolinians must brace themselves for a long resistance [...] The separation of races in public schools, in the circumstances that exist in South Carolina, is necessary. It is not evil or immoral. It does not deprive Negroes of their rights" ("Boarder States Yielding," 1956). In August of 1955, the paper encouraged whites to resist: "the will to resist goes deep into the fabric of the Southern people [...] They do not intend to yield their principles so long as they draw breath" ("The Southern Resistance," 1955). The state responded and Governor Byrnes organized a legal strategy to resist desegregation on multiple fronts, which only strengthened the resolve of the state's emerging rights movement. Byrnes organized a special committee to study alternatives to the court-ordered desegregation. This 15-member committee, which took the name of its chairman, Senator Marion Gressette, worked to create more legally defensible justifications for segregation. The committee first recommended that the legislature amend the South Carolina constitution, removing the requirement that the state maintain public schools. The measure appeared on the ballot of the November 1952 general election and passed unanimously (Edgar, 2012, 100; Smyth, 1991, 106). The state legislature, led by the Gressette's segregation committee, found other ways to avoid desegregating schools. In 1955, the state legislature passed a pupil-placement law, similar to those used in nine other Southern states. South Carolina's pupil-placement law "gave local school boards the discretion and power to assign pupils in the best interest of education" (Baker, 2006, 135).

Charleston schools also used standardized testing to justify giving black students a lesser education; the state already had experience of testing teachers to determine pay through the use of the racially motivated NTE. The use of "objective" standardized testing based on skewed social scientific evidence created an academic tracking system that systematically placed students in vocational or college preparatory tracks, depending upon their score. In 1957, a three-tier tracking system entered the high schools in the CCSD. In Burke High School and Rivers High School, for instance, students' test scores determined whether they were assigned to the honors track, the general track, or the remedial track. Evidence of testing shows that the majority of black students were placed in the remedial track, while the honors track was overwhelmingly white (Baker, 2006, 137).

As the state Supreme Court adopted an equalization strategy, state legislators in Columbia and the local educational authorities began adopting movements toward privatization. Setting the trend of avoiding integration through any means possible, the College of Charleston, under the leadership of President George Grice, began discussions about becoming a private institution. On April 19, 1949 the Charleston County legislature passed a bill returning the College of Charleston to private control, placing the college under the direction of the Board of Trustees (Morrison, 2011, 44; Baker, 2006, 70). Rather than create a local college for African-American students, the city of Charleston offered to provide scholarships for black Charlestonians to attend college at South Carolina State, an offer it hoped would uphold the separate but equal clause. Anticipating the move towards private education in Charleston, in 1958, seven citizen's council groups conducted an architectural survey of Charleston's buildings to determine which could be considered as potential private schools (Hawkins, 2009, 232).

As the inevitability of desegregation became increasingly clear, Gressette's Segregation Committee investigated other methods to support privatization. At the committee's recommendation, the state passed a tuition grant bill in May of 1963, which allocated funds to parents who chose not to enroll their students in public schools. The bill provided $155 per pupil per year to families who chose to enroll their children in private schools. In order to maintain the separation of church and state, however, the bill contained a stipulation that the funds could not be given to students who attended religiously affiliated schools (Baker, 2006, 159–162; Hawkins, 2009, 234). Encouraged by the state's tuition grant act, passed in May of 1963, white parents turned towards private education to avoid desegregation. Following the 1963 decision, five separate groups began discussions to form private schools in Charleston (Hawkins, 2009, 238). The *News and Courier* ran advertisements for several of these schools, including the catholic-sponsored "Marian School."[9] In September of 1964, five segregated academies opened in Charleston, including the College of Charleston-sponsored College Preparatory Academy, which inhabited the building that is presently the Jewish Studies Center (Baker, 2006, 160). During the 1965–1966 school year, just two years after 11 students desegregated the school district, 32 all-white private schools opened their doors in South Carolina (Hawkins, 2009, 239). Such actions paved the way to the proliferation of private schools during the 1960s and 1970s.

---

[9] Bishop Paul J. Hallinan. Letter to parents 18 Aug 1961. Catholic Diocese of Charleston Archives, Charleston, SC. Box 22 Folder 707.1.

Desegregating Charleston and the Experiences of "First Children"

Despite intimidation and white legislators' attempts to preserve a system of segregated schools, local activists demanded integration and equitable opportunity. The pressure to move beyond desegregation was constant, particularly after the NAACP's nationwide strategy targeted the desegregation of schools. The shift in Charleston to demand desegregation, as opposed to equalization, came once the NAACP filed *Briggs v. Elliot* (1952). The case originated in Clarendon County and became one of the cases that comprised the *Brown v. Board of Education* (1954) lawsuit in which the Supreme Court ruled that school segregation was unconstitutional. To build upon the momentum of the *Brown* case, local black Charlestonians petitioned the school board to move beyond equalization and to desegregate the public schools. "As you undoubtedly know," a petition organized by J. Arthur Brown—the father of Minerva and Millicent Brown, one of the students to eventually desegregate Rivers High School, and married to J. Arthur Brown, president of the Charleston branch of the NAACP— stated, "the United States Supreme Court on May 17, 1954, ruled that the maintenance of racially segregated public school is a violation of the Constitution of the United States [...] We, therefore, call upon you to take immediate steps to reorganize the public school under your jurisdiction on a nondiscriminatory basis."[10] Four years after the *Brown* decision, in 1959 Brown filed a lawsuit for his daughter to attend Rivers High School, the white high school in Charleston. Representatives of the Council of City Parent Teacher Associations, the City Federation of Colored Women's Clubs, and the Charleston Branch of the NAACP led the drive. "The discriminations that we shall outline in this petition have existed too long," the petitioners wrote:

> they have warped and tormented the souls, the minds, the bodies of both races—they have kept our community from the full development of our spiritual and mental potentialities; for discriminations shackle the discriminator as much as it does the discriminated [...] We [come as] intensely interested citizens first petitioning, but firmly resolved to pursue every legal avenue available to secure equal justice under the law.[11]

Others lobbied the Charleston County School Board to equalize the funding going into their schools. Local people sought in particular to address the issues of overcrowding in segregated schools: "We feel that the Negro

---

[10] Petition, Board of Trustee Minute Book, 1951–1957, School District No. 20, CCSD.
[11] "To the School Boards of School District #20," Box 7, Folder 8, Eugene Hunt Papers, Avery Research Center.

community has an undercover resentment to overcrowding, and particularly to double sessions."[12]

The Supreme Court's decision established the framework for desegregation and ensured that the process would be implemented within local parameters. The *"Brown* II" decision, released in 1955, enacted a plan that desegregated schools across the South with "all deliberate speed," which was to be determined at the local level under local conditions. Southern policymakers interpreted this as an opportunity to legally forestall desegregation. Judge Martin's decision, handed down in August of 1963, gave the Charleston County school board a full year to develop a plan for integration, a window which it used to develop a strategy to impede complete desegregation. In 1964, Judge Martin approved District 20's plan, which kept elementary students in the school they had attended the year before. This effectively made black students going into high school the only pupils eligible to apply for a school transfer. The "freedom of choice" plan that Judge Martin approved stymied desegregation because it merely granted pupils a right to apply to transfer to another school rather than the right to attend that school. The school board could still deny black students' requests on grounds such as overcrowding, that the student lived closer to a black school, or that it was not in the best interest of the student to transfer. This was problematic because it placed the burden for desegregation on the black community and effected very little change. While the plan did achieve insignificant desegregation of white schools, it achieved no desegregation of black schools. Also, it only applied to School District 20 and did little to implement desegregation in the rest of Charleston County. District 20's plan followed the pattern of school desegregation across the region during the first 15 years following the *Brown* decision. By developing "freedom of choice" plans, Southern states were able to maintain segregation in nearly all schools except for the small handful that were legally forced to accept a token number of black students (Jenkins, 2009, 34; Bolton, 2005, 61–95).

The petitioners in Charleston illustrate how equalization gave way to demands for desegregation at the local grassroots level. Educators demanded equal salaries, the NAACP litigated these demands for equalization while white legislators sought to equalize the system of education, working under the "separate but equal" doctrine established since the *Plessy v. Ferguson* (1896) decision. The work of educators and the NAACP to equalize salaries constituted an attempt to provide a quality education within the parameters of Jim Crow policy. The state of South Carolina adopted similar means to equalize schools, but with a much different goal, that of preserving a segregated system. The lexicon of educational reform shifted once parents,

---

[12] Constituent District #20, Board Minutes, 1958–1978, Reel 212, CCSD.

students, and civil rights organizations began to demand access to previously all-white schools in the early 1950s. Rather than pursuing a quality education through equalization, activists and legal architects behind the *Brown v. Board of Education* (1954) decision demanded a quality education through desegregation. The move toward desegregation signaled controversy and a significant point of departure from an earlier phase of the burgeoning Civil Rights Movement. The decision to desegregate challenged the segregationist ethos and the rationale of Jim Crow that determined the Southern "way of life." The movement invited intense resistance, violence, and disparaging rebuffs from those who challenged it. Demanding desegregation invited fierce resistance, particularly after Southern legislatures began to equalize facilities in the hopes of maintaining a segregated system even after the *Brown* decision.

A shift toward desegregation signified an ideological shift within the Civil Rights Movement. "Desegregation" marked a clear departure from equalization, but it did not encompass the ultimate aims of those who demanded a quality education, through both legal and political grassroots methods. Kenneth Clark, the psychologist who provided counsel to the legal staff of the NAACP during their preparation for *Brown v. Board of Education* (1954), insisted upon the use of the term "desegregation" as opposed to "integration." In a paper he published based on the research he and other social scientists used in the case, he noted:

> The term *desegregation* is used in this report to describe the process of change in social situations or institutions from a system of organization in terms of separate facilities for whites and Negroes, exclusion of Negroes, or a deliberate restriction of the extent or area of participation of Negroes to a system wherein distinctions, exclusion, or restriction of participation based upon race no longer prevail. Desegregation seems a more descriptive term for the actual process which this report is concerned with than is the term racial integration. Desegregation is a more objective and empirical term and does not imply the complexity of social and individual adjustments and attitudinal factors which are inherent in the more evaluative term integration. (Kenneth Clark qtd in Klein, 2004, 225)[13]

As the lead counsel for the NAACP on the use of social scientific research to prove the inequality inherent to segregation, Clark, and other social scientists,

---

[13] The quote is taken from Clark's "Desegregation: An Appraisal of the Evidence" (1953). Michelle Purdy builds upon the premise that "desegregation is not synonymous with integration, though they are often used as such. Integration or racial integration refers to a transformed society, and desegregation is one step towards fulfilling that transformation" (2011, 2). For further discussion of the distinction between the two terms, see Adair (1984, 181, 183); Powell and Spencer (2003, 344).

was in a position to influence the use of the term "desegregation".[14] Desegregation, as noted by Clark, was more concerned with the "objective" process by which institutions provided equal access to all citizens. Desegregation was simply the *process* through which institutions changed to include, rather than exclude, especially on the basis of race. Desegregation, in other words, was the means to a greater end goal and larger objective that encompassed integration and a quality education for *all* students.

Those involved with the process of desegregation from both a legal and a grassroots perspective drew a distinction between desegregation and integration, though the terms have since been conflated. In contrast to desegregation, integration dealt with "social" and "attitudinal factors," with ideological and personal subjectivities more fully aligned with the ideals expressed in the Civil Rights Movement. Activists sought quality education through desegregation, but this was the legal or political means to achieve true integration. Integration, as Clark noted, was much more complex and deeply rooted in religious convictions often encapsulated in notions of a "beloved community." This notion of the "beloved community," a community that extended integration beyond race to include class, gender, age, "and every other distinction that tends to separate us as human beings rather than bring us together" was articulated by James Lawson, a theologian and Southern director of the Congress of Racial Equality (CORE), and by John Lewis, former chair of the Student Nonviolent Coordinating Committee (SNCC) (Lewis with D'Orso, 1988, xvii).

For many activists, desegregation was the legal or political means to achieve a greater end, not an end in and of itself. White segregationists apprehended this and maintained that desegregation symbolized the end of a cherished way of life.[15] Yet in the 20 years following the *Brown* decision, the courts and legal activists were concerned with attempts to achieve desegregation. Therefore, the courts never focused on implementing integration in the schools, thereby impeding the realization of the movements' other goals (Patterson, 2001, 118–146; Klarman, 2007, 41–46, 175–212; Baker, 2006, 139–157).[16]

---

[14] For a comprehensive discussion of the role of social scientists in the *Brown v. Board of Education* decision, see Jackson (2001).

[15] Indeed, by the late 1960s, activists began arguing that "community control," as opposed to desegregation, constituted a more effective means to achieve a truly high-quality education. The "strike that changed New York" illustrates the tensions between white liberals and black activists who demanded that they control the provision of public education, much to the dismay of whites who had been long sympathetic to the movement. For an eloquent and insightfully analytical account of the strike, see Podair (2002); Perillo (2012).

[16] For a history of desegregation's impact on the contemporary movement for multicultural education, see Banks (2004, 3–29).

As the movement to desegregate schools gained momentum, young people still in middle and high school emerged as key actors. They did the radical work of college students in towns like Charleston, where the College of Charleston excluded students of color. College students across the country captured national attention by organizing sit-ins, first in Greensboro, North Carolina on February 1, 1960. As the sit-ins spread across the country, middle and high school students in Charleston, and other towns across the South without a historically black college, organized their own sit-ins as a way to connect with the nonviolent demonstrations sweeping across the nation. On April 1, 1960, 24 students, 16 boys and eight girls from all-black Burke High School, sat-in at the S.H. Kress lunch counter.[17] The student-led protests applied consistent and grassroots pressure on the local and state governments not only to desegregate, but to respond to the larger national movement as it dramatically unfolded across the nation. As the NAACP continued to demand desegregation, young people orchestrating nonviolent direct action protests maintained momentum for the movement.

One of the most visible forms of young people's activism was the historic desegregation of white schools for the first time in South Carolina. While Minerva Brown's case was pending in the courts, she and other students applied to the school board to transfer in the fall of 1960. Brown, then a twelfth grader, and Ralph S. Dawson, a ninth grader, were denied admission to Charleston High School. Oveta Glover, the first-grade daughter of Reverend B.J. Glover, was denied admission to Julian Mitchell Elementary School. In a *News and Courier* article dated October 11, Reverend Glover stated that his daughter's request for transfer had been approved, but the name for the school to which she was admitted had been omitted from the certificate ("Negro Children Denied Admission," 1960). On October 15 of that year, 15 students applied for transfer, instigating a two-year application process. The school board maintained, however, that it could place students in a school that suited it, using "intelligence and cultural tests" to gauge aptitude. Additionally, the school board rejected the idea that placing a black student in a white school was "in the best interest of the child to be transferred." Even after the NAACP selected some of the brightest students to desegregate white schools, school officials often interrogated students in an attempt to intimidate them into withdrawing their request to transfer.[18]

---

[17] Minerva King, interview with the author, December 12, 2011. See also Hale (2013, 4–28); "24 Arrested Here in Demonstration" (1960); Baker, 2006, chapters 6, 7, and 8.

[18] Millicent Brown, the first student to desegregate a school in South Carolina, recalled one such test. The Charleston County School Board requested an interview with her to "test" her integrity in moving forward to desegregate schools. As Brown recalled, "I can

Ongoing pressure generated from the local movement sustained commitment among local people to demand equality which, along with a national movement toward desegregation, pushed local governing officials to act. On August 23, 1963, Judge Robert Martin handed down the inevitable decision that Charleston County schools must desegregate. In *Millicent Brown et al. v. Charleston County School Board, District 20*, Judge Martin ruled that the 12 plaintiffs' requests for admission to white schools must be approved. Because the decision was handed down so close to the beginning of the school year, Judge Martin permitted the school board to limit desegregation to the 11 plaintiffs who were still in school for the 1963–1964 school year (one had recently graduated), delaying total desegregation for a year.

The first day of desegregation was not easy for the first 11 students. Clarice Hines Lewis desegregated Memminger Elementary along with Gerald and Cassandra Alexander. Clarice was in seventh grade, Gerald in second, and Cassandra in third. Mrs. Hines-Lewis remembers being escorted to school by Reverend C.L. Grady, the pastor of the Morris Brown A.M.E. Church.[19] Millicent Brown, a sophomore, desegregated Rivers High School along with Jacqueline Ford, who was in eighth grade. A bomb threat marred their first day (Stambaugh, "Bomb Scare," 1963; "School Integration Begins," 1963, Section A, p. 1; Millicent Brown Papers, Avery Research Center, Charleston, South Carolina). Jacqueline's sixth-grade sister, Barbara (now Morrison) desegregated James Simons Elementary along with her younger sister Gail and Oveta Glover, both in fourth grade.

For students of color, the first day of school was just the first of hundreds of daily battles. Clarice Hines Lewis recalled being taunted by a group of boys every day on her way home:

> every day after school there were either two or three boys on the corner of Coming and Wentworth or St. Phillip and Wentworth that would be waiting for me to pass by [...] and they would either spit on me or they would hit me in the back of my head [...] and I had been told regardless of what they did to ignore it and just keep on walking.[20]

The daily struggle forced the young Clarice Hines Lewis to take "one day at a time," remaining diligent in her studies and her prayers. Even after she

---

remember being hammered with questions. 'Why would you want to leave? Don't you like your school?' [The board members] were very specific [...] I just knew that they were going to try to get to me to say something that would negate why I was supposed to be going to this school" (Millicent Brown, interview with the author, November 29, 2011). See also Baker (2006, 145).

[19] Clarice Hines Lewis. Interview with the author, February 13, 2013.
[20] Clarice Hines Lewis. Interview with the author, February 13, 2013.

had transferred to the white Charleston High School for eighth grade, the same challenges remained:

> We still had young men that would say things and do things [...] we would be walking up the steps or down the steps and they would throw papers or rocks or whatever at us, but then I remember a few young men that did start to talk to us and start to talk to me in certain classes and that we could maybe do assignments together.[21]

Millicent Brown faced challenges both in and outside of school. She faced taunts in the hallways and the bathrooms of Rivers as well as social ostracism from her white classmates, who ignored her throughout the long school days. Barbara (Ford) Morrison recalled her feelings of anxiety during her first days at James Simons: "When I walked in everybody just stared. Some people snickered. I didn't have a very friendly class at all."[22] Millicent Brown also recalled being ostracized by her black peers. Brown remembered attending a basketball game at Burke High School, the institution she had attended before enrolling in the all-white Rivers High School, and experiencing rejection there as well (Baker, 2006, 164; Millicent Brown, interview from Jewish Heritage Collection).

Charleston's "first children" speak collectively of the solitude they felt during their experiences of desegregating all-white public schools. Although there was more than one black student in each of the desegregated schools that year, the young people who were the first to desegregate felt completely alone in their everyday lives. Millicent Brown, Barbara (Ford) Morrison, Clairce (Hines) Lewis, and Oveta Glover all recount feelings of isolation during the school day. At lunch, they sat alone and engaged in very few, if any, meaningful relationships with their white peers. Because the first children were in different grades, for the most part, they had different classes, lunch and break periods, and were therefore often the only student of color in their social and academic circles.

Barbara (Ford) Morrison remembered walking in line to lunch with large gaps between her and the students in front of and behind her. The children, who were supposed to sit in a certain order, would then rearrange themselves so as to separate her from the group. On the playground, her peers isolated her again, except when some of the boys would invite her to play kickball. Unfortunately, she was not very athletic. Barbara did recall one girl who was nice to her in the middle of the year:

> She would come and she told me that her father is a minister and her father said that she had to be nice to me. So she would come and we

---

[21] Clarice Hines Lewis, interview with author.
[22] Barbara Ford Morrison, interview with the authors, October 2, 2013, Charleston, SC.

would be together at recess. First it was everyday then she came and told me that she couldn't play with me every day. That she had to play with her friends so it would be every other day. Then eventually she just stopped playing at all. So during recess I spent a lot of time by myself. I would read and watch other children play. (Millicent Brown, interview from Jewish Heritage Collection)

Barbara Morrison was not alone in her struggles during the free time provided to students. Millicent Brown also recalls the isolation during lunch:

People threw stuff at you in the lunchroom and everything, but mostly it was being alone. Some girls started being friendly to me and after a while I did have some people to talk to me. But they were girls who were social outcasts [...]. I appreciated it, but a couple of them were such losers, socially I mean. I always felt guilty. Yes, I liked that they were my friends and they talked, but all things being equal, these are not the type of girls that I would be hanging with. I had a tremendous amount of guilt about that.[23]

For young people in the often brutal world of adolescence, these social experiences as isolated persons of color were traumatic and left deep emotional scars.

Many of these first students also spoke of the pressure they felt to succeed in school. As a pattern reflected across the country, the NAACP selected students who were accomplished scholars with a demonstrated record of academic quality and merit. This generated a lot of pressure for these young people at a formative age. Millicent Brown recalls the feeling that she was "representing the race." Although her grades suffered during her first semester at Rivers, she managed to improve them, eventually finishing with grades similar to what she would have expected at Burke.[24] Clarice Hines Lewis was also aware of the pressure to do well: "I also knew that I needed to focus. I needed to make sure that my grades were up to par." She did not want to give white parents, educators, and legislatures evidence that black students could not do well in white schools.[25] The pressures of desegregation forced many of the pioneers to act in isolation, which led to loneliness, fear, and traumatic episodes. While desegregation was successful in permitting a small handful of students access to all-white schools, the larger ideal of integration and interracial dialogue, mutual respect and decision-making remained elusive. Token desegregation had been achieved, but the larger goals of true integration remained unrealized.

[23] Millicent Brown, interview from Jewish Heritage Collection.
[24] Millicent Brown, Jewish Heritage interview.
[25] Clarice Hines Lewis, interview with author.

Other students eventually joined in the struggle to desegregate schools. Federal educational policy grew to be much more expansive as it ordered the total desegregation of public schools by the early 1970s. The Civil Rights Act of 1964 contained a provision that denied federal funding to institutions that maintained a system of *de jure* segregation. This provision extended to the public school system when Congress passed the Elementary and Secondary Education Act (ESEA) in 1965. Under ESEA, public schools that received federal support, which included all public schools in the South, had to maintain desegregated schools in order to retain financial support. The Supreme Court rendered decisions that further sped up the pace of desegregation. The *Green v. New Kent County* (1969) and *Alexander v. Holmes* (1970) decisions demanded that stalled desegregation plans be implemented with "all deliberate speed."[26] In anticipation of this decision in the Lowcountry, Judge Martin ruled that Charleston's plan for desegregation did not "comply with the court's directives" and did not meet "minimum constitutional requirements" (Baker, 2006, 166). Charleston's plan for the 1967–1968 school year allowed each student in the district to apply to the school they would like to attend for the upcoming year. This achieved notable desegregation of white schools but, still, no desegregation of black schools. During this period, the school board received over 1,000 applications to transfer, mostly from black students requesting to go to white schools (Baker, 2006, 166). Rather than use the ESEA funds as they were intended, Charleston used them to again equalize white and black schools. Influenced by PTA lobbying on both sides of the color line, Charleston used these funds to equalize black facilities, eliminating tangible inequalities, yet further polarizing school children. If the facilities were tangibly equal, the school board reasoned, blacks would remain in a black school (Baker, 2006, 167).

The state government was satisfied with token desegregation so long as it could be proven that black students legally had the option to attend school with whites. If they did not take the opportunity, the school board reasoned, that was the students' and their families' prerogative. In July of 1967, state senator Charles "Mack" Gibson proposed legislation for a consolidated school system. His plan, passed as S.C. Act 340, created the CCSD. Act 340 consolidated the eight Charleston area school districts into one financial district but one that maintained district lines for enrollment. Gibson claimed that the purpose of the act was "not to move kids but to take the money and move the money." This new equalization scheme promoted racialized districts. Although it sought to provide adequate school funding

---

[26] On federal legislation and the desegregation of Southern schools, see Bolton (2007, 122–126); Crespino (2007, 173–176).

for all eight of the constituent districts, the act also maintained lines for enrollment, which encouraged whites to move to certain districts while avoiding others (Baker, 2006, 170–171; Jenkins, 2009, 40–53).[27]

When the larger goal of integration and a truly high-quality education is considered, the ideals of the *Brown* decision remained elusive; the history of education reform in Charleston illustrates the ongoing struggle for quality education. On January 9, 1981, Richard Ganaway II and numerous other plaintiffs filed suit against the CCSD, the State of South Carolina, and other government officials involved with the provision of public education. The plaintiffs used the equal protection clause of the Fourteenth Amendment to claim (1) that the CCSD remains "substantially segregated by race"; (2) that "intentionally discriminatory legislation and actions" by both the CCSD and the state had caused this racial segregation; and (3) that the intent of Act 340, which combined the eight Charleston County school districts into constituent districts under the CCSD, was to maintain this segregation.[28] The case remained lost in the labyrinth of the legal system for seven years. In September of 1989, the district court of South Carolina ruled that Act 340 was constitutional and that the CCSD fulfilled its requirement under *Brown* to eliminate dual systems. The Court reasoned that because each constituent school district in the CCSD operated a unitary school system, there was no instance of legal segregation despite evidence suggesting otherwise.[29]

In 1984, South Carolina had passed the Education Improvement Act, one of the most comprehensive pieces of education legislation to date (Kirk, 1985, 132–145). This act established a penny sales tax to help improve education, which was expected to generate $217 million in 1984–1985. These funds were to be used primarily to provide basic skills remediation, which included reading, math, writing, and science, increases to teacher salaries, and more resources to the development of school facilities. The eight sections of the act focused on: (1) raising student performance by increasing academic standards, (2) strengthening the teaching and testing of basic skills, (3) evaluating the teaching profession, (4) improving leadership, management, and fiscal efficiency, (5) implementing quality control and rewarding productivity, (6) creating more effective partnerships among schools, parents, community, and business, (7) providing school buildings conducive to improved student learning, and (8) providing the financial support needed to improve South Carolina's schools through the one cent additional sales tax (Kirk, 1985, 135–145).

---

[27] *United States, Plaintiff, and Richard Ganaway, II, et al. v. Charleston County School District and State of South Carolina* (856 F.Supp. 1060 1994).
[28] *Ganaway v. CCSD.*
[29] *Ganaway v. CCSD.*

Though comprehensive in its requirements, reformers argued that the state still denied a sizable minority of students in South Carolina a "minimally adequate" education as guaranteed by the state. In response to ongoing and systemic inequities, 40 of the poorest school districts in South Carolina and 20 of their taxpayers filed suit against the state and its funding formula for school education in *Abbeville v. State of South Carolina* in 1993. The challenge focused on Article XI, Section 3 of the South Carolina State Constitution, which reads: "the General Assembly shall provide for the maintenance and support of a system of free public schools open to all children in the state." The plaintiffs argued that the state was required to fund a "minimally adequate" system of public education yet failed to do so. The plaintiffs claimed that the present school funding formula in South Carolina violated the state and federal constitutions' equal protection clauses, the South Carolina Education Finance Act, and the constitutional provision for a system of public education. After the case vacillated between the state Supreme Court and the District Court, the Third Judicial Circuit Court issued a reconciliatory judgment in 2005, agreeing with both plaintiffs and defendants. The court took no issue with the school facilities, teacher licensure, core curriculum, or revenue for education. It did rule, however, that funding for an early childhood education program was necessary to help close the achievement gap experienced by children growing up in poverty. As a result, South Carolina created a pre-kindergarten program for the plaintiffs' school districts, which would serve as an experiment to determine its effectiveness (see Fogle, 2000; Weiler, 2007, 3–9). The state determined that early childhood education would equalize education in the affected districts.

By the close of the twentieth century, 50 years after the monumental *Brown* decision, educational reformers continued to focus upon the issue of educational funding to achieve a quality education in South Carolina. Indeed, the demand for an equal and quality education in the 1990s in the face of continual economic and political barriers constitutes a perennial theme in the history of South Carolina. The legal challenges bound to the provision of an education illustrate the contested nature of quality education today, nearly 150 years after its origins during Reconstruction. The movement of the first half of the twentieth century ultimately dismantled the legality of *de jure* segregation, but systematic inequalities continued to plague students who remained enrolled in the state's public school system decades later. The work of educational reformers illustrates a direct link to the movement's antecedents in the first decades of the 1900s that led to the push to equalize salaries and the distribution of school resources.

Far from achieving an integrated or quality education, the ongoing struggle of education reformers in South Carolina shows the tenuous nature of desegregation to improve the quality of education for all students. The long history of the struggle for quality education demonstrates the dynamic interplay between grassroots activism and the larger federal context that forced recalcitrant Southern states to desegregate. The dynamic has still not reconciled the constant tension among factors of race and class, and discourse around public, private, and "unitary" school districts. Issues such as the school-to-prison pipeline, funding disparities across the state, and privatization, among other legal quandaries, suppress the provision of quality public education to all students. Though legal and grassroots movements have challenged the state to provide a more equitable education in cases such as the *Abbeville v. South Carolina* (2014), these tensions continue to define the provision of public education and the ongoing struggle to realize the promises of quality education in South Carolina.

Works Cited

"24 Arrested Here in Demonstration." *News and Courier* (Charleston, SC). Apr. 2, 1960.

Adair, Alvis V. *Desegregation: The Illusion of Black Progress.* Lanham, MD: University Press of America, 1984.

Baker, R. Scott. *Paradoxes of Desegregation: African American Struggles for Educational Equity in Charleston, South Carolina, 1926–1972.* Columbia, SC: University of South Carolina Press, 2006.

Banks, James A. "Multicultural Education: Historical Development, Dimensions, and Practice." In *Handbook of Research on Multicultural Education.* San Francisco, CA: Jossey-Bass, 2004.

"Boarder States Yielding to Pressure but Deep South Can Win Race Battle." *News and Courier* (Charleston, SC). Sept. 14, 1956.

Bolton, Charles. *The Hardest Deal of All: The Battle Over School Integration in Mississippi, 1870–1980.* Jackson, MS: University Press of Mississippi, 2005.

Burton, Orville Vernon, Beatrice Burton, and Simon Appleford. "Seeds in Unlikely Soil: The *Briggs v. Elliot* School Segregation Case." In *Toward the Meeting of the Waters: Currents in the Civil Rights Movement of South Carolina During the Twentieth Century.* Ed. Winfred E. Moore and Orville Vernon Burton. Columbia, SC: University of South Carolina Press, 2008: 176–200.

Charron, Katherine Mellen. *Freedom's Teacher: The Life of Septima Clark.* Chapel Hill, NC: University of North Carolina Press, 2009.

"City's Newest School, East Bay Negro Elementary, To Open Monday." *The News and Courier* (Charleston, SC). Feb. 1, 1955.

Clark, Kenneth B. "Desegregation: An Appraisal of the Evidence." *Journal of Social Issues* 9 (1953): 1–12.

"Court Orders Negro Teacher Pay Equality." *The News and Courier* (Charleston, SC). Feb. 15, 1944.

Crespino, Joseph. *In Search of Another Country: Mississippi and the Conservative Counterrevolution.* Princeton, NJ: Princeton University Press, 2007.

Crespino, Joseph. *Strom Thurmond's America.* New York: Hill and Wang, 2012.

Davies, Gareth. *See Government Grow: Education Politics from Johnson to Reagan.* Lawrence, KS: University of Kansas Press, 2007.

Dobrasko, Rebekah. "Architectural Survey of Charleston County's School Equalization Program, 1951–1955." University of South Carolina Public History Program, April 2005.

Drago, Edmund L. *Initiative, Paternalism, and Race Relations: Charleston's Avery Normal Institute.* Athens, GA: University of Georgia Press, 1990.

Edgar, Walter B. *South Carolina in the Modern Age.* Columbia, SC: University of South Carolina Press, 2012.

Fogle. Jennifer L. "Abbeville County School District v. State: The Right to a Minimally Adequate Education in South Carolina." *South Carolina Law Review* 51 (2000): 1–2.

Hale, Jon N. "'The Fight Was Instilled in Us': High School Student Activism and the Civil Rights Movement in Charleston, South Carolina." *The South Carolina Historical Magazine* 114.1 (2013): 4–28.

Hawkins, J. Russell. "Religion, Race, and Resistance: Evangelicals and the Dilemma of Integration in South Carolina 1950–1975." PhD dissertation, Rice University, 2009.

Jackson, Jr., John P. *Social Scientists for Social Justice: Making the Case against Segregation.* New York: New York University Press, 2001.

Jenkins, Katherine. "Desegregation Not Integration: Charleston County Schools and the Struggle over Consolidation, 1963–1980." MA thesis, College of Charleston, 2009.

Kirk, L. Roger. "The South Carolina Education Improvement Act of 1984." *Journal of Education Finance* 11.1 (1985): 132–145.

Klarman, Michael J. *Brown v. Board of Education and the Civil Rights Movement.* Oxford: Oxford University Press, 2007.

Klein, Woody, ed. *Toward Humanity and Justice: The Writings of Kenneth B. Clark, Scholar of the 1954* Brown v. Board of Education *Decision.* Westport, CT: Praeger Publishers, 2004.

Lassiter, Matthew, and Joseph Crespino, eds. *The Myth of Southern Exceptionalism.* Oxford: Oxford University Press, 2010.

Lewis, John, with Michael D'Orso. *Walking with the Wind: A Memoir of the Movement.* New York: Simon & Schuster, 1988.

Moore, Winfred E., and Orville Vernon Burton. *Toward the Meeting of the Waters: Currents in the Civil Rights Movement of South Carolina during the Twentieth Century.* Columbia, SC: University of South Carolina Press, 2008.

Morrison, Nan. *A History of the College of Charleston, 1936–2008.* Columbia, SC: University of South Carolina Press, 2011.

"Negro Children Denied Admission." *News and Courier* (Charleston, SC). Oct. 11, 1960.

Patterson, James. *Brown v. Board of Education: A Civil Rights Milestone and its Troubled Legacy.* New York: Oxford University Press, 2001.

Perillo, Jonna. *Uncivil Rights: Teachers, Unions, and Race in the Battle of School Equity.* Chicago, IL: University of Chicago Press, 2012.

Petition, Board of Trustee Minute Book, 1951–1957, School District No. 20, Charleston County School District Archives, Charleston, SC.

Podair, Joseph, *The Strike that Changed New York: Blacks, Whites, and the Ocean Hill-Brownsville Crisis.* New Haven, CT: Yale University Press, 2002.

Potts, John F. *A History of the Palmetto Education Association.* Washington, DC: National Education Association, 1978.

Powell, John A., and Marguerite L. Spencer. "Response: *Brown* is not *Brown* and Educational Reform is not Reform if Integration is Not a Goal." *New York University Review of Law and Change* 28 (2003): 343–352.

Purdy, Michelle. "Southern and Independent: Public Mandates, Private Schools, and Black Students, 1951–1970." PhD dissertation, Emory University, 2011.

"School Integration Begins Calmly in South Carolina and Baton Rouge." *New York Times.* Sept. 4, 1963: Section A, 1.

Smyth, William D. "Segregation in Charleston in the 1950s: A Decade of Transition." *South Carolina Historical Magazine* 92 (1991): 107.

"The Southern Resistance." *News and Courier* (Charleston, SC). Aug. 24, 1955.

Stambaugh, Barbara. "Bomb Scare Mars Mixing of Schools: FBI, Police Keep Close Watch." *News and Courier* (Charleston, SC). Sept. 4, 1963.

"Statement of Governor James F. Byrnes, July 22, 1952," James F. Byrnes Papers, Series 7, Box 12, Folders 1–13, Strom Thurmond Institute archives, Clemson University.

"To the School Boards of School District #20." Box 7, Folder 8, Eugene Hunt Collection, The Avery Research Center for American History and Culture, Charleston, SC.

Tushnet, Mark. *The NAACP's Legal Strategy against Segregated Education.* 2nd ed. Chapel Hill, NC: University of North Carolina Press, 2004.

Yarbrough, Tinsley E. *A Passion for Justice.* New York: Oxford University Press, 1987.

United States, Plaintiff, and Richard Ganaway, II, et al. v. Charleston County School District and State of South Carolina (856 F.Supp. 1060 1994).

Weiler, Spencer Charles. "*Abbeville v. the State of South Carolina*: A Case Study." PhD dissertation, Virginia Polytechnic Institute and State University. 2007.

Index

Abbeville v. State of South Carolina (1993) 171–172
abolitionism 41, 87– 88
Abtey, Jacques 17–18
Aciman, André 71
activism
   Afro-Chilean 137–153
   Baker, Josephine 11–32
   desegregation 164–165
   motivation for 146–148
   Pan-African 33–56
   public representation 127
adoption, notion of/of children 24–26
advocacy 52, 53
African agency 96, 98
African-American theater 94–114
African Americans
   cultural values 95–96, 111–112
   depictions of 39
   homebuyers 133
   media representations 20
   subjectivity 40
African descent
   belonging and 141
   Latin American populations 142
   location and 144n9
   national identity 145
   racism and 137–138
   violence and 33–34

African diaspora
   in Chile 139
   insider/outsider concept 58
Afro-Chilean activism 137–153
Afro-Colombians 138
Afro-Latin America 137–153
Afro organizations, Chile 138–139
Afrocentric Theater 111–112
Afrocentric Theater (Molette and Molette) 94, 96
Afrocentricity 95, 107
afrodescendiete term 138n1, 144–145
"Afrophobia" 101
AFSC *see* American Friends Service Committee
agency 13, 85, 96, 98
alienation 62
American culture, representation of 11, 19
American Friends Service Committee (AFSC) 117–118, 124–125, 128, 133–134
American Negro Exhibit, Exposition Universelle 35–40, 47
ancestral homeland *see* homeland concept
Andrews, George Reid 141
"animator" model 86n11
anti-discrimination laws, Chile 138
Antillean peoples 61–62, 68

apathy, effects of 127, 130
appropriation strategy 67
area housing groups 121
Arica, Chile 144–145, 149n15
Arthur's dying speech 79–81, 84, 86
"ascent narratives" 77n2
assimilation 63, 67n12, 104
Atlanta, US, arts initiatives 97
Atlantic world, mobility 11–32
authenticity 78
author model 86n11
authorship, dying speeches 83–89
autobiographies, use of 12

Baker, Josephine 5, 11–32
Baldwin, James 101
Barkun, Michael 118, 131–132
Bayton, Ruth 12
Belgian colonialism 3
Belleville, Paris 59
belonging 11–32, 64, 137–153
"beloved community" notion 164
Beyala, Calixthe, *Loukoum* 57–74
Black Aesthetic 96–97
Black Arts 96, 98–99
black audiences
    dying speeches 83–89
    ritual drama 102
"black community" 22, 105, 109–110
black enclaves 119
black home-buyers 133
black masculinity 89, 90
black narratives, dying speeches 77–93
black otherness 57–74
black populations, Chile 141, 144
black power movement 21, 22, 96–97
black students 125, 158, 169
Black Theater Movement 96, 99, 107
Black Theater: Premise and Presentation (Molette and Molette) 94
black women, rape of 90

blackness
    Afro-Latin America 151
    decentering scholarship of 143
Boer peoples 43–46
bond elections 158–159
Bonilla-Silva, Eduardo 4
"borderland conflict" 64
borderland-hinterland distinction 142n7
borders of belonging 137–153
Bouillon, Jo 19, 25, 27
Bourne's vision 27–28
Brazilian African descendants 141n5
Briggs v. Elliot (1952) 156, 161
British Empire World's Fairs 42–43, 45–46
broadsides, dying speeches 79, 87
Brown, J. Arthur 161
Brown, Kimberley N. 28
Brown, Millicent 165n18, 166–167
Brown, Minerva 165
Brown v. Board of Education (1954) 154–156, 159, 161–164, 170–171
Bruce, John Edward 36n8, 52n33
Buffalo Pan-American Exposition 46–53
Byrnes, Governor 157, 159

CAAR *see* Collegium for African American Research
call and response 128
Calloway, Thomas 35–36, 38, 40
Caribbean 3, 137
Carter Harrison, Paul 111
Carter, June 125
cautionary tales 84–85
Charleston, South Carolina 154–174
children
    adopting 24–25
    education achievement gap 171
    migratory spaces 66
    see also school desegregation
Chile, activism in 137–153

Index

Chile-Peru border 145
Christianity 41, 81–82, 88
church support, Summer Project 122–123
citizenship 51
civil rights movement
   Black Theater 99
   desegregated schools 163
   housing discrimination 131–132
   impact of 2
   mobility/resistance and 15–21
the civilized and the savage 33–34
civilizing mission, British Empire 45
Clark, Kenneth 163–164
class issues 109–110
Clifford, James 23
closed housing practices 118, 133
closed societies 126–127
Coe, Kay 122
Coe, Reverend Buckner 122–123, 132
Cohen, Daniel 85–86
Cold War politics 20
collective organization 139, 148, 151–152
college students 125, 165
   see also student-led protests; student volunteers
Collegium for African American Research (CAAR) 1
Colombians in Chile 138
colonialism/colonialization
   European 3–4
   French immigrants 58
   Mexico 2
   Senegal 72
   see also imperialism
color line 40–42, 46, 51
communal identity, immigrants 60
communication
   cultural difference 72–73
   otherness and 65–66
"community control" 164n15
community identity, migrants 60

community, sense of 99
confession and conversion narratives 77–93
consolidated school system 169
consumption, access to 104–105
contended slavery notion 48
court debate, integration/desegregation 164
court-ordered school desegregation 159
criminal conversion narratives 77–93
Cuban exhibit, Exposition Universelle 35
cultural difference, experience of 71–73
cultural identity, immigrants 63–65
cultural invisibility 142
cultural literacy 16
cultural mobility 14–15, 23–24
cultural privileges, French peoples 60
cultural reality, Afro-Chileans 139
cultural revivalism 107–109
cultural values, African-Americans 95–96, 111–112

dance groups 149
Darkest Africa exhibit, US Exposition 48–49
Davis, Reverend Emory G. 123, 132
de Almagro, Diego 143
de Gaulle, Charles 18
de jure segregation 169, 171
demand for education 154–174
democracy, participatory 126
Democratic Party policies 157
demographics, Afro-Latin America 141–142
descent notion 139, 147
   see also African descent
desegregation
   education 154–174
   integration distinction 163–164
diaspora *see* African diaspora

difference basis of immigration 58, 66, 71–73
discriminatory housing policies 117–136
discursive agency 85
diva persona, Baker, Josephine 28–29
Dixiecrats 157
domestic practices, Baker, Josephine 25–26
Dominican Republic 4–5
dominion movement 42–43
"double audience" notion 83
double consciousness concept 38, 83n9
double-narration technique 71–72
Douglass, Frederick 2
Du Bois, W.E.B. 35–36, 38, 40–42, 98
Dudziak, Mary 20
Duvall v. J.F. Seignous et al. (1943) 155
dying speeches/confessions 77–93

Earl's Court, London 42
EBT *see* electronic benefit transfer cards
Eburne, Johnathan P. 24–26
economic status, immigrants 60
education
    demand for 154–174
    experiments in 25
    racial inequality 6
    Westernized 61
Education Finance Commission, US 157–158
Education Improvement Act 170
Edwin, Shirin 63
electronic benefit transfer (EBT) cards 105n5
Elementary and Secondary Education Act (ESEA) 169
Elizabeth I, Queen 3
empathy 89–90
Empress Theatre, London 42–44
ENSBR *see* Evanston-North Shore Board of Realtors

entertainment, dying speeches as 83, 85, 87–88
equality, criminal conversion narratives 88
equalization in education 155–158, 160–163, 166, 169, 171
ESEA *see* Elementary and Secondary Education Act
ethnic groups 140, 150
ethnic identity, immigrants 63
"ethnic ventriloquism" 86n12
"ethnographic other" 33–56
ethnographic projects, Chile 139n2
Euro-American control 33–34
Europe
    Baker's representation 11
    racism 3–4
    whiteness characteristics 140
evangelism 85
Evanston-North Shore Board of Realtors (ENSBR) 119–120
Evanston suburb, Chicago 121, 130, 132, 134
evolutionary superiority 47
exclusion critique, otherness 65–70
exclusionary practices 51
executions 77–78, 81, 84
Exeter Hall 46n21
Exposition Universelle, Paris 34–40

fair housing project 117–136
family, role as head of 16–17, 27
fascism 18–19
The Feminist and Scholar Online journal 13
Filipino peoples 47–48
financing
    area housing groups 121
    desegregated schools 169
    see also funding education; sponsorship
"first children", school desegregation 161–172

first-generation immigrants 66
first-person narratives, dying speeches 78, 88
fiscal measures, black community 105
Fisher Fishkin, Shelley 16
For Real Estate Equality (FREE) 134
formalism in drama 101
Fortis, Edmund 80–82, 86
France
   Caribbean population 3
   colonial immigrants 58
   German occupation 18
   legal system 64
   as the *Métropole* 57–74
   US contrast 20–21, 23
   see also French culture–immigrant culture; French language; French resistance; Paris, France
francophone narratives 57–74
FREE *see* For Real Estate Equality
freedom 78–80, 88, 101
Freedom Centers, Summer Project 122–123, 128
French culture–immigrant culture 63
French language 71–72
French resistance 12, 16–18
funding education 157–158, 171–172
   see also financing; sponsorship

Gaines, Robert 158–159
gallows literature 89n15
gender and crime 79–81, 88–90
gendered drag 79n6
generational immigrant experience 65–66
generational narrative 110
geographic hinterlands 142, 144
German-occupied France 18
ghettos *see* black enclaves; urban ghettos
Gibson, Charles "Mack" 169
global color line 40–42, 46, 51
global community, communication 73

Gossett, Neely 109
government relations, Summer Project 131–132
graduate student volunteers 129
Grandon, Lissette Sierra 137–138
grassroots movements 122, 156, 172
Gray, Thomas 87n14
the Great Awakening 85–86
the Great Migration 118–119
Greater Britain Exhibition 42–44, 48
Greenblatt, Stephen 23–24
Gressette, Marion 159–160
group formation, Chile 148–149
Guterl, Matthew Pratt 12–13n5, 14, 21

Haitian Revolution 2
Hawaiian exhibit, Exposition Universelle 35
heartland of Chile 151–152
heroism, language of 110
high-quality education 154–174
high-rise apartments 119
hinterlands
   Afro-Latin America 137–153
   borderland distinction 142n7
Hobson, J.A. 45–46
"home"
   nostalgia for 67
   sense of 61
homeland concept 57–74
homeowners 127–128, 129
"honor" 107–108
honors track, education 159–160
HOP *see* Housing Opportunity Program
host culture, immigrants 63–65
housing arrangements 60
housing discrimination 6, 117–136
Housing Opportunity Program (HOP) 117, 119–122
human rights 53
humanizing slaves 89

"I Have a Dream" speech (King) 1, 110
iconography 11–12
identity
   collective organizations 151
   individualist 60
   migration and 57, 63
   otherness and 62
   see also national identity
illiterate audiences, dying speeches 79
"imagined community" 22, 27
immigration
   backlash against 5
   categories of immigrants 66n11
   francophone narratives 57–74
imperial progressivism 34, 41, 47–48, 51–52
imperialism 34, 42–44
   see also colonialism/colonialization
in-betweenness, "borderland conflict" 64
incarceration of black men 90
inclusionary practices 51
indigenous populations, Chile 140
individualized identity 60
insider/outsider dichotomy 58
institutional racism 104, 106
integration
   desegregation distinction 163–164
   homeowners' opposition 130
   rejection of 95, 108
   school system 161
interfaith ceremonies 128
international race relations 36
intra-racial issues 102
invisibility
   Afro-Chilean 139, 147
   Afro-Latin Americans 142–143
Islamic code 63–64, 66

Jahn, Jahnheinz 111–112
Jim Crow laws 119, 125, 163
Johnson, James Weldon 83
Jules-Rosette, Bennetta 16, 20
Juletane (Warner-Vieyra) 57–74

killing speeches 90
King, Adele 61
King, Martin Luther 1, 26, 110, 117–118, 127, 131, 134
Kinship (Molette and Molette) 95

labor pools 119
language use 62, 71–72, 97, 107, 110
Latin American activism 137–153
Laurenti, Luigi 129
law/laws
   anti-discrimination 138
   education strategy 158–160
   equalization strategies 155–156
   housing discrimination 119
   legitimacy of 110
   open housing 117
   pupil-placement 159
   see also Jim Crow laws; legal discourse, dying speeches; legal movements, education; legal status; legal systems
law enforcement 4, 84, 127
law schools 156–157
Legacy (Molette and Molette) 95, 107–109
legal discourse, dying speeches 89
legal movements, education 164, 171–172
legal status
   Afro-Chileans 150
   slaves 80
legal systems 64, 89, 170
Les Milandes *château* 13–14, 21–27, 29
Levine, James 118, 131–132
Lewis, Clarice Hines 166–168
Lewis, John 132
Lion, Jean 17
literacy 16
literary trope of migration 59–62

local governments 131–132
location concept 96, 98, 144–145
London, World's Fairs 34, 40–44
loss, sense of 60–61
Loukoum: The "Little Prince" of Belleville (Beyala) 57–74
lowcountry, South Carolina 154–174
Lowen, James W. 119
lynching practices 36
Lyon, Janet 12

Mapuche peoples 140
March on Washington 20–21
marginalization 16, 21, 29, 63
marriage 64, 68
   see also polygamy
Martin, Judge 162
masculinity 89, 90
Matabele War, Rhodesia 43
media relations 123
media representations 19–20, 120
Meigs Damman, Grace 125
mestizo populations 137, 140, 142n7, 144, 147
Métropole (France) 57–74
Mexico 2, 141n5
migration
   francophone narratives 57–74
   from Caribbean 137
   the Great Migration 118–119
   literary trope of 59–62
   see also immigration
"Militant Theater" 94
Mina, Gloria Maria Grueso 137–138, 140, 147
ministers' authority 86
minority housing 119
minstrel performances 106
Mississippi Freedom Summer Project 126–127, 133
Mitten, Jean 128
mixed societies *see mestizo* populations; mulattos

"mobilities paradigm" 23
mobility in Atlantic world 11–32
"mobility turn" 15
modernity and secularism 41–42
Molette, Carlton and Barbara, plays 94–114
Momeyer, Rick 125–126
morality in activism 51
moreno (brown-skinned) 147
Morrison, Barbara (Ford) 167–168
motherhood 21–28
Moyer, William 117–118, 122, 126
mulattos, Chile 141, 144
multicultural communication 72
muntu being 111–112
murder narratives 80–81
Musée Social, Paris 35–36, 38
music 149–150
Muslims 63
   see also Islamic code

NAACP education campaigns 155–156, 159, 161–162, 165
narrative ventriloquism 86
"narratives"
   criminal conversion 77–93
   immigration 57–74
   of otherness 65–70
"narrow nations" 140–141
National Association of Dramatic and Speech Arts 97
national belonging 21
national identity 145–146
NEC *see* Negro Ensemble Company
Negro Ensemble Company (NEC) 99
"negro problem" 36, 38, 40n12
Netherlands 3
"new mobilities paradigm" 15
New Right 154, 156–160
The Night of the Broken Glass performance 17
Noah's Ark (Molette and Molette) 95, 104–105, 106–107

nommo (word power) 111
North Africa, Second World War 18
The 1965 North Shore Summer Project, Chicago 117–136
nostalgia 67

Obama, Barack Hussein 4
objectification 38, 40
The Old Plantation exhibit, US Exposition 48, 50
Olds, Sally 123, 134
open housing laws 117
open market, housing 128, 130
Oro Negro organization 148
otherness 13, 33–56, 57–74
outsider/insider dichotomy 58
overcrowding, segregated schools 161–162

Palacios, Nicolas 146
Palmetto State Teacher's Association (PSTA) 155
pamphlets, dying speeches 79
Pan-African activism 33–56
Pan-African Conference of 1900, London 34, 40–42
Pan-American Exposition, Buffalo 46–53
Paris, France
    Exposition Universelle 34–40
    German occupation 18
    migration to 57–74
    US race relations 47
participatory democracy 126
paternalism 41, 48
patriarchal system 61–62, 63, 68
Patrimonial Slave Route 150
personhood, slavery and 89–91
Peru-Chile border 144–145
phenotypic characteristics, whiteness 140
phenotypic invisibility 142
phenotypic reality, Afro-Chileans 139

Philippines 47–48
picaresque novels 83, 84n10
place
    awareness of 5
    sense of 61
plantation slavery 89
plays, African-American 94–114
Plummer, Jonathan 81, 82, 86–87
political activism 13–17, 20, 23, 28–29
political rights 41–42
polygamy 62, 63, 66
Pomp's dying speech 80–82, 85–87, 88
postcolonial migration 59
Powell, Enoch 3, 5
"primitive" cultures 11
principal model 86n11
print culture 52
printer's role, dying speeches 86
privatization of schools 160
progressivism 34, 38, 41, 47–48, 51–52
property, slaves as 89–91
property values 129
protest dramas 98–99
protest groups 121, 165
protest marches 134
Prudence (Molette and Molette) 95
PSTA *see* Palmetto State Teacher's Association
public dramatization, housing discrimination 127, 130–132
public education 154–174
punishment 88–99
pupil-placement law 159

quality education, demand for 154–174

race
    conception of 108–109
    crime and 88–89
race relations 36, 40, 47
racial discrimination 19, 133

racial equality 26, 34, 47
racial identity, alienation 62
racial inequality, education 6
racial justice, housing 134
racial passing motif 79n6
racial purity myth 108
racial segregation *see* segregation
racial whiteness 140–141
racialized structures, United States 20
racism
    African descendants 137–138
    Baker against 18–21
    discriminatory housing policies 118
    Dominican Republic 4–5
    in Europe 3–4
    pervasiveness 2
    protest marches against 134
    struggle against 7
    theater and 101, 104, 106
radicalism 22
Rainbow Tribe (Baker) 21–28
rallies, housing discrimination 132
rape 36, 79–81, 90, 100–101
"rape complex" 80n7
la raza chilena race 146
readership, dying speeches 79, 83–89
reading as transformative experience 72
real estate agents 119–120, 123, 127–128, 132
redemption 85, 89–91
religion
    activism and 41
    language and 72
    see also Christianity; Islamic code
religious affiliation, schools 160
religious conversion 77, 78, 81–82, 85
religious organizations 122–123, 128
remedial track, education 159–160
Republican Party, rise of 156–157
residential segregation 120

resistance 15–21, 127
    see also French resistance
"revolutionary diva" concept 28–29
revolution, Black Arts 99
rhetorical skills 97, 107
Rhodesia, Matabele War 43
ritual dramas 101–102
"Rivers of Blood" speech (Powell) 3
rootedness 11–32
Rosalee Pritchett (Molette and Molette) 94–95, 98, 100–104, 106, 109

salary equalization, teachers 155
sales tax 157, 170
Salgado Henriquez, Marta 147–149
Santiago conference (2000) 148
the savage and the civilized 33–34
Savage South Africa show 42–46
savagery concept 38, 48
school desegregation 154–174
Scottsboro Boys 123n9
Second World War 4, 16–18
secularism 41–42, 86
segregation
    African Americans 20
    educational 154, 156, 161–162, 169–171
    housing 118–120, 123–124
    legacy of 108
self-determination context 52
Senegal, colonization 72
sensationalism 83, 87–88
servants 119
sexual assault *see* rape
Sheller, Mimi 15n7, 16
Sikkink, Kathryn 53
sit-ins 165
slave law 89
slave narratives 77, 87n14
slavery 48, 78–93, 97, 108–109, 141–146, 150
Smith, Stephen 81–82, 84, 86

social mobility 15
social whiteness 140
sociological theories 38
sociopolitical hinterlands 142, 144
South African War 40, 42–46
South Carolina, education in 154–174
southern traditions 107–109
Spanish American republics 143
"speaker" model 86n11
spiritual conversion 82–83, 85
sponsorship 122, 128
    see also financing; funding education
spy role, Baker, Josephine 16, 17–18
standing vigils 130–131
state, role as head of 16–17, 23
stereotyping 69, 112
strategic appropriation, migrants 67
strike action 164n15
student-led protests 165
student volunteers 123–127, 129, 133
subjectivity 40, 47
suburban housing 117–136
Summer Project, North Shore, Chicago 117–136
Surinamese in Netherlands 3
survival mechanisms 107
symbolism 25–26, 106

taxation 157, 170–171
teacher salary equalization 155
Tee-Shirt History (Molette and Molette) 95, 110–111
ten-minute plays (Molette and Molette) 110–111
testing system, education 159–160
theater, African-American 94–114
Theater of Cultural Revivalism 107–109
"Theater of Experience" 111
Thurmund, Strom 157
time–theater relationship 112

token desegregation 168, 169
transatlantic slave trade 143
transformative experience
    communication 72–73
    migration 67, 70
    reading 72
    theater 94–114
transnational American studies 16
transnationalism 15, 23, 27, 53
Treaty of Vereeniging 46
tuition grant bill 160
tumba carnaval dance group 149
Turner, Nat 87n14

Ugolani, JoAnn 125
United States (US)
    African-American theater 94–114
    blackness studies 143
    Buffalo Pan-American Exposition 46–53
    educational desegregation 154–174
    Exposition Universelle 35–40
    France, contrast to 20–21, 23
    "imagined community" 22, 27
    law enforcement 4
    racialized structures 20
    "universal brotherhood" creation 26–27, 29
uplift mission 34
urban ghettos 120
US *see* United States

value systems 64–65, 95–96, 111–112
"veritable revolution" term 51n30
vigils 130–131
violence
    Euro-American control 33–34
    narratives of 68, 70
    white men 100–101
voluntary housing project 120, 123–129, 133
voyeurism 83, 88
vulnerability 69–70

War of the Pacific (1879–1883) 145
Warner-Vieyra, Myriam, *Juletane* 57–74
Washington, March on 20–21
Webb, Christy 82
WEPPEO term, white supremacy 97
Westernization
  education 61
  value systems 64
white audiences, dying speeches 83–89, 90
white men's violence 100–101
white schools' desegregation 165, 167–169
white supremacy 46, 82, 97, 109, 112
white women
  housing projects 118
  rape 79–81
whiteness
  construction of 47
  dominion movement 43
  global color line and 42, 46
  imperial progressivism 48
  racial 140–141

"whites only" communities 121
WIC *see* women, infants, and children program
will and criminality 89
Williams, Henry Sylvester 45
Williams, Mance 102
Winchell, Walter 19
women
  fair housing projects 122
  migratory spaces 66
  organizations 148
  see also black women; gender and crime; gendered drag; white women
women, infants, and children (WIC) program 105n5
women's theater 98
word power (*nommo*) 111
World's Fairs 33–56
Wrighten, John H. 156
writing strategy 69–70

young people in migratory spaces 66

zoning laws 119